THE GOVERNMENT OF FRANCE

Gwendolen M. Carter

Northwestern University

The Government
of
France

Harcourt, Brace & World, Inc.
New York / Chicago / San Francisco / Atlanta

JN
2594.2
·C 33
1967

The contents of this volume are reprinted from
Major Foreign Powers, Fifth Edition,
by Gwendolen M. Carter and John H. Herz.

COVER PHOTOGRAPH   *Sue McCartney, Photo Researchers, Inc.*

Library of Congress Catalog Card Number: 68-14375

Printed in the United States of America

Contents

Charts and Maps

THE GOVERNMENT OF FRANCE

1. The French People and Their Politics

1. PARADOX AND PROSPECTS

That France has reestablished itself as a major international influence is a new factor in world affairs. Exhausted by war, torn by internal divisions, defeated in one colonial struggle after another, and hampered by an unstable political system, France in the fifties seemed to be sinking into insignificance. Even in that decade, however, France was making its way toward a healthy settlement with its former colonial possessions and was building a firm basis of political and economic cooperation with its Western European neighbors. Moreover, under the brilliant leadership of Jean Monnet, France was laying the foundations for the economic revival that has transformed the nation.

The de Gaulle Republic, under the direction of a highly competent bureaucracy, has pressed ahead the modernization of France's economy. To this economic revolution, the Fifth Republic has added a political one: the transformation of an unstable, Assembly-oriented system into a semiauthoritarian structure with strong executive leadership supported by a loose conglomeration of interests and groups committed to de Gaulle's leadership. Whether or not these political characteristics and alignments can be maintained, French politics can never return to what they were in the past. Nor can the French economy. This at least is predictable about France's future.

France and the World

What happens in France has a critical influence on the rest of the world. For many centuries *la grande nation* has been the most influential country of Western Europe. Its literature, philosophy, and political ideas have affected the thinking of civilized men everywhere. The triumph of revolutionary France in the late eighteenth century carried democratic ideals to much of the rest of Europe; in the mid-twentieth century the de Gaulle regime has given many former French African states a pattern for consolidating power under a strong president. France has played a crucial role in organizing Western Europe into a prosperous economic unit, and it is France that will decide whether the European Economic Community shall admit the United Kingdom into the Common Market. The United States and the United Kingdom often complain that France's external policies seem directed only by its leader's view of national interest—what is sometimes called "the cult of independence." Yet France's prosperity and renewed self-confidence have contributed notably to stability in Western Europe.

2. THE LAND AND THE PEOPLE

The Land

Geographical Influences

In comparison with the United States or the Soviet Union, France is small in area; yet it is larger than any other Western or Central European country. Its territory of 213,000 square miles (somewhat smaller than the state of Texas but almost two and one-half times the size of Great Britain) contains a population (in 1966) of just over 49 million people (in comparison with Great Britain's 54 million). Its climate is temperate, its landscape for the most part is gentle

FRANCE

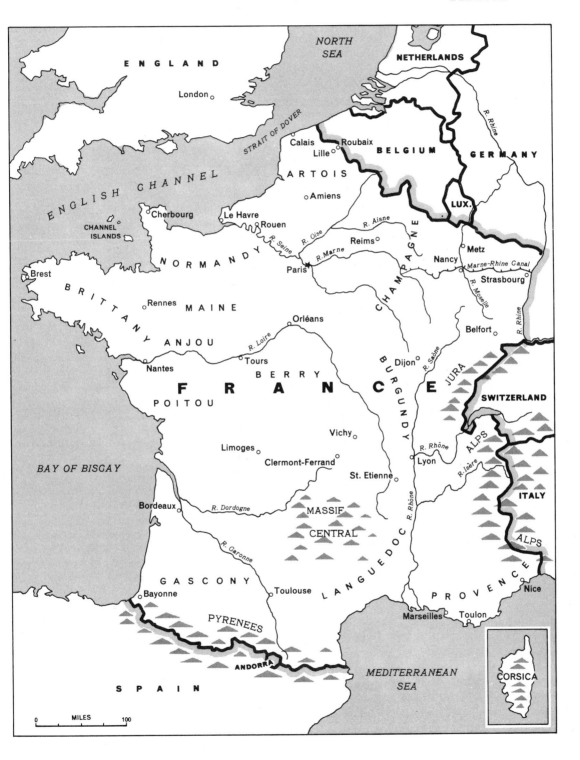

E N G L A N D

NORTH
SEA

NETHERLANDS

London

STRAIT OF DOVER

Calais   Roubaix
Lille

BELGIUM   GERMANY

ARTOIS

R. Rhine

Amiens

LUX.

E N G L I S H   C H A N N E L

Cherbourg   Le Havre
Rouen

CHANNEL
ISLANDS

R. Aisne

R. Oise

R. Seine

Reims

Metz

Nancy

C H A M P A G N E

R. Marne

Paris

Marne-Rhine Canal

Strasbourg

R. Moselle

N O R M A N D Y

Brest

B R I T T A N Y   M A I N E

Rennes

Orléans

R. Loire

Belfort

R. Rhine

BAY OF BISCAY

A N J O U

Nantes   Tours

B E R R Y

F R A N C E

P O I T O U

Vichy

Limoges

Clermont-Ferrand

St. Etienne

Bordeaux

R. Dordogne

MASSIF

CENTRAL

R. Garonne

G A S C O N Y

Bayonne

Toulouse

P Y R E N E E S

ANDORRA

S P A I N

B U R G U N D Y

Dijon

R. Saône

J U R A

SWITZERLAND

R. Rhône

Lyon

A L P S

R. Isère

ITALY

A L P S

L A N G U E D O C

R. Rhône

P R O V E N C E

Nice

Marseilles   Toulon

MEDITERRANEAN
SEA

CORSICA

R. Rhine

MILES
0   100

though varied, and its beauty and fertility have long been proverbial.

A variety of geographical influences have contributed to French national unity. At its farthest extremes the country is not much more than 600 miles across, and most of France lies within a few hours' train travel from Paris. With the exception of the Vosges Mountains (which separate Alsace from the rest of France) there are no barriers dividing one section of the country from another. On the contrary, the great river systems—the Seine, the Loire, the Rhône, the Gironde, the Garonne—link the coast with the interior regions and the different parts of the interior with one another. Certain uplands exist, as in Brittany and the *Massif Central* of south-central France, but they do not interfere with easy communication from south to north and west to east.

France's sense of national unity has also been encouraged by the existence of natural boundaries that cut it off from other lands. Of its six sides, three are bounded by water (the English Channel on the north, the Atlantic Ocean on the west, and the Mediterranean Sea on the south), and two by mountains (the Pyrenees in the south, and the Alps and the Jura Mountains in the east). Only on the northeastern frontier is there an absence of natural barriers. French history for centuries has been dominated by the struggle first to establish a northeastern boundary and then to maintain it against attack. On this frontier France has had to meet invasion three times in the last century. It is only in very recent years that firm cooperation between Western European countries has eliminated the fear of aggression.

Regional Variations

Despite its compactness, France is a land of many distinct regions and attitudes. Far more than in England, differences have survived in costume, dialect, and way of life. According to popular stereotypes, the dark-haired son of the Midi (the south of France) is noted for his eloquence, his excitability, his religious indifference, and his political radicalism; the blond Norman for his reticence, shrewdness, and conservatism; the Breton, for his mystical piety; and the Lorrainer for his steadfast patriotism.

More important are the political and economic contrasts. The north and northeast, where some 80 percent of French industry is concentrated, are politically conservative but economically progressive. The west, center, and southwest are politically to the left but slow in introducing economic innovations. But France's economic revolution is now bringing new industry to these latter areas, often under government stimulus, with a consequent lessening of the restrictive influence of small landholders and businessmen.

The People

Nationality

As in Great Britain, the earliest inhabitants of France of whom we have historical record (the Gauls) were Celts. As early as 600 B.C., however, the Greeks had founded a colony at Marseilles on the Mediterranean coast, and in the second and first centuries B.C. this region (whose modern name, Provence, is derived from the Latin word *provincia*) opened the way first to Roman influence and then to Roman conquest of all Gaul. But in contrast to Great Britain, where the Roman influence was neither profound nor permanent, Roman influence on France was both powerful and continuous. The Gallic peoples adjusted themselves to their conquerors with exceptional ease, and the impact of Roman language and law still is apparent. As a result, it is common to speak of France as a "Latin" country.

Early in the fifth century A.D. France was invaded and conquered by a succession of Germanic tribes—the Visigoths, the Burgundians, and the Franks—but the Teutonic conquerors did not, as in England, destroy the earlier way of life. The fighting in France between Celt and Teuton was less bitter than in England, and particularly in the southern half of the country the conquerors tended to accept the language, law, and religion of the people they conquered.

In the centuries that followed there were few infiltrations or additions of new blood. The Northmen who invaded Normandy quickly adopted the language and institutions of the natives, and only Brittany (which offered a haven to Celtic refugees from the British Isles) and Alsace (which was not acquired until the seventeenth century) contain a significant number of people who speak a language other than French. There are, however, a small Basque-speaking minority in the south and a small Flemish-speaking minority in the north. With the possible exception of Alsace (where the inhabitants, though generally loyal to France, continue to speak a Germanic dialect and at times press for a certain degree of autonomy), there is no problem in continental France of national minorities: the tension between people of different nationality, which has complicated the political life of such countries as Belgium, Czechoslovakia, Canada, and the Soviet Union, has no counterpart in French politics.

Population Trends

France's particular population problem has been its birth rate. In the days of Napoleon, France was the most populous European country apart from Russia. It was outstripped by Germany in 1870, by Great Britain at about the turn of the century, and even by Italy in 1930. While the rest of Europe experienced a phenomenal population increase, France suffered a steady decline in birth rate throughout the nineteenth century. To translate the end result into military terms: France, which had the same number of men of military age as Germany at the time of the Franco-Prussian War (1870), had less than half as many as Germany at the outbreak of World War II. Being also less urbanized and industrialized meant that France's economic power was much below that of its neighbor.

After World War II, however, the French population suddenly began to grow more rapidly than ever before in its recorded history— at a rate, moreover, considerably higher than those of several of its neighbors. The increase of 5 million from 1949 to 1954 was almost as great as the increase during the whole nineteenth century. By 1960 the proportion of young people in France had outstripped the proportion in West Germany—24.5 percent of the French population was under 15 as compared to 21.5 percent in West Germany. Indeed, even their numbers were greater. Today the increasing youthfulness of France's population is matched by the rapid modernization and rationalization of industry, a potentially powerful combination.

Religion

France, traditionally "the eldest daughter of the Church," is overwhelmingly Catholic. Of its 49 million inhabitants (1966), 40 million are, in some degree, attached to the Roman Catholic faith; fewer than a million are Protestant; some 300,000 are Jews; the rest are atheists or freethinkers. Potentially, at least, France provides a powerful basis for a political party promoting Catholic ideals and interests.

Yet if eight out of ten Frenchmen are Catholic in form, fewer than three in ten are deeply devoted to the interests of the Church. Most Frenchmen are Catholic in the sense that many Americans are Protestant: they attend the great church festivals, and they use their churches for baptisms, weddings, and funerals. But they resent the interference of the Church in politics, and it is not unusual for a Frenchman to be both Catholic and anticlerical.

Nevertheless, and in great contrast to Great Britain, where in recent generations religion has not been a major political issue, the position of the Catholic Church in France was until quite recently a subject of bitter political controversy. Before the Revolution of 1789 the Church was closely allied with the monarchical regime, which vigorously persecuted heresy (notably Protestantism) and religious and philosophical speculation. But this very persecution aroused the enmity of liberal intellectuals against the monarchy and against the Church as well. This enmity was slow to die. Restrictive pro-clerical measures under the Bourbon monarchy, a reaction to the excesses against the Church during the French Revolution, convinced many nineteenth-century Frenchmen that no one could be both a devout Catholic and a good republican. Although the latter years of that century saw a lessening of tension between the Church and the Republic, the Dreyfus Affair (see Chapter 2) and legislation separating Church and State revived the earlier bitterness. Thereafter and until World War II, the Church avoided overt political action. The fact, however, that Marshal Henri Pétain's Vichy regime, which appeared to collaborate with the Nazis, bestowed special privileges on the Church and that some of the highest church officials supported him again aroused republican suspicions.

Even after the war the relationship of the Catholic Church to French political life remained complex. With the liberation of France, Catholic leaders of the Resistance formed a new party, the *Mouvement Républicain Populaire* (MRP), of whose devotion to democracy and social progress there could be no doubt. Initially, the MRP captured over a quarter of the country's votes and was one of its three major parties. But the most troublesome of postwar religious issues, that of state subsidies to church schools (see Chapter 8), subsequently drove a wedge between the MRP and its natural allies on the left, helped to weaken the MRP itself, created crises in both the Fourth and Fifth Republics, and further complicated ideological divisions within France. Thus the religious issue in France in the past has disrupted the relations of groups with similar economic and social objectives in a way almost inconceivable to Americans or Britons.

The French Way of Life

Frenchmen are often portrayed as fiercely individualistic, argumentative and inflexible, bitter over distinctions of class and wealth, antiforeign, and resistant to change. André Siegfried wrote in 1930: "An anarchic individualism characterizes the Frenchman; he is hostile to the state; he is unwilling to associate himself with it; he does not want others to interfere with his affairs."

These characteristics have been somewhat modified by the recent impact of technology, radio and television, by growing affluence, the movement to the cities, increased travel, and the postwar flood of foreign products, which are still resented but universally displayed. Yet Frenchmen, and even more so, Frenchwomen, retain many of their traditional characteristics: their pride in France, particularly in French culture, language, art, and science; their independence, individual and national; their peasant mentality, which leads to an abhorrence of waste and a passion for concealing their wealth in order to avoid taxes; and their desire for perfection, whether in cooking, art, or the turn of a phrase.

Traditionally France has been a country of small farms and *paysans*. The 1962 census disclosed that 21 percent of the French working population were still farmers—as compared to 5 percent of the British and 6 percent of the American. Moreover, most French farms are still minute by American standards, with 79 percent under 50 acres and 56 percent under 25 acres; farms in the United States, in contrast, average over 300 acres. But the high costs of inefficient farming, coupled with the expansion of industry, are bringing to France the same changes that Great Britain and the United States underwent at an earlier period. Between 1954 and 1962, 1,300,000 Frenchmen left the land, reducing the percentage on farms from 28 to 21; in another decade it will be down to 15 percent. The few French farms over 1,000 acres in size and the 4 percent over 120 acres—those that can use mechanization efficiently and often draw cheap labor from Spain and Italy—are those that will reap the benefit of the great agricultural opportunities of the increasingly tariff-free Common Market of Western Europe (see Chapter 9). In the meantime, the French peasant protests, even riots against changes, but will soon no longer be the distinctive feature of French life.

This trend in agriculture is related to what is happening in industry. (Again we find similarities between what is taking place in France today and what took place earlier in the Anglo-Saxon countries.) The number of small craftsmen-employers in the towns has gone down by 25 percent since 1954. The number of independent traders is lower by 6 percent, although urban employment has increased by 9 percent. Between 1954 and 1962 those earning wages and salaries outside of farming increased by 1.6 million. At the same time there was a marked shift to employment in services (insurance, banking, trade) and away from traditional industries—like textiles, clothing and leather—and also, most dramatically, by 22 percent (204,000 workers) from mining to newer fields like building, chemicals and engineering, particularly electrical engineering.

These rapid shifts in occupation are a result of France's unprecedented economic growth after 1950. In the 12 years to 1962, total consumption (by 1956 prices) rose 76 percent, and consumption per capita rose about 57 percent. Since 1957, consumption has grown about 6 percent per annum. The transformation of French society is uneven, but it is clearly well under way. Moreover, the full impact on social mobility of the postwar population increase will be felt only in the coming decade.

Although France is being transformed from a semirural to an urbanized society, significant differences still persist between the character, size, and distribution of French cities and British cities. Few facts have affected French history more than the overwhelmingly dominant position of Paris, with its 8.5 million people (in 1965), almost 18 percent of the whole population. The other French cities are far less populous. France's second and third cities, Lyons and Marseilles, have just over 900,000 and 800,000 respectively; the next largest are Bordeaux and Lille, with under half a million. Only 12 other cities had a population greater than 250,000 in 1962. Thus there are no large cities outside the capital to act as counterpoles of attraction as there are in Great Britain.

As a result, Paris is the locus of a striking amount of the country's productive activity. Sixty-four percent of the country's companies have their head offices in Paris; one-quarter of all industrial workers, one-third of all college and graduate students, and 65 percent of all artists and writers are centered there.

Another marked feature of uneven distribution of wealth and activity in France lies in regional disparities: in particular, between the heavily industrialized northeast and the well-developed east on the one hand and the much less industrially advanced west, center, and south. The northeast has two advantages: its coal and iron deposits and its proximity to the heavily populated region around Paris. Within the northeast, which covers only 20 percent of the nation's territory, 38 percent of the population produces 46 percent of the country's industrial and agricultural output, and at a 25 percent higher productivity rate than the national average. In comparison, the western part of the country (the area west of a line drawn from Le Havre to Marseilles) is falling behind in agriculture and is experiencing relatively slight industrial development. The most recent French Plan (see Chapter 6) is intended to reduce this serious imbalance, but it will be a long-term process.

The political significance of France's uneven growth is masked by the diversity of support enjoyed by General de Gaulle. This support spans urban and rural areas and both the industrial northeast and the undeveloped west. The maps in Chapter 3 show some new voting alignments, but it is not clear how much these alignments result from the Gaullist mystique and how much from economic and social factors. Pockets of dissatisfaction show themselves from time to time in angry eruptions and demonstrations, almost always in the less-developed areas of the country, which were once staunchly Gaullist. In contrast, the Communists, who might be expected to thrive on discontent, continue to enjoy considerable support in sections of affluence and high development. In this period of political mobility, after the relative political apathy in the first years of the Fifth Republic, so many factors affect political attitudes that it is difficult as yet to generalize about the sympathies of its different groups.

Despite the rapid economic and social changes that are taking place in France, disparities in income and opportunity have not sharply segmented its population. In Great Britain the lines between farmer, worker, and professional and business middle class are relatively clear (though less so than they used to be). In France, however, many members of both the farming class and the working class are also middle class, in the sense that they own property, employ themselves, accumulate savings, and, unlike the workers to whom Marx appealed, have much more than their chains to lose. The ranks of the middle class also include the large number of Frenchmen who own their own shops and businesses, the professionals, and the increasingly large number of white-collar workers.

Clearly France, more than most modern countries, is dominated by a property-holding middle class, which, since the days of Aristotle, has been regarded as the foundation of social order and constitutional government. Thus, despite the response of one-fifth to one-quarter of all French voters to the appeal of the Communist party as a party of dissent (not only to those who are dissatisfied with their own lot but to those who cherish some high though vague goal of domestic or international perfection), France's unevenly developed but generally affluent society possesses great stability.

Interest Groups

To say that there is a strong middle class in France is not to say, however, that bitterness does not exist among and even within segments of society or that special-interest groups do not compete vigorously and often acrimoniously with one another. Frenchmen have a particular attachment, in fact, for whatever group they feel represents their own special interest or special point of view. This feeling has often led them, particularly under the Fifth Republic, to rely on pressure groups or their own direct action instead of what are demonstrably rather ineffective political parties. Thus latent tensions created by bitterness over inequalities in income between large and small businessmen, businessmen and labor, large farmers and landless tenants, or over policies toward Algeria have led from time to time to the sudden rise to prominence of such groups as the army, and to continuous pressure by trade unions, agricultural groups, and business associations.

The Army

The role of the army in France has been quite different from the role of the army in Great Britain or the United States. Either by active participation or by studious noninvolvement, the army has often turned the course of French history. The new national army of the Republic protected the nation from invasion, brought Napoleon I to power, and under his command marched across Europe imbued by ideological zeal. But under the Restoration and throughout the nineteenth century, the army was used to suppress social upheavals and became the guardian of order rather than the defender of freedom. Yet, though the army supported Napoleon III in his revival of the Empire, it did not promote General Boulanger's abortive attempt to overthrow the Third Republic in 1889 nor aid Marshal Pétain in 1940. In 1958, however, the army's open support of General de Gaulle was a major contribution to the demise of the Fourth Republic.

Humiliated and defeated in Indo-China by 1954, the army struggled for seven years to keep Algeria French. During those years, however, the French public became increasingly outraged by the brutality the army used against partisan bands and French liberals in Algeria. Many senior army officers, from their side, became infused with a political passion to keep Algeria French. When they realized that de Gaulle, far from advancing the purpose for which they had supported him, intended to give Algeria independence, they mutinied, in April, 1961. Later, others attempted de Gaulle's assassination. But even those who unwillingly accepted the army's withdrawal from Algeria to France posed a great danger to the nation, from which the military appeared to have become chronically alienated.

De Gaulle's foreign policy has been molded in large measure by the priority he has given to the task of controlling and then reintegrating the army into France. His reaction to the 1961 mutiny was swift, stern, and decisive. Nine generals and eight other high officers were tried and convicted by the High Military Tribunal. The Ministry of the Armed Forces was put under the direction of trusted Gaullists, and the General Staff was overhauled. But de Gaulle also believes that the only way to keep the army permanently out of politics is to preoccupy it fully with its professional task of protecting France. Hence he insists on equipping the army with the most up-to-date and powerful weapons, including the independent nuclear deterrent. Thirty years earlier General de Gaulle had written that the French army needed new morale, a precise function, and, the prerequisite for both, effective equipment. To provide them has been one of his most congenial tasks. Whatever the impact of this policy on international relations, it may have saved the unity of France.

Organized Labor

Compared to the dramatic role of the army in French politics between 1958 and 1961, the activities of more orthodox interest groups may seem tame. Yet in the postwar years these groups played highly influential roles in French life that at times seemed almost as decisive.

The leading organization of French workers has long been the *Confédération Générale du Travail* (CGT). Traditionally, this organization, in accordance with the independence that characterized the old French working class, had held aloof from politics and, unlike the British trade unions, had refused to identify itself with any political party. Instead, the union put its trust in "direct economic action," confident that the general strike, in particular, constituted a more effective weapon than any amount of parliamentary chatter. Following the foundation of a French Communist party in 1920, however, those workers who were under Communist influence seceded from the CGT and formed the *Confédération Générale du Travail Unitaire* (CGTU), which maintained an independent existence until 1935 when, as part of the Popular Front movement for common action of all leftists against fascism, the two labor organizations were reunited.

During the Pétain regime in unoccupied France from June 1940 to November 1942 (see Chapter 2) this organization like other workers' organizations was banned, but its members regrouped themselves underground and emerged after the Liberation, unchanged in name and with a larger membership and greater power than before. There was, however, an extremely important change in the nature of the resurrected CGT, for during its years as an illegal organization the Communists had succeeded in capturing control. Under their leadership, the union dropped its old attitude of noninterference in politics. Communist leaders explained that the economic powers of the government were now so great that the unions could not refrain from attempting to guide it. However, anti-Communists charged that another motive was at least as important: the desire to use the trade unions as a weapon for the Communist party's own political purposes.

At first glance, the relationship between the Communist party and organized labor might not seem very different from the relationship of the Labor party and British trade unions. In reality, there is a fundamental difference. The British trade unions look on the Labor party as an instrument for the peaceful attainment of economic reform; the party is useful to the unions only to the extent that it can persuade a large part of the electorate voluntarily to vote for its candidates and program. But in France the position of party and unions is reversed. The party controls the CGT and uses it as a weapon to coerce the voters who might not otherwise accept the Communist candidates and program.

In the fall of 1947 the Communist party called

what was virtually a general strike, ostensibly to bolster a legitimate demand for higher wages, but actually to force a change in government and to prevent France from cooperating with the European Recovery Program as proposed by U.S. Secretary of State George Marshall. Only the government's decisive measures to maintain order, the good sense of French workers, and the opposition to the strikes by the moderate reformist wing of the CGT prevented the plan from succeeding. In December 1947 a large number of workers, including both those who were sympathetic to the Socialist party and those who wished to return to the old nonpartisan tradition, broke away from the CGT and formed a new organization, the *Confédération Générale du Travail—Force Ouvrière* (FO—Workers' Force). Nonetheless, the CGT at the behest of the Communist party launched a second crippling strike in October–November 1948, this time concentrated on the coal mines. Once again courageous action by the government, combined with the support of other workers, proved that the Communists could not dominate the nation's economy. But though this experience reduced Communist influence within France as a whole and particularly within the labor movement, the CGT has remained the dominant organization among industrial workers; in not a single basic industry has its supremacy been shaken.

The French trade union movement is now divided into one major, two minor, and several smaller groups. The CGT, with its nearly two million members (in 1946 it had 5.5 million), is by far the largest and, indeed, has more members than all French political parties put together. The much less numerous Catholic trade unions are strongest among white-collar workers in private industry. Originally united in the *Confédération Française des Travailleurs Chrétiens* (CFTC—French Confederation of Christian Workers), they are now split between a very small union that keeps the original name to preserve the reference to Christianity, and a larger union that has replaced the word Christian by Democratic (CFTD). Still smaller is the *Force Ouvrière*, which includes most unionized civil servants and state-employed workers. Both the FO and CFTD insist they are not allied to a particular political party, but they are inevitably associated with the Socialist party and the MRP respectively. Thus, in practice, they lose both the influence that British trade unions possess through affiliation and the influence that American trade unions possess through their political independence.

One of the most widely unionized groups in the country is that of the teachers, some 80 percent of whom are represented in the Autonomous Teachers Union. Between 40 and 50 percent of civil servants are unionized. But in total, and particularly when compared with Great Britain, France has a relatively small percentage of trade unionists. Moreover, the continued adherence to worn-out myths of class warfare, and the control of the CGT by the Communists, have led the workers' movement into an essentially negative role. Prosperity seems to have done little to change this situation. A new generation that is free of the historical stereotypes of exploitation may be necessary before French labor can assume the forward-looking attitudes now prevalent in so much of the rest of the economy.

Organized Farmers

In agriculture, traditionally a far more individualistic occupation, attempts have been made to produce a counterpart to the organization of industrial workers. Before World War II certain pressure groups promoted the interests of particular types of agricultural producers—winegrowers, sugar beet growers, and so forth—but there was no single powerful channel for the exercise of the farmers' political influence. Following the Liberation, an association of large farmers was formed under Socialist leadership; it became the postwar *Confédération Générale de l'Agriculture* (CGA). It had a brief political success in 1951 when 27 of its leaders were among the 59 farmers who became rightist deputies; the farmer-deputies temporarily occupied a strategic position from which they could control the destinies of any center coalition. By November 1951, however, the Peasant group had split, and its days of particular prominence were over. Less politically oriented than the CGA (which no longer exists) is the *Fédération National des Syndicats d'Exploitants Agricoles* (FNSEA), which is more important than was the former as a farmers' association but takes no stand on other than agricultural issues.

Temporarily significant was the effort of the extreme rightists, the Poujadists, in the later years of the Fourth Republic to enroll small farm-owners and landless tenants in their protest movement against economic change. Changing their name from *Union de Défense des Commerçants et Artisans* to *Union et Fraternité Française,* the Poujadists posed briefly as champions of the more stagnant areas of French agriculture. Poujade's rapidly diminishing political influence coincided with improved agricultural conditions. But French agriculture is still far from healthy, and angry farmers often demonstrate fiercely against government policies to develop more efficient agriculture.

Organized Business

Much more united than French farmers, and even more so than French labor, are French employers. But the progression which led to the present efficiently organized employers association, the *Conseil National du Patronat Français* (CNPF), was a slow one. The ineffectiveness of the original employers association, the *Confédération Générale de la Production Française* (CGPF), established in 1919 in response to government urging, became obvious in June 1936 when political pressures from the Popular Front and a wave of sit-down strikes forced employers to conclude the humiliating "Matignon Agreement" with the CGT. This agreement transformed what had been technical rights into genuine protection of the kind normal in an industrial state: freedom for workers to organize and bargain collectively, minimum wages, the forty-hour week, and holidays with pay. Its disclosure of out-of-date working conditions, and the inefficiency of the CGPF, led to demands for tighter organization. Although it proved impossible to develop any genuine unity of policy among employers prior to the Fourth Republic, organized business was strong enough to prevent any further advances by labor before the war.

Scornful of the vacillations of parliamentary government in the Third Republic, the French business community as a whole supported the Vichy regime, particularly in its early stages, and approved its emphasis on labor discipline and a government-directed economy. As a result of this apparent collaboration with Vichy, organized business was virtually ostracized during the early days of the Liberation. The cohesion employers had developed during the war aided them, however, in organizing the CNPF in the first half of 1946, while their wartime experience predisposed them to a controlled economy dominated by businessmen.

The CNPF is a loose, decentralized federation of trade associations, but its executive body is capable of swift and decisive action in the interests of employers. Its tactics do not differ distinctively from those of other pressure groups. The CNPF has not demonstrated, however, such forward-looking attitudes as have either British or American employers' associations. It tends rather to act defensively and in short- rather than long-range terms. Thus, though French heavy industry and large-scale business have achieved a remarkable degree of prosperity and economic progress in recent years, there has been a continuation of the mutual suspicion of capital and labor that has long bedeviled French society and reached a stage of dangerous tension under the Fourth Republic.

The vigorous economic and financial policies of the de Gaulle government have built on the economic accomplishments of the Fourth Republic. Despite their efforts through the Poujadist movement, small, inefficient enterprises had proved unable to slow up the process of change, even though at times they threatened the political structure of the country. Today, even small business is convinced of the value of the freer economy of the Fifth Republic and the Common Market. It is doubtful that the growing sense of mutual interest between large and small enterprises, and between employers and employees, is yet strong enough to stand the strain of a serious economic reverse. Nevertheless, continued prosperity is likely to strengthen harmonious relations.

The National Economy

Despite strains, pressures, and disparities in growth among and within regions, the French national economy is remarkably strong. This is the more striking because it had been virtually static in the years before World War II. The original credit for the improvement must be given to Marshall aid. Subsequently, government planning for economic growth has been supported by its judicious injections of capital into selected areas of the economy. More recently the Common Market and other external arrangements have provided considerable stimulus. The results of these efforts and opportunities have been that industrial production has risen decisively, diversification has become common, French products can now compete with those of France's neighbors, and the nation enjoys a comfortable trade surplus.

France's large measure of self-sufficiency has made it easier for its government to plan for economic growth than it is for the British government. The French economy benefits from an unusual balance between industry and agriculture. In addition, France is rich in certain resources: it produces 9.7 percent of the world's supply of bauxite (the principal ore of aluminum); it is the world's third-largest producer of iron ore (after the U.S.S.R. and the U.S.); and it is the world's leading exporter of potash.

Despite these advantages and France's remarkable recent advances in production and distribution, there are still problems for its economy. A larger and better-trained labor force is needed. It is proving difficult to persuade backward areas of the country to accept new techniques and the dislocations that accompany them. What has already been accomplished, however, makes it clear that France's economic growth is sound and that French prosperity is likely to become more evenly distributed as industrialization proceeds.

3. ORGANS OF POLITICAL OPINION

The Press

In France, as in Great Britain, the chief source of political information and analysis is the press. In France, however, there is a sharper distinction between what is called the "press of information" and the "press of opinion." The former devotes itself ostensibly to reporting events, to entertaining its readers, and to providing literary and artistic criticism. The press of opinion, in contrast, consists of the journals of political parties and makes little pretense of being objective.

The Prewar Press

In the years before World War II the ethical standards of the French press were low. Many, indeed, attributed the collapse of French morale and of the government itself, in the summer of 1940, to the press's insidious work.

Unlike British newspapers, many of which (largely because of income from advertising) are highly profitable enterprises, the French press has always had difficulty supporting itself. In the prewar period many newspapers sought other sources of revenue. Large economic interests, such as the *Comité des Forges* (an organization of the great iron and steel manufacturers), subsidized individual newspapers. Foreign governments at times spent large sums to influence the French press in favor of their policies, and the French government itself was known to use "secret funds" to win the support of influential papers.

The Postwar Press

Following the Nazi victory in 1940, some newspapers ceased publication, some collaborated actively with the Germans, some tried to continue publication while cooperating with the authorities as little as possible, and some published underground. After the Liberation, those newspapers that had published beyond a certain date during the German Occupation were suspended or condemned, and a special commission was set up to lease their property to authorized newcomers. Moreover, in response to the urging of leftist parties that "the reign of money" must not be allowed to return, newspapers were restricted to certain forms of income. Political parties were allowed to subsidize newspapers, but nonparty newspapers were required to support themselves by sales, advertising, job printing, and similar methods.

For a time these restrictions plus the general interest in political events gave the party press the largest circulation. But as interest in politics diminished, the party press, especially of the left-wing, suffered. By the spring of 1948, four of the ten Communist dailies had ceased publication. In 1953 *Ce Soir* went off the stands, and

L'Humanité became the only important Communist daily left. The Socialists have had to struggle hard to save their great Paris daily, *Le Populaire.* The left-wing daily *Libération,* founded clandestinely in 1941 in Vichy France, closed in November 1964. *Combat,* the most brilliant journalistic offspring of the Resistance, has survived only because a group of businessmen took it over in 1961.

Though private money once more plays a significant role in the French press, France has few press lords in the British sense. Most of the money to finance papers comes from other sources. *France-Soir,* a Gaullist paper which has the largest circulation of all French dailies (1,250,000 in 1966) is associated with the firm of Hachette, the dominant distributor of papers and books. Two of the main Parisian dailies, *Le Figaro* (500,000) and *L'Aurore* (425,000), independent and moderate rightist respectively, receive support from the textile industry. Only with the greatest difficulty was *Le Monde* (300,000), the pride of French journalism, able to resist the efforts of a group of businessmen to take it over. By giving shares to the editorial staff, *Le Monde* now ensures its editor tenure for as long as his staff supports him.

Government pressures, and outright coercion, have also harassed the left-wing press and, under the Fifth Republic, the right-wing press as well. During the Algerian war the government frequently seized issues of dailies and weeklies that contained unpalatable comments or news. Between 1955 and 1962 there were over two hundred seizures in mainland France and many more in Algeria. The Socialist-led government of Guy Mollet (1956–57) attacked weeklies of the democratic left and even tried to put pressure on *Le Monde* by threatening to withdraw state-controlled advertising, a very significant source of revenue. The Fifth Republic has been no less restrictive, particularly by an unprecedented use of an old law that makes it possible to punish certain kinds of attacks on the head of state.

Whenever the press has stood together against government efforts to exert or extend control, the authorities have backed down. United press opposition stopped Premier Debré's attempt in 1960 to force the chief French news agency, *Agence France-Presse,* to submit to closer government supervision. At that time, following widespread protests, the government disavowed rumors of a "reform" of the press laws. But only *Le Monde* has consistently condemned seizures of newspapers, whether of the left or of the right, and not until March 1965 did the French Publishers' Association speak out against government censorship of books.

Although many Frenchmen read a wide range of newspapers, the total circulation of dailies is proportionately lower than in either Great Britain or the United States. Greater Paris, with its 8.5 million people, has 12 dailies with a circulation of just over 4.5 million. Metropolitan New York, with over 10.5 million people, has fewer dailies—four in all—but they have a total circulation of over 12.5 million. London far outstrips both. The provincial press in France, on the other hand, with its 95 dailies, some 20 of which cover large areas, is much more significant than is the provincial press of Britain and commands over 60 percent of the total daily circulation in the country. Most of the editorial matter in the provincial newspapers comes from Paris, it is true, but the Paris press itself is no longer so widely read as before World War II.

The Paris Press

In the shifting pattern of press popularity, the press of opinion, especially left-wing opinion, has suffered the greatest losses. *L'Humanité*, the official Communist newspaper, which had over half a million circulation in May 1946, had leveled off at about 180,000 by 1966. The Socialist journal *Le Populaire*, which sold a quarter of a million copies a day in 1946, has had a hard time maintaining a circulation of 13,000. Even *La Nation*, however, the organ of the ruling Gaullist UNR party, could sell only 20,000 copies a day in 1966, an indication that Frenchmen are tired of partisan papers. *La Croix*, a liberal Catholic paper, has fared better, but its circulation of 133,000 (1966) was below what it was in 1951.

Next in circulation to *France-Soir* in 1966 was *Le Parisien Libéré* (915,000), which is independent and right of center. It is followed by *Le Figaro* and *L'Aurore*, the Gaullist *Paris-Jour* (350,000), and *Paris-Presse* (97,000). Thus apart from *L'Humanité*, *La Croix*, and *Le Monde*, the most substantial circulations are of rightist papers.

By far the most outstanding paper in France (some say in Europe) is *Le Monde*, the nearest equivalent to the *Times* of London. The completeness and accuracy of its news, its brilliant, sometimes witty, political analyses, its hospitality to nonconformist views, its restrained reporting of unpalatable realities, and the excellence of its foreign correspondents attract a wide group of influential readers. Half of its readers are said to be professional people, businessmen, high administrators, and political figures. Alone among Paris dailies, *Le Monde* has a substantial circulation outside the capital: some 80,000 in the provinces and 20,000 in North Africa.

Radio and Television

The brilliant use of radio and television made by the candidates in the presidential campaign in 1965 vastly accelerated the political and newscasting importance of these media. Though since mid-1964 they have been technically a public utility—*l'Office de la Radiodiffusion et Télévision Française* (ORTF)—the Fifth Republic, like earlier regimes, has used them without restraint to advance the purposes of its leaders. Thus it has staged presidential news conferences, or limited or ignored the speeches of opposition leaders, when these tactics suited government purposes.

As with party leaders in Great Britain, however, all the presidential candidates in 1965 were given radio and television time during the two weeks of the official campaign. Senator Jean Lecanuet, ex-President of the MRP, used his time to present the issues to the voters with such skill that he drew de Gaulle into an unplanned degree of active campaigning on these media. Moreover, after the election public figures from all the parties continued to receive an opportunity to present their special points of view.

Actively competing with the official French radio are Radio Luxembourg, the Saar's Europe No. 1 station, Radio Monte Carlo, and the BBC (which retains its wartime popularity, particularly in newscasts). These stations are said to have won over a high proportion of French listeners to their more popular programs. French television has a monopoly, however, and at least half the French population can be reached through the six million or more TV sets now in use.

The French government justifies its partisan use of programs by citing the press support enjoyed by the opposition. Yet the bias of the French media is in marked contrast to the political impartiality of British radio and television.

The Effect of French Organs of Opinion

A particular virtue of the French press in relation to democratic government used to be the fact that most of the major political groups and interests of France possessed their own organs of opinion. As a result, especially in Paris, the reader had a greater choice of papers and opinions than does the average Englishman. Foreigners were often bewildered and frustrated by the lack of objectivity of most French newspapers. The Frenchman knows, however, that party papers are political weapons and that he must adjust himself to the bias of the particular paper he reads.

Nonetheless, the sharp drop in the circulation of the party press suggests that Frenchmen became bored in their reading, as in their politics, by excessive partisanship. They also grew weary of the excessive conformity of the press. Yet there are encouraging signs in radio, television, and the press that these organs of opinion are responding to the new spirit of political questioning that appeared in the 1965 campaign for the presidency. Thus, as with so much else in France, the organs that mold political opinion are themselves being molded by change.

2. The French Political Heritage

1. ANTECEDENTS OF THE REPUBLIC

Perhaps the most striking difference between the political history of France since 1789 and that of Great Britain and the United States in the same period is the lack of constitutional continuity. Since the Glorious Revolution of 1688 Great Britain has had no political revolution and has made no violent change in its government. Since 1789 the United States has had only one constitution and has had no successful rebellion. But the story of modern France is largely one of recurrent revolutions and threats of revolution. In contrast to Anglo-American political continuity, France since 1789 has had eleven constitutions: three constitutional monarchies, two empires, one semidictatorship, and five republics. Moreover, most of these changes have been effected by violence. Thus it is not unnatural that talk of achieving further change by revolution seems far more realistic in France than in the United States or Great Britain, and that the French take their political institutions far less for granted than do the other great democracies.

Such frequent and drastic changes inevitably have had a profound influence on the nature of French politics. In order to understand contemporary France, therefore, it is essential to have some knowledge of the earlier regimes.

The Heritage of the "Ancien Régime"

Modern France's chief inheritance from the ancient monarchy is the tradition of a highly centralized, hierarchical administration, a tradition that is all the stronger because of the long and painful struggle required for its establishment. The power of the medieval Kings of France was far more severely restricted than that of their English counterparts. For many years the frequent wars with England (culminating in the Hundred Years' War, from 1337 to 1435) divided the country; and even after the invaders had been expelled, the French King was unable to exercise effective authority over such powerful nobles as the Dukes of Burgundy and Brittany. Louis XI (1461–83), through the skillful, Machiavellian use of his power, reduced their authority substantially. But throughout the sixteenth century great nobles (frequently identifying themselves with the Protestant party in the wars of religion) intrigued and fought against the royal authority. Only in the seventeenth century did a succession of great ministers of the King—Richelieu (who crushed the last vestiges of Protestant military power and political autonomy), Mazarin, and Colbert—unify the country politically and establish a centralized administrative hierarchy that was dependent solely upon the authority of the King. Today it is still popular to say that, whatever else has changed in France, the system of monarchical administration still is recognizable. That system has been transformed, however, under the Fourth and Fifth Republics into a modern, efficient technocracy.

The *ancien régime* also had an important negative influence upon succeeding governments by impeding and delaying the growth of a tradition either of constitutionalism or of parliamentarism. During the Middle Ages there had been a strong belief both in France and England that the King's power was subject to the inherited customs and law of the kingdom. But in the seventeenth century the Kings of France, partly through the use of the great military force needed to defend and extend the land frontier, established the kind of divine right monarchy that the dazzled Stuart monarchs had tried in vain to introduce in England.

The Middle Ages had also seen the growth of an embryonic French parliament, the Estates General, representing the nobility, the clergy, and the growing middle class. This body, however, met only when summoned by the King, and from 1614 to 1789 it was not summoned at all. In consequence, when the French people finally overthrew the monarchy, they had none of the experience in the conduct of parliamentary institutions and in self-government that made possible the orderly supplanting of the royal authority in England. Early nineteenth-century attempts to introduce a parliamentary system based on the British pattern failed: the experience, customs, and habits of mind essential to the success of such institutions could not be carried across the Channel with them.

The keeping of social peace in France was impeded by another characteristic of the ancient monarchy: the maintenance of a sharp distinction between the nobility and the middle class. In Great Britain the younger sons of the nobility regularly became "commoners," and the most distinguished of the commoners often acquired titles. Consequently, the nobility and the upper-middle class were far from hostile. But in France, class lines were maintained with considerable strictness, and the privileges of the nobility (which seemed unjustified once the nobility abandoned the rigors of military service for a pleasant but parasitic life at court) aroused great resentment.

As the middle class grew more numerous, more prosperous, and better educated, it regarded with ever increasing animus the high taxes (from which the nobility were exempt), the financial ineptitude of the government, the class barriers to careers in the army and administration, the absence of organs for the representation and defense of their economic and political interests, the restrictions on industry and trade, the arbitrary exercise of the royal authority, and the limitations on freedom of thought, expression, and political action. Thus the Revolution of 1789 was a violent reaction of the middle classes against many of the outstanding characteristics of the monarchy—but a reaction which, by its very violence, produced what

has proved to be an enduring cleavage in French national political life.

The Revolutionary Heritage

The great French Revolution started out, in 1789, as an attempt to reform the monarchy; it ended, in 1792 and 1793, by abolishing the monarchy and executing the King. As the Revolution advanced, it was marked not only by foreign war and by civil strife between Royalists and Revolutionists but by a struggle among the Revolutionists themselves. A Reign of Terror followed in which the Revolution devoured many of its own children—first those who had been more moderate and finally the terrorists themselves. In 1795, in reaction against both the excesses and the idealism of the preceding years, power was entrusted to the five-man Directory, a government characterized by weakness, mediocrity, and corruption. There was little popular desire to defend so uninspiring a regime when Napoleon Bonaparte, one of the distinguished generals of the Revolutionary armies, attacked it, proclaimed the Consulate (with himself as First Consul) in 1799, made himself Consul for life in 1802, and established an empire (with himself as Emperor) in 1804.

But if the life of the First French Republic was short, agitated, and bloody, it had enduring consequences. The work of unifying the country was completed by sweeping away all internal economic barriers and by proclaiming the French Republic to be, in the famous phrase, "one and indivisible." Moreover, this unity found a powerful spiritual reinforcement in the growth of a fervent sentiment of national patriotism, symbolized in the *Marseillaise* and the deep attachment to the tricolored flag which, at least until the Popular Front of the mid-1930's, overrode the divisions of religion, class, political outlook, and economic interest.

In addition, the Revolution abolished the reign of privilege and established, as an enduring principle of French government, the "career open to talent." The partial destruction and division of the great estates of the nobility and the Church helped to create the powerful, property-owning rural middle class in which the Republic, in later generations, was to find its strongest support. And the noble, if unrealized, aspiration toward political liberty and self-government, as expounded in the Declaration of the Rights of Man and of the Citizen, provided an ideal and a precedent for subsequent, and more successful, struggles for human freedom.

The Influence of the Empire

Napoleon's success in destroying the Republic led to one stream of thought in France that was marked by the fear of any strong leadership and by a certain distrust of even the people themselves as a bulwark of democracy. Each of Napoleon's successive usurpations was ratified in plebiscites by an overwhelming majority of the people; and it was evident that the great majority of Frenchmen were ready to exchange a perilous liberty for personal security, political order, and military glory.

Yet if Napoleon destroyed the Republic, subverted political liberty, and concentrated unlimited power in his own hands (and in this sense was a forerunner of modern totalitarian dictators), it was not forgotten that he also maintained and consolidated many of the social and economic gains of the Revolution: the elimination of privileges based on class, the destruction of provincial barriers to trade, the freeing of the people from feudal tithes and duties, and the distribution of property among the peasants. Moreover, he added certain contributions of his own. His codification of the law and reorganization of the administration determined the form of two institutions that remained essentially unchanged through all the political vicissitudes of the coming generations and that have had a profound effect upon French political life. De Gaulle's semiautocratic leadership in the Fifth Republic has been both criticized and endorsed for much the same reasons.

Experiments with Constitutional Monarchy

The defeat of Napoleon in 1814 and 1815 and the restoration of the Bourbon monarchy under Louis XVIII provided France with its second opportunity to develop constitutional monarchy and parliamentary government on the British pattern. The ancient nobility and the higher clergy, however, were reluctant to adjust themselves to the new political code. The accession of Charles X in 1824 inaugurated an era of re-

action that precipitated the revolution of July 1830 and the substitution of a new monarch, Louis Philippe of the House of Orleans.

The new "citizen king" was pledged to constitutional government and to moderate policies, but there was still no clear acceptance of the principle of ministerial responsibility and, therefore, of popular supremacy; further, the Orleanist monarchy's prosecution of its political opponents was taken as additional proof that monarchy could not be reconciled, as in Great Britain, either with political liberty or with democratic government. In 1848, with surprising ease, the King was dethroned and France began its second republican experiment.

The Second Republic

The life of the Second Republic was short and agitated. From the very beginning, there appeared a cleavage between the moderate men of the middle class who favored republican government but feared social upheaval, and the radical working class of Paris, which was primarily responsible for the Revolution. The two elements came to blows in the bloody "June days" of 1848, and the moderates, who controlled the government and who were supported by the provinces (which looked upon "red Paris" with great distrust), triumphed over their opponents.

Their victory, however, was short-lived. In the presidential election of December 1848 the candidates of both moderate and radical republicans were overwhelmed by the tremendous popular vote for Louis Napoleon Bonaparte, the nephew of the great Napoleon—whose orderly and glorious government appeared in retrospect as something of a golden age. Imitating his uncle, "Napoleon the Little" in December 1851 dissolved the legislative assembly, seized its leaders, and won the consent of the people (in each case by an overwhelming vote), first to an extension of the presidential term of office to ten years and then to the establishment of an empire to be ruled by Louis Napoleon under the title of Napoleon III.

Thus for the second time a Republic that lacked internal cohesion was overthrown by a strong, popular leader with monarchical ambitions.

The Second Empire

The first years of imperial government were marked by the vigorous persecution of political opponents and the concentration of great power in the person of the Emperor. Yet it was symbolic of the cleavage between those who were interested primarily in political liberty and those who were chiefly devoted to social justice that certain socialists supported the Empire in its early years in the hope that it would introduce economic and social reforms.

As popular dissatisfaction with the imperial government increased, an attempt was made to transform the regime into a "liberal empire," although the problem of whether a Ministry's first responsibility was to the legislature or to the Emperor was never clearly resolved. The disastrous Franco-Prussian War of 1870 intervened before the new constitutional experiment could be carried very far. In September a new revolt in Paris overthrew the government and established the Third Republic.

Thus the agitated years between 1815 and 1870 had brought no clear agreement on fundamental political principles and institutions; if anything, the political problem had grown more complicated. The supporters of both monarchical and republican government were divided among themselves into supporters of Bourbons, Orleans, and Bonapartes, those who favored a moderate republic, and those who favored radical social reform. Yet there was one gain: each of the different regimes had experimented with some form of parliament. Thus, even though the problem of the relation of executive to legislature had never been worked out, a considerable degree of familiarity with parliamentary institutions had been gained, and the new Republic could draw upon a valuable store of political and parliamentary experience.

2. THE POLITICAL HERITAGE OF THE THIRD AND FOURTH REPUBLICS

Early Crises of the Third Republic

For many years after the collapse of the Empire, the life of the Republic was anything but secure. The first elections actually resulted in the victory of a royalist majority; and it was only because the monarchists could not agree which king to restore that the Republic, more or less by default, was permitted to survive. In addition, in 1871, the city of Paris, which had precipitated every successful revolution since 1789, again revolted and established a government known as the Commune. This time, however, the revolt was mercilessly crushed, and the very vigor with which the provisional government suppressed the Communards reassured the mass of non-Parisian voters that a republican government could also be conservative and stable. Yet the new prestige of the Republic was purchased at the price of bitter hatred, and the memory of the martyrs of the Commune is still cherished by Paris workers.

It was not until 1875 that France acquired the makeshift constitution under which the country lived, somewhat to its own surprise, until 1940—a far longer period of existence than any other French constitution. The new constitution was really a series of three laws—on the organization of the public powers, the organization of the Senate, and the relations among the public powers—passed by a combination of republicans and moderate royalists who were tired of long delay, eager for some kind of definite political order, and willing to compromise on a set of laws that could easily be adapted to a restored monarchy. According to these laws, a bicameral parliament was set up consisting of a Chamber of Deputies to be elected by universal suffrage and a Senate chosen by indirect election. The two chambers meeting in joint session (under the title of National Assembly) had the power to elect a President of the Republic for a term of seven years. When each chamber had adopted a resolution to that effect, the National Assembly could amend the constitutional laws by a majority vote. Ministers were collectively responsible to the chambers for the general policy of the government, and individually responsible for their personal acts. With the consent of the Senate, the President could dissolve the Chamber of Deputies before the expiration of its term of office (four years) and call new elections.

The Sixteenth of May

It was not long before these laws met their first severe test. The President of the Republic, Marshal Marie de MacMahon, was a royalist and a strong partisan of the Church. When the Chamber of Deputies (of which the republicans had control) passed an anticlerical resolution, MacMahon rebuked the Chamber. On the famous Sixteenth of May, 1877, Premier Jules Simon resigned in protest, as MacMahon had hoped he would. When the President appointed a pro-clerical Ministry that lacked the confidence of the Chamber of Deputies, he was felt to have attacked parliamentary principles; and when he proceeded to dissolve the Chamber of Deputies, with the consent of a bare majority of the Senate, many believed that the Republic was in extreme danger. MacMahon's supporters were decisively beaten, and in 1879 the President resigned his office.

The episode had an enduring effect on the Third Republic. From that time on, the dissolution of parliament in case of disagreement between the Ministry and the parliamentary majority was not considered to be a normal part of the parliamentary process, as it has been in Great Britain, but rather as a weapon that would be used only by a potential destroyer of the Republic.

MacMahon's successor, Jules Grévy (1879–87), was authentically republican and sufficiently colorless to prevent anyone from fearing his aspirations. During his period of office the Republic further strengthened itself by instituting a system of universal, free, and lay education, which was intended to be secular and neutral toward religion. In practice, however, the teaching was ardently republican, and the survival of the Republic was often attributed to its prowess in the battle for the minds of the children.

The Boulanger Episode

The colorlessness as well as the corruption of the Grévy administration explain to some extent the phenomenal growth in popularity, in 1886, of General Georges Boulanger, the Minister of War, a young man of dashing appearance but questionable character. Having won dramatic expressions of support in different parts of France, Boulanger finally succeeded in sweeping the city of Paris, the old stronghold of radical republicanism. When his friends urged him to overthrow the government by force, however, his nerve failed, he fled the country, and in 1891 he committed suicide on the grave of his mistress. While this fiasco made Royalists and clericals appear absurd, good republicans shuddered at the thought of what an able adversary might have done with the opportunities Boulanger had squandered.

The Dreyfus Affair

In 1892 Pope Leo XIII called upon French Catholics to accept the republican government, but unfortunately such efforts at reconciliation (which might have simplified French politics by eliminating the religious issue) were doomed by the crisis known as the Dreyfus Affair.

A financial scandal involving high government officials and Jewish bankers had shaken the Republic and raised the issue of anti-Semitism. To this fire, fuel was added by word that a young Jewish army captain, Alfred Dreyfus, had been found guilty of selling military information to Germany and had been condemned to imprisonment on Devil's Island. By an extraordinary series of coincidences and accidents, however, Dreyfus' family and friends learned that top officers of the French army knew that the real culprit was not Dreyfus but probably a cosmopolitan adventurer, Major Charles Esterhazy, the nephew of General Walsin. Largely to conceal the corruption, intrigues, and chaos that ruled in the Ministry of War, officers had connived to suppress and ultimately to forge evidence against Dreyfus.

The charges against the army created a national crisis. Most royalists, clericals, militarists, and superpatriots, as well as those who hated Jews, Protestants, and foreigners, felt that an attack on the army was an attack on France itself, and that it was far better that an innocent Jew should suffer than that the integrity of military commanders should be questioned. Most of the staunch republicans, the anticlericals, and the socialists saw the struggle as one between intolerance and reaction on the one side, and justice and liberty on the other. Intellectuals like the writers Émile Zola and Anatole France and the painter Claude Monet, together with many scholars and teachers, deserted their studies and studios and joined with such practical politicians as Clemenceau and Jean Jaurès to clear Dreyfus' name.

Esterhazy and the forger, Henry, ultimately confessed, and Dreyfus was liberated and restored to the army. Even so, many anti-Drey-fusards refused to believe the evidence or insisted quite frankly that justice was less important than order and national power. Thus the case intensified divisions that had seemed on the point of lessening.

The Anticlerical Reaction

Some of the republicans who triumphed in the struggle over Dreyfus were as fanatical as their most reactionary opponents, and they now turned their fury against the Church. The Combes Ministry, which came into office in 1902 (Combes himself had been trained for the priesthood), led the attack. Government officials and army officers were discriminated against if they went to Mass or sent their children to church schools; and in 1905 the famous *Separation Law* not only revoked the government's power over the appointment of bishops (a change that the Church welcomed) but deprived the Church of all financial support from the government and vested ownership of all churches in the government, although religious congregations were permitted to continue to use them without payment. Although the government soon relaxed the rigidity of enforcement, the provisions of this law were bitterly resented and resisted by faithful Catholics.

The Interwar Period

World War I did not shake the stability of the Republic. Though the country passed through a series of financial crises from 1924 to 1928, it was not until the economic depression of the early 1930's coincided with the rise of fascism in Germany and with new financial scandals that the Republic again came into danger. In January 1934 the suicide of Stavisky, a Jew of Russian origin (and therefore an apt subject for anti-Semitic and nationalist propaganda), led to the disclosure of financial malpractices that could have been carried on only with the friendly tolerance of high government officials. The Cabinet of Premier Camille Chautemps, by trying to hush up the scandal, gave ammunition to those who charged that the government from top to bottom was corrupt and that it was conniving with swindlers and thieves. On February 6, 1934, a great mob, predominantly fascist, with a sprinkling of royalists and Communists, attacked the Chamber of Deputies. The police, with great difficulty, held the mob in check, but the Cabinet resigned.

The Popular Front

In the face of the depression and the menace of fascism, the three great parties and organizations of the left—the Radicals (the moderate lower-middle-class party, often called the Radical Socialists), the Socialists, and the Communists—drew together in the Popular Front of 1935. Forming a common front, they won a substantial though not overwhelming victory in the election of 1936, and León Blum, the leader of the Socialist party and a Jew, became Premier (a fact that gave further encouragement to anti-Semitism among the rightists).

The Blum government, concentrating at first on social reform, passed a series of laws providing for collective bargaining, the raising of wages, nationalization of the munitions industry, the forty-hour week, aid to farmers, and the reorganization of the Bank of France. In economic and social life it created a veritable watershed in French development.

But the reforms of the Popular Front took place in an atmosphere of great social tension, and the outbreak of the Spanish Civil War intensified the bitterness between the right and the left and to some extent revived the clerical issue. Despite its far-reaching program, the Popular Front developed serious cracks within a relatively short time and was obliged to resign after one year in office.

The End of the Third Republic

In the following months no government provided the firmness and leadership needed to meet the succession of crises that set in, and there was an increasing tendency for emergency powers to become a regular and necessary part of the political order. The most shattering evidence of cabinet instability was the parliamentary crisis in March 1940 (the month Hitler's armies invaded Norway). The country was on the verge of a second parliamentary crisis when the Germans invaded the Low Countries in May. Thus the government had neither the confidence nor the support of the country at the time of its greatest trial. France's subsequent military disaster was intensified by the absence of effective political leadership.

On June 16, 1940, a new Cabinet was formed under the leadership of Marshal Henri Pétain, a hero of World War I, who was looked on, even by the left, as a model military man. Only when in power did he display his clerical and authoritarian sympathies. Pétain promptly opened negotiations for an armistice with the Nazis. Signed on June 22, it divided France between an occupied northern zone and an unoccupied southern zone. The National Assembly (the Chamber of Deputies and Senate in joint session) convened at Vichy, the capital of the unoccupied zone, and by 569 votes to 80 gave "all power to the Government of the Republic under the authority and signature of Marshal Pétain." The Third Republic was at an end.

The Vichy Regime

Until November 1942 (when the entire country was occupied by German troops) France was thus divided. The German army occupied the northern half of the country and a strip along the Atlantic coast, while the remainder of the southern half (unoccupied, or Vichy, France) retained a semblance of independence under Marshal Pétain.

Pétain was supposed to frame a new constitution (to be ratified by popular vote) guaranteeing the rights of "work, family, and native country"—a vague but significant substitution for the traditional republican trinity of liberty, equality, and fraternity. But the constitution was never promulgated. Throughout the life of his government its only legal basis was in the provisional grant of powers. Pétain did, however, issue a series of "constitutional instruments" that repealed the constitutional provision for the election of a President, abolished the responsibility of the government to the legislature, and ended the latter's legislative powers. From this time on Pétain himself held all legislative power, and the ministers were responsible to him.

The announced aim of the Pétain government was to bring about regeneration and to free the nation of the vices that were thought to have destroyed France under the Third Republic. Masonic lodges (which were regarded as a republican political machine) were dissolved and their members deprived of government office. Organizations of workers and employers were disbanded, and state organization of industry was introduced under organizing committees, which rapidly fell under the control of big business. Attempts were made to introduce religious education into the schools, and subsidies were given to Catholic schools. In addition, under pressure from the Nazis, the government introduced anti-Semitic policies of such severity as to evoke formal protests from both Catholic and Protestant leaders.

The Resistance and the Liberation

From the moment of the fall of France, General de Gaulle, at the time relatively unknown to the masses of the French people, rallied a group of "Free French" in London and appealed to the people of his country to resist. At first he had little popular support, but as the Pétain government revealed its undemocratic character, as the Germans drafted labor for work in Germany, and as the stubborn British defense showed that the war was not over, the Resistance movement became stronger. Many young men escaped to join de Gaulle's army, and many more joined in the work of the underground. After the German attack on the Soviet Union in the summer of 1941, the French Communists took an outstanding part in the Resistance movement. The movement always included men and women of all political opinions, however, from extreme rightists to liberal Catholics and Socialists. Workers and members of the professions provided the most recruits.

The political and economic program of the National Council of Resistance (which combined all the leading resistance groups) called for a provisional republican government headed by General de Gaulle; the reestablishment of democracy with full freedom of thought, conscience, and expression; full equality of all citizens before the law; and the institution of social and economic democracy through the destruction of the great "feudal" economic and financial interests and through a planned economy under which private interests would be subordinated to the general interest. About the political ideas of General de Gaulle himself, there was considerably more doubt. It was known that he was a pious Catholic, and as an army officer he was naturally suspect to many good republicans. Yet he proclaimed his loyalty to the Republic, and as the day of liberation approached he came personally to symbolize the spirit of the Resistance.

With the Liberation of France in 1944, General de Gaulle became head of the provisional government. An assembly existed, but it was purely consultative. The Cabinet was chosen by de Gaulle and was responsible to him alone. Thus the regime in the first fourteen months following the Liberation was rightly called a "dictatorship by consent."

The Constitution of the Fourth Republic

It was obvious that France must have a new constitution, and when the first legislative assembly was elected in October 1945, the people, by a vote of 18.5 million to 700,000, decided that one of its tasks should be to frame such a document. Thus France was governed for several months by a combined legislature and constitutional convention known as the "Constituent Assembly."

But although the people were agreed on the need for a new constitution, they were not agreed on its nature. Conservative quarters called for a strengthening of the executive according to a somewhat incongruous blending of American and British practices. Most leftists, however, were opposed to any strengthening of the President or Premier and maintained that parliament alone should represent the national sovereignty.

The First Version

As a result, the first version of the constitution, a leftist draft that was presented to the voters in May 1946, placed almost complete authority in the hands of a single chamber called the National Assembly. General de Gaulle, who had resigned as President in January 1946 following a series of controversies with the left, maintained silence on the issue of ratification. But the Catholic MRP (*Mouvement Républicain Populaire*) and the few remaining Radicals, as well as the rightist political organizations, urged a negative vote. The Communists and Socialists naturally urged ratification, as

did the Communist-controlled CGT. To the general surprise, however, the constitution was rejected by a narrow margin—10,584,539 votes to 9,454,034.

The Second Try

In the new Constituent Assembly, elected in June 1946, the MRP replaced the Communists as the largest party, but the Communists and Socialists, when supported by deputies from Overseas France, were still able by a very slight margin to outvote their opponents. As a result, the second version of the constitution was very much like the first. Though a second chamber, the Council of the Republic, was added, power continued to be concentrated in the National Assembly, and the executive remained very weak. Nonetheless, the MRP (even while announcing its intention to seek amendments) decided to join with the Communists and Socialists in urging the voters to accept the constitution. General de Gaulle, however, demanded that it be rejected, and in this attitude he was supported by the Radicals and the parties of the right.

The results of the election were curiously indecisive. In the referendum of October 1946, 9,297,470 voters supported the constitution; 8,165,459 voted against it; and 7,775,893 eligible voters stayed away from the polls. Thus the constitution of the Fourth Republic came into being with what General de Gaulle and his supporters claimed was the support of only a little more than a third of the population.

The Balance Sheet of the Fourth Republic

The paradox of the Fourth Republic is that, despite the slim margin with which it came into existence, and the almost universal opprobrium with which it ended thirteen years later, it encompassed a period in which a newly vigorous France came into being. By 1958, France had its highest birth rate in a century; much of its industry had been modernized, and its industrial production had expanded since 1953 as quickly as that of Germany and far faster than that of either Great Britain or the United States. The French standard of living had improved markedly, partly because of economic growth and partly because of the enlightened social security system established after the Liberation. Moreover, France under the Fourth Republic undertook a farsighted and generally successful policy of closer relations with its Western European neighbors, culminating in the acceptance of the Common Market and Euratom in mid-1957.

Why, then, was the Fourth Republic written off as a failure in 1958, both at home and abroad? Partly it was because France's parliamentary regime had found itself increasingly handicapped by the presence on both the extreme left and the extreme right of large groups that rejected the parliamentary system in the form in which it existed and thus forced the moderate parties that lay between them into a constant series of expedients to maintain effective government. Because of this handicap, the Fourth Republic never succeeded in enforcing a genuinely equitable social distribution of the national income; it proved incapable of resisting the pressures of special groups (such as those producing alcohol); it failed to cope with the problems posed by the poverty of the Catholic schools in which one-fifth of the children of France were being educated; and it could not tackle effectively the urgent needs of tax reform and improved housing. But beyond this, the Fourth Republic was weakened irreparably by the dismal succession of defeats in France's overseas possessions and the costly and long-drawn-out war in Algeria. It was crisis in Algeria that brought de Gaulle to power once more in 1958 and led to the Fifth Republic.

The twelve-and-a-half-year period of de Gaulle's political semi-isolation saw shifting party alignments as confusing as those of the Third Republic. When de Gaulle resigned from office in January 1946, he had left the political field to three large, well-disciplined, but ill-mated political parties: the Communists, the Socialists, and the new socially progressive Catholic MRP. Their uneasy partnership lasted less than a year. In May 1947, the Communists voted against the government and were ejected from it; an ensuing wave of revolutionary strikes led by the CGT was ruthlessly broken. Already on the right had appeared de Gaulle's new political organization, the RPF (*Rassemblement du Peuple Français*), which he intended to be above parties but whose parliamentary representatives

were soon playing the parliamentary game. At first RPF votes combined with Communist votes to thwart the Socialist-MRP alignment, and the latter was forced to rely increasingly on the Radicals and Independents.

The new electoral law of 1951, by aiding electoral alliances, weakened the proportionate strength of the Communists and RPF in the Assembly. Coveting a share in power, many former Radicals and Independents, who had gained their seats as representatives of the RPF, now moved into the central coalitions. In 1952, the RPF split openly; in 1953, de Gaulle renounced it. In 1954, a new alignment of Radicals and Socialists helped Pierre Mendès-France displace the MRP and Independents. He replaced the latter's do-nothing policies with a whirlwind attack on France's major external issues. He settled the war in, and withdrew from, Indo-China; he gave internal autonomy to Tunisia; and he forced the project for the European Defense Community to a vote, in which, however, this was rejected. In the election of 1956, Mendès-France's new Left gained strength, the MRP and Independents held their own, and a new anti-democratic rightist group, the Poujadists, a protest movement of small shopkeepers and backward farmers against the dislocations of modernization, appeared in the chamber. But despite his apparent electoral success, Mendès-France was gradually isolated, and the Socialists and MRP combined under the former's leader, Guy Mollet. On February 6, 1956, however, Mollet capitulated to riots organized by French *colons* (settlers) against a liberal settlement of the Algerian question. In so doing, he made it virtually impossible for any other leader of the Fourth Republic to work out an acceptable solution in Algeria.

3. THE MAKING OF THE FIFTH REPUBLIC

The Fifth Republic was born out of violence and the need to reestablish political unity and stability. It has rightly been called the de Gaulle Republic, for de Gaulle has molded its constitution and its policies to his own view of the country's needs in a way no other Frenchman has been able to do since the days of Napoleon I.

Whether in so doing de Gaulle has provided the permanent base of stability in France that he seeks is uncertain. What is certain is that he has forced French politics and institutions into radically new patterns.

The war that destroyed the Fourth Republic was a colonial-type struggle, the Algerian revolt. Guy Mollet's swing to the side of the *colons* led to the pitting of 350,000 French soldiers against some 15,000 active Arab rebels. But as warfare descended into barbarism on both sides, the French became increasingly sick of the sacrifices, uneasy about the tactics, and insecure at home. In the autumn of 1957 there was no government for five weeks because none could secure a majority. When the government fell again in April 1958, it took a month to patch another one together. As Pierre Pflimlin prepared to present his Cabinet to the Assembly on May 13, the extremist Europeans in Algeria, fearful that he would propose negotiations with the rebels, broke into a frenzy. A self-elected revolutionary committee took office in Algiers under the benevolent eye of the army. Ten days later the extremists had seized control of Corsica. France itself appeared imperiled.

In fact, a stalemate had set in. Whatever the leaders of the army might have desired, it was questionable if the young conscripts would have marched on Paris. But the politicians in Paris were paralyzed. Only de Gaulle was clear about what should be done.

On May 15 de Gaulle publicly announced his readiness, if he was called upon, to assume power. After a tense period of waiting, President René Coty acted. Pflimlin resigned and de Gaulle was appointed Premier. On June 1, the Assembly accepted him by a majority of about a hundred, mainly from the right but including Radicals and Socialists. The Communists voted solidly against him. De Gaulle's condition for accepting office was the power to rule by decree for six months, at the end of which time he promised to propose a new constitution for the country's vote.

Those who supported de Gaulle in this time of crisis were motivated by various expectations. The Gaullists saw the chance at last for strong executive leadership; many who disliked de Gaulle's principles and personal authority saw them as the only way out of France's current im-

passe but looked on them as a temporary evil; those leading the revolt, especially the "colonels," could not believe that a general did not share their view of how to maintain the glory of France. Only the Gaullists were to be satisfied.

De Gaulle used the six-month period of decree power to push through a host of reforms. A new constitution was formulated, under the direction of Michel Debré. This constitution changed the balance of French political life. It vested legislative leadership in the executive and played down the role of the Assembly. It made a post in the Cabinet incompatible with membership in the Assembly. The choice of Premier henceforth rested with the President. The presidency, clearly designed for de Gaulle himself, emerged as the balance wheel in the constitutional system. Although the presidency was not yet the popularly elected office de Gaulle ultimately made it, the President in the Fifth Republic from the start was clearly intended to stand out as the representative of the nation selected, as he was, by a strikingly large and broad electoral college of local government representatives.

In September 1958, in a referendum in which the French territories in Africa and elsewhere as well as metropolitan France voted, the constitution of the Fifth Republic was accepted by an overwhelming majority of the voters—30,708,438 to 5,394,970. Metropolitan France voted 17,688,790 to 4,624,511. The constitution of the Fourth Republic, as we have seen, had been greeted by marked lack of enthusiasm. That of the Fifth Republic, for all its novelty, or perhaps because of it, was launched on a wave of overwhelming approval.

The Political System of the Fifth Republic

The most striking characteristics of the Fifth Republic have been the length of time—from June 1958, when de Gaulle took over power, to December 1965, when he was forced to participate in a second ballot to win the first direct election for the President of France—that de Gaulle's dominant leadership received overwhelming support from the French electorate; the use of the referendum as an institution and source of authority; the emergence and apparent persistence of a Gaullist coalition or association that has produced a dominant, even majority party, the UNR (*Union pour la Nouvelle Republique*), in the National Assembly for the first time in the history of republican France; the new political personnel that has carried on and added to the technical revolution that has been transforming France; and the widespread character of social and economic change.

It is these facts, spelled out in detail in succeeding chapters, rather than the constitution itself, that are the significant factors in the making of the new France. Yet it has been the de Gaulle constitution, as modified at his own insistence, that has provided the framework within which the forces of contemporary France have been at work. It is necessary, therefore, to look at the constitution of the Fifth Republic, particularly in the perspective of those of the Third and Fourth Republics, to understand the France of today.

The Constitution of the Fifth Republic in the Perspective of Those of the Third and Fourth Republics

Partly by design, but partly also because of its dual parentage, the constitution of the Fifth Republic is a hybrid of presidential and parliamentary government. De Gaulle saw strong executive leadership as the primary objective and insisted that the President, far from being the choice of the legislative chambers and with no legislative role, as he had been under the Fourth Republic, should be a national figure both in manner of choice and in authority. But Michel Debré, with his training in law and political science and his experience in the Fourth Republic's second chamber, possessed the perspective of a parliamentarian and the temperament of a reformer. The structure he designed, therefore, was a reformed parliamentary system in which the former excessive power of the National Assembly and the consequent instability of the Cabinet would be curbed by constitutional restrictions.

The power to dissolve the legislature has always been looked on as a major means of maintaining executive leadership in a parliamentary system. It was determined that there should be a major change in the Fifth Republic in regard to the use of this power. We have seen that after the MacMahon intervention on the famous Sixteenth of May, 1877, the use of dissolution had lapsed in the Third Republic; it was so hedged with restrictions under the Fourth Republic that it played little role. Thus the Premier was left at the mercy of the competing interests and ambitions of the members of the lower house, who, in contrast to the relatively clear-cut divisions characteristic of British and American politics, were divided into a spectrum of political ideologies and groups extending from the far left to the far right. French governments in the Third and Fourth Republics were always coalitions, therefore, that depended on the support of several parties, and often the withdrawal of a single parliamentary group would mean the fall of the Ministry. Whereas British Prime Ministers could commonly count on being in office for four or five years and could thus make long-range plans, a French Premier was lucky if he could survive for a year. While the same person often retained a ministry through several governments, top leadership was subject to frequent changes. Sometimes, as we have seen, the country was left for weeks on end without a Cabinet in office.

Under the Fifth Republic, the power of dissolution, as a reinforcement of executive leadership, was specifically written into the constitution. But rather than being at the disposal of the Premier, as in effect it is in Great Britain, the right to dissolve the French chambers is vested in the President, and in practice has been exercised at his discretion. Thus when Debré wanted the chambers dissolved at the end of the Algerian war in mid-1962, at a time when de Gaulle's prestige was particularly high, his request was refused. It was Debré himself who lost his position, being replaced as Premier in April 1962 by Georges Pompidou, who had never been even a member of parliament or of a political party.

This illustration of how de Gaulle as President overrode the advice of his Premier is characteristic of the way in which he systematically eroded the parliamentary features of the constitution in favor of presidential leadership. The constitution declares that the President is responsible for "the regular functioning of the governmental authorities, as well as the continuance of the state," and also for "national independence, the integrity of the territory, respect for . . . treaties." Under the Fourth Republic, the Premier and Cabinet were in control of foreign affairs, but from the start de Gaulle insisted on determining foreign policy. On May 15, 1962, for example, he publicly described his European policy even before informing the Cabinet, five of whose members, those from the MRP, promptly resigned.

Indeed, de Gaulle has maintained an important role in regard to all major policy decisions. He referred those concerning Algeria to referenda rather than the legislature. Despite charges of unconstitutionality he also insisted on a referendum on the issue of direct election of the President. Beyond these specific issues, de Gaulle has also molded those economic and social decisions, particularly of an unpopular character, for which the Cabinet has had to take public responsibility. Moreover, when the military putsch in Algiers took place in April 1961, he used his emergency powers to govern the country until the autumn, preventing the chambers either from legislating or introducing motions of censure against the government.

The greatest change in the functioning of the political system under the Fifth Republic has been the relative powerlessness of the chambers. For this situation there were many reasons. One dominant reason has been the personality and towering presence of de Gaulle, particularly in contrast to the transitory, often fumbling leadership of the Fourth Republic. The other was the awareness of the tightrope to be walked if the army was to be made to accept Algerian independence (which was not proclaimed until July 1962). Throughout, de Gaulle's position has been buttressed by the unswerving personal loyalty first of Debré and then of Pompidou, by the limited time—five and a half months in the year—in which the chambers can be in session, and by the remarkable strength of the Gaullist alignment in the lower chamber.

One cause of the instability of the Cabinet during the Third and Fourth Republics had been the divided and shifting character of the party system. On the left were three large parties: the Radicals (the loosely organized party of the anticlerical lower-middle class—that is, the small shopkeepers, the less successful professional men, and the small farmers); the better or-

ganized Socialists; and the tightly controlled Communists. In the Fourth Republic, as we have seen, there was also a new socially minded Catholic party, the MRP, which, except for its Catholicism, often seemed more to the left than the Radicals. On the right the political situation was less clear, for there the groupings were looser and the organizations less highly developed. In general, the right was conservative in economic matters but was divided between those who were anticlerical and strongly republican and those who were pro-clerical and socially conservative.

Under the Fifth Republic, the number of parties was no less (indeed a small new party, the PSU, appeared in 1958 between the Communists and the Socialists). But there was a decisive difference: the parties aligned themselves either for or against de Gaulle's policies instead of trying to devise policies of their own around which to organize enough support to control the chambers. The Communists have always been bitterly opposed to de Gaulle, but in any case their numbers in the National Assembly were reduced by a return to voting through single-member constituencies. The Socialists supported de Gaulle's accession to office in 1958 and endorsed the Algerian settlement, but they criticized almost everything else. The Radicals, the "vital center" in the Third Republic and a balance wheel in the Fourth, were decimated in the November 1958 Assembly elections although they retained strength in the Senate and in particular areas of France. The MRP supported de Gaulle during the Algerian war but broke with him over his European policy and his authoritarian attitudes toward parliament. The Independents (the term in France is synonymous with conservative) in the Assembly opposed the Algerian settlement, although their ministers reluctantly accepted it. Most significant, however, the amorphous UNR, despite its slight organization and program, began to bring France some semblance of a three-party system: the UNR, ordinarily with certain other support; the rest of the non-Communist parties; and the Communists, who formed a bloc of their own.

The National Assembly has not been acquiescent in the reduction of its status and authority. Even during the Algerian war, its deputies tried to resurrect the process of interpellation, which had been used with deadly effect under the Fourth Republic to destroy Ministries. The deputies were stopped in this effort only by the action of the Constitutional Council, the official guardian of the functioning of the constitution. Debré had to force bills through parliament four times by staking the life of his government on the outcome. In 1961, all parties except the UNR walked out of the Assembly in protest against the curbing of their legislative powers during de Gaulle's assumption of emergency powers. In 1962, as will be described in detail in Chapter 4, the "old parties" battled fiercely with de Gaulle, who not only overrode both the Assembly and the Senate but also the Constitutional Council and the Council of State (see Chapter 6) in his determination to take his own route to establishing the direct election of the President. Thus the opposition deputies have tried, repeatedly but unsuccessfully, to recapture the role the Assembly played in the past.

Basic to the realignment of executive-legislative relations under the Fifth Republic is the fact that the President, General de Gaulle, and not the Premier, controls the executive power. And the only way in which the Assembly can influence the President is through the Premier and the Cabinet. As Debré envisaged the government of the Fifth Republic, and indeed as it appears in the constitution, executive-legislative relations would be those of a traditional parliamentary system, except that the rule-making functions of the Assembly were restricted and those of the Premier and his Cabinet specified. Under those circumstances, the President would have remained above the political battle, in the role he himself once described as "a national arbiter far removed from political struggles." But circumstances—in particular the Algerian struggle and the dangers posed by an alienated army—and de Gaulle's determination to dominate policy have led the political system of the Fifth Republic to operate much more in presidential than in parliamentary terms.

Nonetheless, the provisions of the constitution, the ill-concealed impatience of the deputies over their subordinate role, and the renewal of political concern throughout the country suggest that the balance has not been established permanently. The surprising fact that de Gaulle had to enter a second ballot in the first direct election for the President, in December 1965, marked his first setback after a series of overwhelming plebiscitary victories. Despite his efforts and the great authority that has accrued to the presidency, it is not the role of the President as such but of President Charles de Gaulle that has molded the Fifth Republic. There is reason to wonder, therefore, whether the Fifth Republic, or the type of presidential leadership that distinguishes it, can survive its dominant figure.

Emergency Powers: Article 16

The most controversial clause in the constitution of the Fifth Republic is Article 16, under which the President can assume emergency powers at his own discretion. The constitution provides that he shall consult the Premier, the chairmen of the two chambers, and the Constitutional Council before declaring such a state of emergency. It defines the conditions that constitute a state of emergency as a threat to the institutions of the Republic, the country's independence, or the fulfillment of its international commitments. Nonetheless, the clause leaves the President full freedom to make the ultimate decision on his own judgment and thereby legalizes his use of full powers.

Behind de Gaulle's insistence on the insertion of this provision in the constitution was the break in the continuity of the French political system in 1940, with the Nazi invasion. It was not another war, however, but an ill-planned coup on the part of certain French officers in Algeria that gave rise to the declaration of an emergency in April 1961. No one in France disputed the need for and the use of these powers at that moment but the deputies of the older political parties grew restive and bitter over being kept so long from exercising their normal legislative functions.

The Referendum

While Article 16 permits the executive to bypass parliamentary procedures in times of extreme crisis, the process of referendum throws certain crucial decisions to popular vote. The constitutions of both the Fourth and the Fifth Republics were legitimized by being accepted by majority vote in a referendum. Indeed, the first draft of the constitution of the Fourth Republic was rejected by the voters on May 5, 1946, and the second draft was accepted five months later. The constitution of the Fifth Republic was accepted by referendum on September 28, 1958.

Whether other types of decision should be made by referendum has been a matter of controversy. The referendum has been a favorite means for General de Gaulle to capitalize on his popularity and on the widespread belief, particularly in the early days of the Fifth Republic, that he was indispensable. His use of the referendum to win support for Algerian independence was widely accepted as the best way of keeping this controversial issue out of the party arena. But there was great hostility on the part of the "old" parties and tacit, if not explicit, opposition from the Constitutional Council and the Council of State to his use of the referendum, rather than the regular amendment procedure, to institute the choice of the President by direct election.

De Gaulle justified the use of this procedure by referring to Article 11 (under which the referenda on Algeria had been called), which permits use of the referendum "on the proposal of the Government during sessions." His opponents pointed out with still more cogency, however, that Article 89 specifically provides for the amendment process and for the participation of the chambers therein. Whatever may have been the merit of instituting the process of direct election for the office of President, the fact that de Gaulle insisted on using a referendum on October 28, 1962, to validate the new procedure weakened its constitutional legitimacy and provided a somewhat dangerous precedent for the future.

The Constitutional Council

Neither in the Fourth nor in the Fifth Republic has the body set up to supervise the constitutionality of executive and legislative acts been effective. The Constitutional Committee of the Fourth Republic was created in 1946 to protect the second chamber, the Council of the Republic, from encroachment on its limited powers by the National Assembly. The Committee's jurisdiction was to determine the constitutionality of a measure challenged by a majority of the second chamber and the President.

On one occasion, but on one only, the Committee gave slight protection to the Council in a matter of procedure.

Little more useful has been the Constitutional Council set up under the Fifth Republic, even though it was supposed to have more responsibilities and more power than the earlier Constitutional Committee. The Constitutional Council must be consulted on whether organic laws and the standing rules of the Assembly are in conformity with the constitution, but the Council can do no more than give its opinion and leave action to the relevant body, the Cabinet or the Assembly. The Council has three other functions: to supervise elections and decide any disputes arising out of them; to advise the President on the existence of an emergency and the measures he should take to handle it; and, if asked, to give advice on the boundaries between executive and legislative competence, and whether proposed laws (other than organic laws) or treaties are in conformity with the constitution. But it is clear that the right to advise is far different from the power to decide—and that, in practice, the Constitutional Council is hardly more effective than its predecessor.

The Process of Amendment

The 1958 constitution, like that of 1946, has a relatively simple formula for amendment. The constitutional provisions of Article 89 are that the President, on the proposal of the Premier or a deputy, may make the initial proposal; the proposal must then be adopted in identical terms by both chambers and ratified by a referendum or, if the President so decides, by a three-fifths majority of both chambers sitting together. This procedure, if used, would provide the Senate with a greater role than did the procedure under the Fourth Republic, in which the Assembly could dispense with the consent of the second chamber if it had a two-thirds majority among its own members. Under the Fifth Republic, however, the amendment process has atrophied, partly because de Gaulle by-passed it when making the most decisive change in the constitutional balance of power, and partly because the sphere of the executive is so great, both through constitutional provisions and through deliberate enlargement by de Gaulle, that the presidency is the molding force in the regime.

4. FRENCH POLITICAL IDEAS

Far more than in Anglo-Saxon countries, political ideas in France have remained the fighting words of political action. While the Fifth Republic has been marked by a diminution of ardor in this respect, much of French thinking is still comprehensible only if one has some knowledge of the great rival political traditions of France.

The Ideas of 1789

The French Revolution, which provided French republicanism with its political creed, shared much of its political philosophy with the American Revolution. Some of its leaders, such as Lafayette, had fought for American independence, and many of its thinkers had been influenced by the Declaration of Independence and the Virginia Declaration of Rights. Both American and French liberals had read the writings of John Locke, and certain Americans, such as Thomas Jefferson, had formed close friendships with the men who prepared the intellectual program of the French Revolution.

The Enlightenment

In contrast to the United States, however, there were two distinct intellectual currents in the French revolutionary stream. The one that ran closer to American thought was that of the philosophers of the Enlightenment, a group of thinkers of the middle and later part of the eighteenth century who believed that man was a good and reasonable creature endowed with inalienable natural rights. According to their creed, man, by using his reason, could discover the principles of a just society and, being good, he would act upon them. Once he was freed from political and religious tyranny, there would be constant progress toward a perfect society. Thus the political philosophy of the Enlightenment was one of reason, individualism, humanitarianism, confidence in human progress and perfectibility, love of mankind, and hatred of religious superstition and political tyranny.

The Influence of Rousseau

The second current, which flowed from the thought of Jean Jacques Rousseau (1712–78),

was also characterized by a passionate hatred of tyrants. But where the philosophers of the Enlightenment exalted reason, Rousseau trusted to the uninstructed instinct of the ordinary citizen; and where the philosophers insisted upon the natural rights of the individual, Rousseau emphasized the interest of the community as a whole. Rousseau believed that the highest authority in any community was the *general will,* the content of which was determined by a direct vote of all citizens. Men were to vote, however, not according to their selfish interests but according to their understanding of the interests of the community. It was inconceivable to Rousseau that a community of free men (for Rousseau, too, believed in the natural goodness of man) should choose to pass tyrannical or unjust legislation. The ordinary citizen might be mistaken in his judgment, but he would always desire the welfare and freedom of all. Therefore, if ever a minority should differ from the majority, the minority should submit; and if the minority refused to submit, it should be "forced to be free." For Rousseau, unlike the authors of the Declaration of Independence, there were no "inalienable rights." Popular sovereignty (that is, government by popular vote) and the rule of the majority were the important considerations. Where the philosophers of the Enlightenment were chiefly concerned with political liberty and its protection against the government, Rousseau was chiefly concerned with political equality and the right of all men to participate in their government.

The Declaration of the Rights of Man and of the Citizen

The French Declaration of the Rights of Man and of the Citizen (1789)—the counterpart of the American Declaration of Independence—contained elements of both philosophies. The preamble, following the doctrine of natural rights, proclaimed that "forgetfulness or scorn for the rights of man are the only causes of public misfortunes and the corruption of governments." The first two articles maintained that "Men are born and remain free and equal in rights; social distinctions can only be founded upon common utility," and that "The aim of every political association is the conservation of the natural and imprescriptible rights of man;

these rights are liberty, property, security, and resistance to oppression."

Article 3, however, introduced a Rousseau-like element: "The principle of all sovereignty resides essentially in the Nation; no body, no individual can exercise authority which does not expressly emanate from it." Article 4 to some extent combined the two schools, declaring that "Liberty consists in being able to do everything which does not harm others: thus the exercise of the natural rights of man has no limits other than those which assure to other members of society the enjoyment of the same rights; these limits can only be determined by law."

Article 6 (apart from its provision for representative government) followed Rousseau: "Law is the expression of the general will; all citizens have the right to participate personally, or by their representatives, in its formation; it should be the same for all, whether it protects or punishes. All citizens, being equal in its eyes, are equally eligible for all dignities, positions, and public offices, according to their capacity, and without other distinction than that of their virtues and of their talents."

Other articles in the Declaration protected men from arbitrary arrest, imprisonment, and punishment; guaranteed freedom of thought, including religious thought; proclaimed "the free communication of ideas and opinions" to be "one of the most precious rights of man"; guaranteed to each citizen the right to "speak, write, and print freely"; and proclaimed property to be "an inviolable and sacred right." Except for the guarantee of property and of the "career open to talent" and a provision calling for popular consent to taxation, the concern of the framers of the Declaration was with political rather than economic rights.

During the French Revolution many of these rights were violated in the most flagrant way. But the "ideas of 1789"—liberty, equality, popular sovereignty, the career open to talent, government under law—remained the heart of traditional republican doctrine in France. The continuing importance of these ideas was indicated by the preamble to the French constitution of 1946, which began with the words:

> On the morrow of the victory of the free peoples over the regimes that attempted to enslave and degrade the human person, the French people proclaims once more that every human being, without distinction of race, religion or belief, possesses inalienable and sacred rights. It solemnly reaffirms the rights and freedoms of man and of the citizen consecrated by the Declaration of Rights of 1789 and the fundamental principles recognized by the laws of the Republic.

The Conservative Reaction

The Early Traditionalists

The French Revolution, with its culmination in the Reign of Terror, brought shock and disillusionment to many of the French people, and it was natural for a school of thinkers to appear who defended the monarchical tradition and challenged the political assumptions on which the Revolution had been based. Never very influential so far as the mass of the French people were concerned, certain of their ideas have nevertheless continued to dominate the thinking of leaders of the upper classes and of literary and intellectual circles.

The most prominent of the early traditionalists were the Vicomte de Bonald (1754–1840) and the Comte de Maistre (1753–1821). The former, challenging the idea that men desired "progress," insisted that their real desire was for the peace, stability, and order of a hereditary society. Men, he believed, were basically unequal. The happiest society is one in which the place of each person is determined by tradition and inheritance and in which each stays in that place. The best society is one in which a hereditary monarch wields the executive power; in which there are permanent social distinctions between a hereditary nobility and the commoners; in which there is an established church; and in which there is a harmonious balance between monarch, nobility, and independent judiciary. Order and authority he regarded as established by God. To revolt against the established order was to resist His will.

Maistre, the more influential of the two thinkers, attacked another pillar of the faith of the Enlightenment: the belief in the power of reason and in the ability of men to use their reason in order to plan and control their destiny. Like Burke he taught that inherited institutions and practices and even inherited prejudices represent a wisdom far greater than that attainable by the use of the human power of reason. Human institutions, instead of being shaped by men, are the product of many different social, economic, and political forces that men cannot control and that mold the minds of men.

In contrast to Rousseau's belief in direct popular government, Maistre maintained that in all governments it is the able and energetic few who rule. Monarchy he thought to be the best of all governments, and government he held to be naturally absolute and unlimited. "There can be no human society without government," he wrote, "no government without sovereignty, no sovereignty without infallibility." And although he agreed that temporal sovereigns, unlike the Pope, were not infallible, he thought a belief in their infallibility to be the only sound foundation for an orderly society.

The Newer Conservatives

Where the earlier post-Revolutionary traditionalists centered their loyalty on a hereditary monarchy, an aristocratic order, and an established church, the later traditionalists (while not necessarily rejecting these ideas) added an extreme nationalism as one of the essentials of the conservative faith. Maurice Barrès (1862–1923), one of the most popular of French novelists, continued the warfare against liberal individualism by insisting that the individual, far from shaping himself, is the product of his ancestry, his national traditions, and his native soil. The man who cuts himself loose from these influences is rootless and self-destructive, denying the core of his own being. Detesting and fearing foreigners, Barrès preached a doctrine of veneration for one's ancestors and one's dead, of reverence for the French language and the French earth. Men were to identify themselves with their families, their villages, and their provinces. Barrès' own affection for his native province of Lorraine, where repeated invasions had encouraged a particularly strong variety of patriotism, led him to believe that the road to French patriotism lay through devotion to one's locality. A religious skeptic, he nevertheless honored and defended the Catholic Church as the religion of his ancestors. In politics his only standard was that of unquestioning nationalism. Whereas the philosophers of the Enlightenment had preached the religion of humanitarianism, of love for mankind, of liberty, truth, and justice, Barrès judged all issues in terms of French power and glory. "Every question," he wrote, "must be solved in sole relation to the interests of France."

A somewhat different brand of nationalism was that of Charles Maurras (1868–1952). Unlike Barrès, Maurras was a native of Provence, that province of France in which the classic influence of Greece and Rome is still the strongest. To Maurras, France was the representative and defender of the classical spirit against the barbarians of the Teutonic and Anglo-Saxon world. Personally a skeptic (the Vatican eventually denounced both him and his organization, the *Action Française*) he saw in the Catholic Church, not the institution of "Hebrew Christianity" (which he detested), but the preserver of the classical tradition of ancient civilization. As opponents of this tradition, he attacked not only those Frenchmen of foreign descent (to whom he applied the Greek word *metic*) but Protestants and Jews as well. To him the Republic and the Revolution were something un-French, the product of a foreign and Protestant tradition (Rousseau had been, in origin, a Swiss Protestant from Geneva). He wanted to restore the old France of the monarchy, classic order, and authority. Stability was more important than justice. At the time of the Dreyfus Affair he declared, "Anything which disturbs the public order is an injustice, so that true justice is to respect public order." And when the army officer who had forged some of the evidence incriminating Dreyfus confessed and committed suicide, Maurras wrote in tribute: "Our bad half-Protestant education has kept us from estimating justly so much moral and intellectual nobility. . . . But your unlucky forgery will be recognized among your finest feats of war." The "unlucky forgery," Maurras insisted, could injure only the enemies of France. The Maurrassian doctrine of "integral nationalism" ("the exclusive pursuit of national policies, the absolute maintenance of national integrity, and the steady increase of national power—for a nation declines when it loses military might") made any conception of universal justice or morality a delusion if not an irrelevancy. Liberty, truth, and similar values became inconsequential in comparison with the worship of national power.

Maurras never commanded a popular following. But the beauty and clarity of his style and the force of his intellect won him authority in French intellectual circles. He lived long enough to be one of the supporters of the antirepublican and antidemocratic government of Marshal Pétain, paradoxically preferring defeat of the Republic to the victory of France, and he was imprisoned for his collaborationist activities. The successors of Maurras have never forgiven General de Gaulle for his opposition to Marshal Pétain, whom they regard as the symbol of religious orthodoxy, political order, and authority.

Socialism and Communism

Early Socialists

Although the industrial revolution came later to France than to England and was never so complete, socialist thought flourished in France from an early date. Before the general ascendancy of Marx, the influence of such thinkers as Saint-Simon (1760–1825), Fourier (1772–1837), Louis Blanc (1811–82), Blanqui (1805–81), and Pierre-Joseph Proudhon (1809–65) extended far beyond French borders.

The teachings of the early French Socialists were highly varied in detail, but the majority of them shared certain general characteristics. For the most part, they were true children of the Enlightenment, believing in reason, progress, and the goodness of human nature. They thought that social evils resulted from the wickedness not of men but of their institutions; yet, with the exception of Blanqui, they desired a peaceful reformation of society. All of them appealed to right and justice (although to Marxists these ideas were simply the reflection of a class interest), and in most instances their concern was with the building of a new society rather than with the violent destruction of the old. Often they believed that specific reforms (the introduction of social workshops as advocated by Louis Blanc, or the organization of model communities known as phalansteries according to the plans of Fourier) would provide the remedy for the worst social evils. Some of them were opposed to any growth in the authority of even a democratic government, and

Proudhon, whose influence was particularly strong among French workers, attacked Communist proposals for state planning and organization. He spoke of these as the "yoke of iron [which communism] fastens upon the will, the moral torture to which it subjects the conscience, . . . [and the] pious and stupid uniformity which it imposes upon the free, active, reasoning, unsubmissive personality of man."

Marxian Socialism

Even after Marxism, toward the end of the nineteenth century, had come to be the predominant type of socialism in France, there continued to be a strong humanitarian and reformist current in French Socialist thinking. Jean Jaurès (1859–1914), who more than anyone else personified French socialism, was ready to acknowledge in orthodox Marxian fashion that political developments were dependent upon economic ones, but he rejected the inevitability of class warfare. He was deeply concerned with the spirit and dignity of man as well as with man's material needs. He thought of socialism not simply as a response to certain economic conditions but as the culmination of all that was best in Greek, Jewish, and Christian civilization and in the thought of the Enlightenment. Economic forces were important, but they operated upon human beings who were infinitely diverse and who could not be understood in terms of a single mechanical economic formula. Rejecting the doctrine of a basic conflict of interests that could be resolved only through class warfare, Jaurès went so far as to recognize the good faith and idealism that had motivated the bourgeoisie (the bogey of all orthodox Marxists) at certain times. He believed that capitalists and workers shared certain interests in common that could be made the basis of a peaceful evolution toward the socialist society.

Jaurès was assassinated at the outbreak of World War I in 1914; in the later years of that great struggle the Socialist movement was seriously divided. Many Socialists supported the war as a battle for democracy, although an increasingly large minority became disillusioned and turned either to an absolute and extreme pacifism or, more significantly, to the belief, propagated by Lenin, that the international war must be turned into a civil war, a class struggle between the bourgeoisie and the proletariat. To this last group, the success of the Bolshevik Revolution in Russia was an inspiration and a source of tremendous prestige. In 1920 the left wing of the Socialists adopted the name of "Communists" and joined the Moscow-led Third International. Most of the leaders of the party, however, remained loyal to the old name and the old program, and in the following years they attracted a greater popular following than did their Communist rivals. This following, however, included not only workers but also a large part of the population of the small towns and countryside, as well as many members of the white-collar middle class, including a high proportion of government employees. As a result, there were several different "chapels," or what the French often call *tendances,* within the Socialist party: one that was devoted to radical social change and the interests of the working class, and commonly called the "doctrinaires"; one that was strongly pacifistic; and one that represented the progressive middle classes who desired moderate social reform within the framework of constitutional democracy. For a time, much of the popularity of the party resulted not from its desire for social reform but from its pronounced opposition to war—for France had almost bled to death in World War I.

Christian Socialism

Throughout the nineteenth century there had been some more or less isolated individuals in France who preached a doctrine of Christian Socialism, believing that democracy and social reform should be achieved through the application of Christian principles and with the help of the Catholic Church. So long as Pius IX remained Pope (1846–78) such movements were frowned upon by the Church; but his successor Leo XIII (1878–1903), while attacking Marxian socialism, urged the passage of social legislation to protect the working class. In France a large number of Catholics, particularly among the younger laity and the lower clergy, gave enthusiastic support to these ideas. Early in the twentieth century the movement known as the *Sillon,* led by Marc Sangnier, a young Catholic who believed devoutly in the Church's social mission, attempted "to place the social forces of Catholicism at the service of democracy." The group was condemned and silenced by the Vatican in 1910 not so much for the content of its social doctrine as for its claim to independence from the authority of the Church. But in the interwar period, a small party known as the Popular Democrats represented a continuation of the doctrine of a democratic and social Catholicism. Its leaders were prominent in the Resistance, and under the new name of the *Mouvement Républicain Populaire,* MRP, the group emerged as one of the strongest, and for a time most influential, parties of postwar France.

French Political Ideas in the Interwar Period

The years immediately before the outbreak of World War II forced a considerable readjustment in the French ideological pattern. Until this time, the parties of the right, in the spirit of Barrès and Maurras, had been identified with extreme nationalism, which often took the form of hatred of Germany, skepticism about the desirability or efficacy of international organization, and bitter opposition to social and economic reform. In contrast, the parties of the left (except for the Communists, who continued, with occasional intermissions, to work for international revolution) adopted slogans of peace and reconciliation, disarmament, and peaceful social progress. In 1933, however, an aggressive Hitler came to power in Germany at the very time when a disastrous economic depression had aroused a demand for sweeping social reform in France. A dilemma for both sides resulted: rightists had to decide whether they hated an aggressive Germany more than they feared social reform at home, and leftists had to decide whether they loved peace and social progress more than they hated Nazism. The result was a shifting of position and a split in both groups. A few rightists maintained the position of traditional French nationalism: Germany, whether monarchist, democratic, or fascist, must be kept powerless. A somewhat greater number, however, felt that France had been too corrupted by Marxism, anticlericalism, and lack of discipline to be able to fight successfully against the fascist powers.

Disunity on the left was just as serious as that on the right. The majority of Radical Socialists and Socialists reluctantly came to the same conclusion as their leaders Edouard Herriot and Léon Blum—that it was necessary to fight German aggression in order to save French democracy. But many Radicals were leaders in the effort to appease Hitler. And while at least half the Socialists resolutely opposed appeasement, most of their deputies voted for Marshal Pétain, though there were forty among them who refused to swing with the majority. The leaders of the Catholic progressives, the Popular Democrats, stood firmly for democracy and against appeasement. But the Communists, after being most vocal in the demand for resistance to Hitler, reversed their position in August 1939 when they received word of the Hitler-Stalin pact and actively opposed French participation in the war.

Finally, on the left, on the right, and in the center, there were masses of people who found it impossible, when confronted by a choice of evils, to choose either alternative with enthusiasm or even with firmness. The state of bewilderment and the lack of conviction of the ordinary Frenchman in 1939 and 1940 undoubtedly were important elements in the German triumph.

The Resistance

In its first months the Resistance movement lacked any clear political philosophy. Its leader, General de Gaulle, a devout Catholic, seemed to some to symbolize the militarism, nationalism, and clericalism which, to an earlier generation at least, marked an enemy of the Republic. However, as the Vichy government revealed its antirepublican and anti-trade union character, and as outstanding representatives of the Church and of big business collaborated with it, the Resistance movement became increasingly leftist in composition. Those Catholics who participated in it generally represented the Christian Socialist element in the Church. And in 1941, particularly after the invasion of the Soviet Union, the Communists took a conspicuous part in resistance activities. The program of the National Council of Resistance, which after 1943

combined all the major parties and organizations of the Resistance, called for radical social and economic reform. When a new constitution for the Fourth Republic was drawn up and ratified, its preamble, after reaffirming "the rights and freedoms of man and of the citizen consecrated by the Declaration of Rights of 1789," set forth a long list of social and economic guarantees.

But if the constitution, in this sense, represented a triumph for the socialist parties, whether Christian, reformist, or Communist, it would be wrong to suggest that traditionalism and conservatism had lost their power. Badly discredited at first by their association with the Vichy government, the conservatives steadily won new strength, partly as a reaction against growing Communist aggressiveness, partly by exploiting General de Gaulle, to his disgust, and partly perhaps because of the natural swing of the pendulum of political success.

In the Fourth Republic France was plagued both by colonial and by Communist problems. In many ways ideology was subordinated to the day-to-day efforts in solving these persistent threats to stability. No other nation in Europe, it may be noted, was faced with both problems at once: Great Britain had the colonial problem, Italy had the Communist problem, but neither had to battle simultaneously on two fronts. The Fourth Republic was able to cope with the Communist problem but not with the colonial one; that problem finally came to an end when the Algerian crisis was solved.

The process of decolonization (the battle in Algeria from 1954–62) led to de Gaulle's return to power in 1958. With his return, his supporters tried to revive Gaullism in a different form from that of the Resistance period. The Gaullists preached a "new France" devoid of the kind of political squabbling that had marked, and sometimes disgraced, the Fourth Republic. This "new France" was to play an important role in international politics and was to transform the nature of French administration at home. De Gaulle himself preached a new kind of nationalism that would restore France to its "rightful place" in the concert of nations: that of leader. To achieve that place, France would have to set an example for the "Third World": in foreign affairs it would be both anti-American and anti-Communist; at home it would evolve a society governed in an ultramodern fashion.

Before France could play the role in world affairs de Gaulle envisaged, he had to liquidate the Algerian war. By 1962 he had freed his hands and could embark upon his mission. His "neonationalism" prevented him from supporting the type of European Common Market that might subordinate France to countries which might be "tools of the United States of America." He thus became the target of the "Europeanists," who wanted France to take the lead in shaping a new European community.

De Gaulle also applied his ideas on government to the French civil service. He tried to popularize certain aspects of the "technocratic ideal." The National Assembly was no longer to play *the* important role in directing France; much more initiative was to be left to the technocrats or specialists who were needed to run the country. Thus he supported the ideology of "effective technocracy": a modern, efficient, active administration that could be trusted to run the country wisely and well.

Today, then, as in the past, there is a conflict of ideas in France. On the right, the bearers of the tradition of order and authority have added efficiency to make a new trilogy. On the extreme left, the Communists, while using the words *freedom* and *democracy,* interpret them in such a way as to justify the use of force and the suppression of the rights of political opponents. Between these two can be found every gradation of political view. In the center are those who hope to combine the philosophy of 1789 and a certain amount of freedom of enterprise with a moderate degree of social reform, and those who wish to combine social reform with loyalty to the Church. On the moderate left are Socialists who, in the tradition of Jaurès, hope to achieve social reform and a planned economy through the use of democratic methods without violating individual liberty. Each of these ideas is represented by an organized political movement or party. To understand both their present and their past appeal, it is necessary to look at these organizations in more detail.

3. French Parties and Elections

1. THE CHARACTER OF THE FRENCH PARTY SYSTEM

The French party system has long challenged the generalizations about political parties that Englishmen and Americans are tempted to make. To them it seems natural that there should be two large parties, that one should rule and the other oppose, and that every once in a while they should exchange positions. The rise of a third party has usually been regarded as a disrupting influence that upsets the entire system. Particularly in Great Britain, government seems possible and comprehensible only when one party is able to take the responsibility for political leadership, and when there is a united and forceful opposition prepared to take power whenever that party is defeated.

In France, however, none of these assumptions seems either natural or obvious. A two-party system, however desirable in theory, has appeared totally inadequate to represent the great variety of French political interests and principles. The characteristic multiplicity of parties in France has made, and still makes, difficult the development of a clear and cohesive majority and/or a responsible opposition. Moreover, the bitter opposition between the extremes of right and left and the antidemocratic tendencies at both ends of the spectrum have created a disturbing absence of the restraint and tolerance that mark the alternation of parties in Great Britain and the United States.

To the foreigner the French multiplicity of parties often seems unintelligible and chaotic. The French are accused of political fickleness and frivolity, with the implication that any solid and sensible people could organize a firm and simple party system. If anything, however, the French people have not been frivolous and fickle enough. The issues dividing them have had an ideological or historical base, and the party groupings reflect these divisive issues. Thus the French have rejected the sort of practical and facile compromise that can unite northern progressives and southern conservatives in a single Democratic party.

In sum, the reflection in the French party system of the cleavages in French society prevented it, prior to the Fifth Republic, from accomplishing what seem to Anglo-Americans the most important functions of a party system: to represent the opinions and desires of the voters, and to provide effective government.

It was to provide effective government that the Fifth Republic shifted from party government to executive government. Paradoxically, one result has been a far stronger trend toward large parties, or toward groupings of parties, under the Fifth Republic than ever before. One main reason has been a new source of division in French politics: that between those supporting and those opposing President Charles de Gaulle and his policies. But whether this new factor, consolidated in party organization, will permanently affect the French party system has yet to be seen.

The Party Systems of the Fourth and Fifth Republics

The party system of the Fifth Republic, like that of the Fourth Republic, is a multiparty system. There is little similarity, however, between the Assembly elected in 1946 and the Assemblies elected in 1958 and 1962. In 1946, the Assembly was dominated by three large, well-disciplined parties of the left: the Communists, the Socialists, and the MRP. There were two parties of secondary importance: the RGR, a union of republican leftists formed around the old Radical party, and the conservative PRL. The Independents were a small and apparently ineffective group. In 1958 and 1962, in striking contrast, two right-wing parties —the UNR and the Independents—won a dominant position in the Assembly, only seventy seats short of a majority in 1958 and eight more than an absolute majority in 1962. The once-powerful left was sharply reduced in strength and is still struggling to build itself into an effective opposition.

The transition from the 1946 Assembly to the 1958 one was less abrupt, however, than their juxtaposition here may suggest. The original coalition of the three leftist parties broke up in 1947 as the result of the intransigence of the Communists; thereafter a series of governmental crises encouraged splinter groups, revived the importance of the rightist parties, and, on occasion, made the votes of the Independents crucial, particularly during the curious situation created by the establishment in 1947 of General de Gaulle's organization, the RPF. The RPF claimed to be above political parties and, in fact, aimed at the total elimination or absorption of its opponents. After spectacular successes in the municipal elections and those for the Council of the Republic in 1947 and 1948, the RPF emerged as a full-fledged party. It contested the national election of 1951 with such effect that the RPF became the largest party in the Assembly.

The fact that the two largest party groupings produced by the 1951 elections, the Communists and the RPF, were the two most antagonistic to each other, and also to the parliamentary party system within which they found themselves, inevitably threw particular weight on the so-called center parties. Since, aside from the Socialists and MRP, these parties all had the loose organization characteristic of the parties of the Third Republic, the Assembly became once more the scene of shifting coalitions. This was still more the case when de Gaulle disavowed and, in a sense, disbanded the RPF in mid-1953, leaving its deputies free to participate in the struggle for political power.

Nor was the pattern changed by the 1956 elections. The RPF had disappeared, and its place on the extreme right was taken by a far less disciplined group, the Poujadists, whose opposition to the parliamentary system was not tempered by the experience with its functionings that so many Gaullist deputies had possessed. The Radicals under Pierre Mendès-France temporarily took a turn toward the left and united with the Socialists to form a governing coalition called the Republican Front—a government held together less by internal cohesion than by pressures from the extremes and by fear of further crises. The political compromises, shifting party alignments, and parliamentary individualism that marked French politics thereafter paved the way for the collapse of the Fourth Republic, the reemergence of de Gaulle, and the establishment of the Fifth Republic.

The marked, though somewhat erratic, trend to the right in French politics was accentuated in the Fifth Republic. The explanation lies both in the continued (though by 1965 diminishing) dominance of President Charles de Gaulle and in the splintered character of the left. So long as the Algerian crisis persisted, de Gaulle received the support of the MRP (which, indeed, drew on a largely conservative electorate despite its socially progressive program), as well as of the newly formed and avowedly Gaullist Union of the New Republic (UNR) and the highly conservative Independents. Significantly, de Gaulle ostentatiously refused in 1958 to have his name associated with the UNR, since he recognized that many of his own supporters were also dedicated to keeping Algeria French. His major objective was to be free to handle the Algerian situation on whatever terms and with whatever timing he himself decided. Hence he kept the Algerian issue as far as possible out of electoral and legislative considerations and used public referenda to register support for his decisions.

In 1962, however, de Gaulle adopted another tactic:[1] a forthright attack on the old parties that were reaching toward a new, if tenuous, unity in opposition to his decision to have presidential elections decided by popular vote in-

---

[1] For a case study of these events see "Presidential Power and the Constitution: de Gaulle Appeals to the People 1962," by Stanley Hoffman in *Politics in Europe: Five Cases in European Government,* edited by Gwendolen M. Carter and Alan F. Westin (New York, Harcourt, Brace & World, Inc., 1965).

stead of by the indirect and traditional process of selection by persons already holding offices. (These were the deputies themselves in the Third and Fourth Republics, and a wide range of local representatives in the Fifth Republic). Declaring scornfully that "to confuse today the parties of yesteryear with France would be simply ridiculous," de Gaulle arrogated to himself in the legislative election of 1962 (as he had in the preceding, controversial referendum on direct election) the perception of France's "true will."

De Gaulle's actions in 1962, combined with the settlement in Algeria, sharpened the line of division between the UNR—Gaullist Independents and the rest. Seeking desperately to reestablish the old solidarity of the left, leaders of the opposition parties face the dilemma posed by the existence of the Communist party on the far left, which still polls some 20 percent of French votes. The Socialists, in particular, are constantly harassed by doubts about their relation to the Communists: should they align themselves with the Communists, as Guy Mollet decided to do in 1962, on the assumption that Gaullism was the greater peril? Or (as does the British Labor party) should they emphasize the difference between their evolutionary socialism and the more radical brand espoused by French Communists?

In addition, of course, the parties of the center and left have trouble even retaining their own cohesion. Yet this very difficulty provides insight into the pressures and trends of opinion within France. So do the sporadic activities (and somewhat diminishing enthusiasm) of the political clubs that sprang up during the early period of de Gaulle's undisputed leadership. Thus the spectrum of French parties is no less important an indicator of the character of French society now than it was in the days when parties played a more important role in shaping French policy.

2. THE PARTY SPECTRUM

Within the French multiparty spectrum, the crucial issue is whether the right, the center, or the left—non-Communist and/or Communist—will form the nucleus around which majority legislative strength can be built. The majority position of the right—which was unprecedented from 1958 to 1966—appeared threatened by the growing strength of the opposition that unexpectedly forced General de Gaulle to enter a runoff ballot in the presidential elections of December 1965. His challenger, François Mitterrand, had wide support among the Radicals and Socialists, and also on the extreme left among the Communists, and oddly enough on the extreme right as well. Jean Lecanuet's brilliant personal success—although he finished third—enabled him to build the Democratic Center that balanced between a rightist and a center-left orientation. Thus the perennial French issues of "who should combine with whom" and "under whose leadership" continue to plague French politics. Thus all descriptions of party stands, organization, and alignment must be viewed as tentative.

The Right

The most significant change on the right during the early years of the Fifth Republic was the advance of the UNR and its allies, the dissident Gaullist Independents, and the resulting reduction between 1958 and 1962 in the strength of the Independents. The new Gaullist right absorbed much, if not most, of the traditional right. Moreover, it won its parliamentary victory in 1962 not only because of its close identification with de Gaulle but also because it appeared to represent a new modernism concerned with industrialism, urbanism, and technology. In contrast, the Independents, whose support dropped from 20 percent of the vote in 1958 to less than 10 percent in 1962, belonged to or represented local notables of a predominantly rural society that was rapidly being superseded in the "new" France.

Thus the basic questions about the future of the right are: Will the UNR's loyalty to de Gaulle provide it with sufficient popularity for it to maintain its dominant position? Will the economic transformation of France help the UNR to develop a greater rationale and cohesion of its own? Or will it be splintered by an opposition that is able to exploit the growing popular dissatisfaction with the authoritative policies of an entrenched executive working closely with a technically minded bureaucracy?

The UNR

The most paradoxical feature of the French party system in both the Fourth and the Fifth Republics is that the only man who can create a mass party drawn from all elements in the population, General Charles de Gaulle, does not believe in political parties, nor perhaps even in the representative system within which they play an essential role. When he formed the *Rassemblement du Peuple Français* in the spring of 1947, it was, he insisted, not a political party but above party, aimed at the political union of all French people. As it quickly gained phenomenal popularity, however, the RPF took on the form of a well-organized political party, and de Gaulle's followers sought ministerial offices as members of the RPF. Disillusioned, de Gaulle renounced his parliamentary followers in April 1953, leaving them free to engage in the parliamentary struggle for power from which he had tried so long to restrain them. Yet the end result was the disappearance not only of the RPF but of most of those who had swept into the Assembly in 1951 under its banner.

The *Union pour la Nouvelle République* was in a sense a reemergence of the RPF. It failed, however, to capture all the supporters of the earlier movement, and its leadership added to that of the former Gaullist groups some of the quasi-fascist elements that had engineered the overthrow of the Fourth Republic in May 1958. Though de Gaulle refused to lend his name to the UNR during the election campaign or to assume active leadership of it thereafter, its success in winning some 20 percent of the votes in the 1958 election and in capturing the major bloc of seats in the runoff contests was clearly attributable to his popularity. So was its even more striking success in the legislative elections of November 1962.

The major areas of Gaullist strength are western, northern, and eastern France; the areas of weakness are the center and the south. However, the Gaullist vote for deputies in 1962 was less decisive in the north than had been the vote for de Gaulle himself in the referendum on the direct election of the President. Nor was it nearly so decisive as was the voting for de Gaulle in the presidential election of December 1965, where again his support clustered in the northwest, the northeast, and the southeast. These areas form a curious melange, for they include both the underdeveloped west, where there have been many antigovernment demonstrations, and the highly prosperous northeast. Thus the voting for de Gaulle himself gives only a rough indication of the strength of the Gaullists.

The UNR prides itself on its loyalty to de Gaulle and publicly disavows any desire to have de Gaulle follow the policies its members most desire. This self-abnegation facilitated de Gaulle's settlement with Algeria, which many members of the UNR found distasteful, and subsequently kept them in line behind economic and social policies that are much more advanced than their conservative bias would suggest.

Few members of the UNR, apart from Michel Debré, are widely known either nationally or internationally. Neither de Gaulle himself nor Premier Pompidou owns a party card. On the whole, the UNR is not yet well rooted in the cities; it does less well in municipal than in national elections. Its success in replacing the Independents in so many areas rests on its position as the party of the government (which, in contrast to the situation in Great Britain, is quite different from being the governing party). Rather unkindly, the UNR has been called a claque rather than a political party. Americans find it easier to understand the party than do the British, for the UNR, like American parties, is a heterogeneous collection of groups of the right and center held together by their acceptance of the national leadership of an outstanding figure, and by their association with, though not possession of, political power.

Such organization as the UNR possesses does not extend beyond its small group of leaders, men like Debré, who are keenly aware both of the party's potential and of its deficiencies. In theory the party is strongly centralized, and its annual conference supreme in defining doctrine and program. A national council, made up of an equal number of persons inside and outside parliament, is said to assume responsibilities between the sessions of the conference. But in practice the secretary-general (there is no president), the twenty-member political committee, and, to a lesser degree, the sixty-member central committee make most of the decisions, including the selection of candidates, particularly for run-off ballots. Local organization is weak and shifting. At the national level, the philosophy of following rather than initiating means that policy decisions are left to the government.

The Independents

The Independents, who are what the French call moderate and what we call conservative, have had a checkered history. Like the UNR, they had predecessors under the Fourth Republic who benefited from the prevailing if uneven trend toward the right. These predecessors consisted of several rather ill-defined parties: the *Parti Paysan* (the Peasant and Social Action Party) and the *Parti Républicain de la Liberté* (PRL), in the First Assembly; the Independent Republicans for Social Action and the Independent Republicans, in the Second Assembly; and the Independents and Peasants for Social Action (IPAS) and the Social Republicans (the remnants of the RPF), in the Third Assembly. Under one designation or another, these groups held between seventy-five and a hundred seats in each Assembly during the Fourth Republic.

Broadly speaking, these rightist groups all stood for the traditional institutions of the family and the Church, urged support for church schools, and opposed nationalization and economic *dirigisme* (planning). Though they inclined toward the right-wing Radicals on economic policy, they were divided from them by the clerical issue. Despite, or perhaps because of, their lack of a precise program, they attracted considerable support. They provided (in March 1952) one of the Fourth Republic's most popular Premiers, Antoine Pinay, subsequently the formulator of the first programs of economic liberalism under de Gaulle. In the 1956 Assembly, however, their opposition to the economic programs of the left and center, and their hostility to concessions on Algeria, caused the fall of Ministry after Ministry and greatly contributed to the collapse of the Fourth Republic.

Nonetheless, in 1958, the Independents

emerged as the second largest party of the Assembly. For a brief span, it appeared as though they might realize their ambition to become the great conservative party of France. The Independents drew strength from small or large, rather than middle-sized communities, they appealed to persons of moderate but comfortable means, and they had the support of local "notables." But, like the Radicals, they were associated with the discredited Fourth Republic and with the values of what was rapidly becoming an obsolete, rurally oriented society.

Moreover, the Independents soon split over de Gaulle's leadership and policies. By 1962 they had disintegrated into three distinct groups: the pro-Gaullist Independents, who linked themselves with the UNR to form a parliamentary majority after the 1962 elections; an anti-Gaullist but constitutional group, which campaigned against de Gaulle's decision to have the President selected by direct election and suffered disastrously in the process; and an anti-Gaullist extremist movement, which bore some faint resemblance to the Poujadists.

Despite this splintering, the pro-Gaullist and the once anti-Gaullist Independents may have key roles to play in the future. Both groups compete with the UNR for the same conservative and clerical electoral support. The Gaullist Independents, led by Giscard D'Estaing, resist absorption but have no other place to go. The formerly anti-Gaullist Independents, however, under the sparkling leadership of Jean Lecanuet, have formed what is called the Democratic Center, which has obvious links through its leader with the MRP but has been tempted by the chance of sharing political power with the UNR.

The Center

The center parties—the *Mouvement Républicain Populaire* (MRP) and the Radicals, in particular—played a crucial role during the Fourth Republic by keeping the French government from falling under the control of either the extreme left or the extreme right. In so doing they frequently had the cooperation of the Socialists. The question continually faced, however, was where the center of political gravity was to be: in the non-Communist left, or the center, or the center-right. Complicating the establishment of any stable alliance was—and to some degree still is—the incompatibility between the traditional anticlericalism of the Radicals and Socialists, and the Catholic base of the MRP.

Under the Fifth Republic the center parties still face the same difficulties, though they have been somewhat ameliorated by a settlement of the issue of state support for parochial schools (see Chapter 8). But they have acquired an even more difficult problem: how to persuade pro–de Gaulle voters that they, rather than the UNR, represent the true center in French politics. The brilliant performance in the 1965 presidential campaign of Jean Lecanuet, ex-president of the MRP, brought the center into a new prominence. Although he finished in third place and was thus eliminated from the runoff election, Lecanuet has continued to exploit his popularity—his TV performances and publicity buildup have sometimes been compared with those of John F. Kennedy—in an effort to develop a cohesive center attractive to those from both sides of the spectrum. Although he has formally separated himself from the MRP, he can count on its continued support in his Democratic Center. This alignment can turn either to the right, as it showed signs of doing late in 1966, or to the center-left. Since Lecanuet refuses to work with the Communists, the possibility of any single anti-Gaullist alliance is eliminated.

The Mouvement Républicain Populaire

The *Mouvement Républicain Populaire* came into existence at the end of the war as one of the two largest parties in France. Its appearance constituted a double phenomenon: the emergence of a large and well-organized party capable of balancing the great parties that traditionally constituted the French left, and the creation of a large party able to combine friendliness to the Catholic Church with a democratic and semisocialist policy.

The leaders of the MRP—Georges Bidault, André Colin, Maurice Schumann, and Robert Schuman—had taken an active part in the Resistance movement, had an excellent record of opposition to fascism both at home and abroad, and were genuinely devoted to social and economic reform. They had joined with Socialists and Communists in drawing up the program of the National Council of Resistance, and they insisted that the MRP was itself a leftist party. Yet they also profited from the prestige of General de Gaulle, a Catholic, who, though conservative, was believed to favor them.

If the position of the leaders of the party was perfectly clear, however, there was considerable doubt about the nature of their following. In the first elections after the Liberation, the party received a tremendous popular vote, but much of this vote resulted not from desire for social reform but from fear of Communism or admiration for de Gaulle. Thus much of its earlier electoral support shifted quickly to the Gaullist RPF or to other conservative parties and never returned.

Yet this rapid drop in electoral support perhaps saved the MRP from becoming much more conservative than its founders desired. It has sought to reflect the progressive social conscience of the Catholic Church, so manifest after World War I, and to attract both the Catholic trade unions and young people. Like the Socialists, its leaders believe that the fullest development of the human personality demands proper economic and social conditions, but they emphasize social rather than economic reform. Like parties further to the right and in contrast to the Socialists, the MRP supports state financial aid for church schools. It has a sense of purpose based on an interpretation of life as concrete as that of the Communists.

It maintains contact with its constituents through Catholic trade unions (though the CFTU is no longer so close to the MRP as it originally was), youth groups (which help at election time), professional associations, and family organizations.

Around this program and through these agencies, the MRP built a mass party that polled between 14 percent and 25 percent of the votes under the Fourth Republic. Under the Fifth Republic its support and its importance have been much less. In 1958 it won fifty-six seats; in 1962 only thirty-six. Its growing disillusionment with de Gaulle—whose sharp words in May 1962 against European integration and the sup-

porters of a supranational community precipitated the resignation of the five MRP ministers
from the Cabinet—was matched by the shift of
its voters to the right. In 1962 it won an even
smaller percentage of votes than the Independents—8.9 percent on the first ballot and 5.2
percent on the second, as compared to the latter's 9.5 percent and 7.8 percent—though it won
one more seat.

All during the Fourth Republic, the MRP was
plagued by the fact that its electorate was more
conservative than its leadership. When this
division was compounded by the split between
the anti-Gaullism of its leadership and the
Gaullism of many of its natural supporters,
the party's future was threatened. In May 1963
its annual congress even voted in support of
merging its identity in a new opposition party,
if such a party showed prospects of securing
majority support. At the same time, the MRP
explicitly rejected any notion of associating itself
with the Communists. This stand seemed to
indicate a hope that the MRP, the Independents,
and the Radicals might form a strong enough
center grouping to offer a hope of electoral success against the UNR. But since these three together polled less than a quarter of the votes
and won less than a quarter of the seats in 1962,
the hope seemed illusory. Moreover the chance
of adding the Socialists to such a grouping was
made much less likely by the explicit exclusion
of the Communists.

In formal structure the MRP consists of sections united into federations that send representatives to an annual congress. There is also
a national committee (which gives special
weight to parliamentarians) and four executive
organs: the president, the secretary-general, the
executive commission, and the bureau. Under
a liberalization of rules in 1959, the president,
who is supposedly the leader in political matters,
cannot be a cabinet minister, nor can he be reelected more than three times. The secretary-
general, who handles organization matters, can
stay in office longer. The bureau, some of whose
thirteen members are now selected by the national committee, is the intermediary between
the secretary-general and the executive commission. These changes were intended to keep the
party leadership more in tune with the membership, but they do not solve the MRP's major

problem: how to make itself a vital part of a non-
Gaullist, non-Communist political grouping.

The Radicals and the RGR

From the beginning of the twentieth century
until the election of 1936, the Radical party
(*Parti Républicain Radical et Radical Social-
iste*), often known as the Radical Socialist party,
was more than any other identified with the
Third Republic. It was the representative par
excellence of the lower-middle classes, which
held the greatest power: small shopkeepers,
farmers, less successful professional men, and in
general those who were suspicious of big men
and big ideas and who were devoted to republican principles (particularly to anticlericalism)
and to the heritage of the French Revolution. Inevitably, therefore, it suffered from the reputation of the Third Republic for inefficiency and
corruption. Although its outstanding leader,
Edouard Herriot, had a stainless record of opposition both to Nazism and to Vichy, the party
as a whole was discredited. Loss of much of its
press added to its weakness. In consequence,
during the early years of the Fourth Republic
the Radicals appeared in parliament only as a
minor group. The center of a loose alliance
known as the *Rassemblement des Gauches Ré-
publicaines* (RGR), it hoped to hold the balance of power between more powerful groups,
although it seemed to have little hope of becoming a leading party itself.

In this perspective the role played by the
Radicals in the Fourth Republic was almost as
striking as the decline of the Socialists. As the
balance of power shifted to the right with the
ousting of the Communists in the spring of
1947, the votes of the Radicals became more
significant. Before long, one of their top figures,
Henri Queuille, formed a Ministry that turned
out to be the only one in the course of the first
Assembly to last longer than a year. By 1950
the Radicals had reestablished their local electoral machines, and in each subsequent election
of the Fourth Republic they increased their representation in the Assembly till they ranked
once more as one of the larger parties. Always
a loosely united party, the Radicals were pecu-
liarly susceptible, however, to internal divisions.
In the early days of the Fourth Republic they
split over the issue of whether to cooperate with

de Gaulle or to work with the democratic parties to the left.

Still more serious was the ultimate effect of Pierre Mendès-France's efforts to reform the party structure and turn the Radicals into a disciplined national party. In his whirlwind attack on France's major problems during his premiership in 1954–55, Mendès-France achieved a settlement in the disastrous situation in Indo-China and secured economic sacrifices in the interests of strengthening France's economic situation. He was finally toppled from office, however, by the withdrawal of the support of the right-wing Radicals. Shortly thereafter, Mendès-France's group displaced the conservative party leaders and secured a seal of approval for a leftist emphasis in economic policy that recalled the early roots of Radicalism and heralded the possibility of an alliance with the Socialists. After the 1956 election, Mendès-France led the Radicals into a coalition with the Socialists (thereby reestablishing an anticlerical left—the Republican Front—for the only time in the history of the Fourth Republic). But the choice of Socialist Guy Mollet as Premier weakened Mendès-France's hold on his own party; he resigned from the Ministry in May 1956 without overthrowing the governing coalition. When, in 1957, he also resigned as leader of the Radicals, he had failed to break the local machines or to institute discipline among the party's parliamentary members. Moreover, the old members had been alienated, and the new ones he had attracted failed to remain constant. Thus the party suffered a striking defeat in 1958, despite the return to the *arrondissement* electoral system (see below) that had once been the basis of their strength.

In 1962, however, the Radicals held their own better than did either the Independents or the MRP. It seems likely, therefore, that the UNR's striking success in that election was largely at the expense of the other two. Moreover, although the Radicals and the other center-left groups of the *Rassemblement Démocratique* (Democratic Rally) associated with them polled fewer votes on the first ballot than the MRP, they gained more on the second ballot and managed to win forty-two seats, six more than the MRP. While this relative success strengthened the hands of those who were eager to

maintain their association with the left, the major objective of the Radicals is still to consolidate all non-Gaullist groups.

The unexpected emergence of François Mitterrand (whose UDSR—the Democratic and Socialist Union of the Resistance—has been loosely associated with the *Rassemblement Démocratique*) as de Gaulle's competitor in the second ballot for the presidency in December 1965 provided the kind of opportunity the Radicals and their associates have sought for their coordinating role. While Mitterrand's inclinations are toward the left rather than toward the MRP and Independents, he has sought associations in both directions. The Radicals would prefer such mobility but have found themselves increasingly impelled toward an alignment with the left.

Like other parties, the Radicals have their departmental federations, national congress, executive committee, bureau, and president. In 1959 the executive committee was cut in size from six hundred to two hundred, and inherited the power of a special group, the Comité Cadillac, to decide whether Radicals should participate in a ministry. The president, who has a two-year term, may now be reelected only once. But regardless of formal provisions, there is relatively little relationship between the party organization and the loosely organized deputies who call themselves Radicals.

The Left

Of all the general designations in French politics, that of "the left" is the most deceptive, the most confusing, and the most troublesome. Surprising to an American, French politicians find it an advantage for their popular image to belong to "the left." Thus center and even some rightist parties include some variant of left or democratic in their name and try to avoid the seats on the extreme right of the semicircular Assembly.

The fact that the Communists are at the extreme left of the political spectrum provides them with an aura unthinkable in most other democratic countries. The most serious weakness in the French party system in both the Fourth and Fifth Republics is that the Communists, an antidemocratic party, have consistently polled at least one-fifth of the votes in each legislative election. The number of seats in the Assembly that the Communists have won in different elections depends on the electoral system in force and the degree to which the non-Communist left and center hold together in run-off contests. But the continuing strength of Communist electoral support confronts the other left and left-center parties with a dilemma. They prove weak when they refuse to work with the Communists, and they face the danger of domination if they associate themselves with the Communists.

To draw distinctions between the Socialists and the Communists is as easy as to differentiate between the Socialists and the Radicals. Yet in both cases there are similarities as well as differences. The Socialists and Radicals are both left of center, and both are anticlerical. They differ sharply, however, in their approach to economic planning, which the Socialists support and the Radicals oppose. Both the Socialists and the Communists are Marxist in ideology, but only the latter are aligned to Moscow.

The Radicals, Socialists, and Communists formed the constructive Popular Front government of the mid-1930's that created decisive changes in France's economic and social structure. The tripartite relationship in which the Communists shared in the first year of the Fourth Republic left a less happy memory. Thus French politicians fear a Communist alliance but see its advantage for forming a strong opposition to the Gaullist UNR.

The presidential campaign of 1965 gave encouragement to those who favor such a left-center alignment. The refusal of Gaston Deferre, the wealthy, popular Socialist mayor of Marseilles, to accept Communist support in his candidacy for president so split his own party that he was forced to withdraw from the race. François Mitterrand, in contrast, although from a splinter center party, accepted Communist as well as Socialist support in his presidential campaign and won the run-off position against de Gaulle. Moreover, thereafter he formed the Left Wing Federation, which grouped together Socialists, Radicals, and political clubs, and opened talks with the Communists over tactics in the 1967 elections. Yet the old problems remain to haunt the Socialists. If they work with the Communists, this left alliance may so frighten the right and right-center as to consolidate the Gaullist majority. But if they ignore the Communists will they be able to gain a sufficient number of seats to play a distinctive role in the Assembly?

The Socialist Party

The tragedy of the Socialist party in France is that it has never been able to command the enduring allegiance of that kind of working-class organization that forms in Great Britain the bulwark of the Labor party. Immediately before World War II the Socialist party (which is often designated by the initials SFIO—*Section Française de l'Internationale Ouvrière*, or French Section of the Workers' International) was the largest of French parties. It had high hopes during the Resistance of becoming the strongest force in the revived French state, just as Labor became in Great Britain in the immediate postwar period, and with much the same kind of program. The first manifesto of the Socialist party announced a reorganization to make it a "great republican, democratic, and revolutionary force in the nation." Yet French Socialists have not been able to overcome the handicap of having a more dynamic group to their left, the Communist party.

In postwar as in prewar France, the Socialist party has been handicapped by the incongruity of its position and its following. In theory, it is a Marxist party, and as such it wants to be the representative of the working class. But, except in the northern regions, the industrial and mining departments of Nord and Pas-de-Calais, the SFIO has never satisfied the deeply felt class consciousness of the French workers, on which the Communists have capitalized so successfully. Fundamentally, French workers mistrust the bourgeoisie; but increasingly both the followers of the SFIO (in particular, teachers, professional and state-employed white-collar workers, and lower-grade civil servants) and its leadership are bourgeois. The British Labor party has been able to draw strength from its combination of working-class and middle-class support; the French Socialist party tends to fall between the two, not wholly trusted by either. Hardly less important is the Socialists' lack of appeal to youth and also, largely because of its anti-clericalism, to women.

Characteristic of the Socialist party is its division into *tendances,* or, as is sometimes said, into little "chapels" beside the big church, Communism. The two chief *tendances* are the doctrinaires, who press the party to adopt a more radical attitude, to return to the purity of Socialist doctrine, and to refuse to cooperate with middle-class parties; and the humanitarians, who emphasize human values and the importance of political and spiritual liberty and are ready to work with those who similarly prize them.

The great fear of French Socialists has been that, like the Liberal party in Great Britain, their support will be whittled away by the counter-attractions of the parties on either side of them. This fear has been intensified by the loss of much of their influence over the industrial working class (the *Force Ouvrière,* with which they have cordial relations, has limited working-class strength) and by the fact that they retain little significance apart from their role in parliament. During the Fourth Republic, the Socialist party alternated between sharing in Ministries—1946–51 and 1955–58—and deliberate self-exclusion from the Cabinet in order not to work with center and rightist groups. Thus the Socialists have been torn between their desire for political influence and their fear of falling into the kind of opportunism that ruined the Radicals in the late years of the Third Republic. Although the Socialists decisively supported de Gaulle in 1958, and although Guy Mollet, their secretary-general, was in de Gaulle's Cabinet until Debré's Ministry in January 1959, they have vigorously criticized all of de Gaulle's policies except his decision to give Algeria independence. Thus they early formed a part of the Gaullist opposition. Throughout the Fifth Republic, however, the Socialists have been more divided than ever, both internally and over their outside alignments.

A small new party that called itself the United Socialist Party (PSU) appeared between the Socialist party (SFIO) and the Communists early in the Fifth Republic. It drew support from both the SFIO and the Communists, from left-wing radicals and various small cliques. At its second congress, in 1963, no fewer than seven factions fell into dispute. The only point on which all its members agreed was that the PSU should try to reunify the Marxist left, particularly by encouraging the SFIO to cooperate both with themselves and with the Communists. The Communists, already wooing the SFIO, ignored the PSU. The SFIO, in turn, believed that the PSU was trying to destroy it.

These maneuvers would not have made so much difference if the SFIO itself had not been split internally between those following Guy Mollet, who favored the leftward alignment, and those who agreed with Deferre that the Socialists should reject the Communist alignment and work for an association with the Radicals and others of the left center. Mollet succeeded in developing an entente with the Communists in the 1962 election (which meant withdrawing competing candidates on the second ballot) that not only saved his own seat but won the Socialists thirty of their sixty-five seats, and the Communists twenty-two of their forty-one.

But while restraint under such circumstances could be mutually rewarding, only one candidate could successfully oppose de Gaulle for the presidency, and the Communists, as the price of their support, demanded a common program for the parties backing an opposition candidate. Deferre refused to consult them as we have seen, and temporarily won his party's endorsement for this stand at the 1964 congress despite Mollet's opposition. Failing, however, in his major effort to create a strong left-center grouping, Deferre retired. Mitterrand then succeeded in securing such support and thereafter built it into working arrangements for the 1967 legislative elections.

The local organizations or sections of the Socialist party are grouped in departmental federations. A federation that includes five sections, or a hundred members, can send representatives roughly proportionate to its members to the annual national congress, which defines basic doctrine and tactics. In the intervals between its meetings, the highest party organ is theoretically the national council, which is composed of one delegate from each departmental federation. The key authority in the party, however, is the executive committee, a body of forty-five members selected by the congress by majority vote (a process that under-represents minorities and entrenches the dominant group). The executive committee selects the five-man secretariat, the other center of power, and also the leader of the youth organization and the editors of the party's newspapers. The secretary-general (parliamentarian Guy Mollet since 1946) directs party organization and election strategy, but he has often not been able to persuade either the executive committee or the parliamentary members of the party to follow his lead. Moreover the party's local organizations often insist on nominating candidates who are not the first choice of the national leaders. Although this can be a source of weakness in its parliamentary representation, the very democracy this practice reflects can also be the party's proudest boast. Nowhere else in the French party system is there so decisive a control of party machinery by its rank and file and, as a consequence, so deep a feeling of genuine comradeship among many of its party members.

The Communist Party

The Communist party is quite unlike any other political group in France. This is partly because it is closely allied, or even perhaps subservient, to Moscow. But it is also true that its inner core of members regards the party as "the model-in-miniature of the new society" that it works to bring into existence, a society the more easily recognized because it already exists in the Soviet Union. Obviously, only a relatively small proportion of those who vote Communist, sign its petitions, and even speak at its meetings look on the Communist party in this light. Only the inner core provides both the strength and the essential characteristics of the Communist party. Whatever policies may be adopted as the result of tactics—and the party has followed highly flexible and varied policies since the Liberation of France—the overriding aim is to subserve the higher purposes of Communism.

Though the ultimate goal of the Communist party, as an exponent of the revolutionary Leninist school of Marxism, is social revolution, its tactics in France have been exceptionally opportunistic. On occasion, the party has promoted moderate and constructive policies aimed, not without success, at winning the support of small farm-owners as well as the landless and small businessmen as well as laborers. Though it tried to cripple the country with strikes from 1947 to 1950, it has more frequently—especially in 1962 and thereafter—bombarded the Socialists with demands for common action.

In the 1962 election, the Communists, through their party newspaper, *L'Humanité,* continually encouraged a rapprochement with the Socialists. Moreover, as we have seen, the Communists entered wholeheartedly into the bargain with the Socialists for mutual withdrawals and gained, as the Socialists did, from the arrangement. In January 1964, the Communists moved closer doctrinally to the Socialists by formally asserting that a one-party regime is not necessary "for the passage to Socialism" and that the transition to Socialism can be achieved by peaceful means. At the same time, the Communists revised their party statutes to provide that all party committees, except the all-important national Political Bureau, should be selected by secret ballot. In addition, under the Fifth Republic, the Communists have behaved in parliament in a much less obstructionist fashion than when they were in opposition in the Fourth Republic. Although they have been unwavering in their opposition to de Gaulle from the genesis of the Fifth Republic, they have demonstrated that opposition through legitimate parliamentary tactics and, on occasion, have even voted for proposals by the non-Communist opposition instead of restricting themselves to parallel action.

The Communist maneuvers over the 1965 presidential election provide a useful insight into their position and into their relations with other parties. Repeatedly they threatened to nominate their own candidate unless some agreement was reached on a common program for the opposition candidate. Thus they used their ability to split the opposition vote to win an affirmation of the acceptability of their support. Their continued opposition to Deferre was an influential factor in forcing his withdrawal, and their votes were important—they claimed decisive—in making Mitterrand's challenge to de Gaulle so effective in the 1965 presidential election. The dilemma of French politics of the left is, therefore, the indispensability of Communist support for electoral success coupled with the suspicion of other parties that any alliance will be turned to Communist advantage alone and that unscrupulous tactics will discredit those who worked with them.

It may be wondered why, in the face of such widespread suspicion of their motives, the Communists continue to poll such extensive support. One important reason is their control of the largest and most vigorous of the trade unions: the CGT. Through the CGT, the Communists maintain constant contact with a major group—the industrial workers—who commonly vote their ticket. They also include in their own estimates of membership civil servants, artisans, shopkeepers, agricultural workers, and teachers. In 1959, they disclosed that over half of their 200,000 to 400,000 members were over forty, and nearly four-fifths of them male. Perhaps only 70,000 of this total membership can be ranked as militants, but this hard core is devoted and disciplined.

The Communists can exploit real, as well as fancied, grievances of members of these groups. Moreover, as indicated, they enjoy an unjustifiable but no less real advantage as a result of their leftist position, which endows them with the aura of the French revolutionary tradition. In contrast to the other parties, with their shifting alignments, "flabby" leaders (to use the Communists' term), and internal splits, the Communists exude energy, and self-confidence. They are dynamic and aggressive, and they present a picture of unity, which sometimes cloaks their own inner struggles. There is no question to which they do not provide a clear and simple—and often destructive—answer.

Like other Communist parties, the French party has a highly disciplined hierarchical structure that gives supreme authority to those at the top. Its foundation is made up of cells of from three to eighty members. There are three types of cell: workplace, home, and rural. The workplace cells (forming 20 percent of the total number in 1955) are preferred for their effectiveness in developing class-consciousness and for being a potential basis for an underground organization. They are, however, difficult to organize in the face of employer opposition and shifting work schedules. The home cells (45 percent) are organized more loosely by streets or communes and thus have less

revolutionary potentialities; the rural cells (35 percent) combine home and workplace.

The cells meet once a week or biweekly to consider national and international news in the light of party doctrine. They are autonomous, and each has its own bureau, or executive. Coordination is secured through the "section," which may include the cells in a large factory or those in a particular area. The sections, in turn, are grouped into departmental federations, one for each department in France. The federations send delegates to a party congress that meets, in theory, every three years and is technically the highest party authority. In fact, its role is educational: to present party orthodoxy to those present. Draft theses or motions may be circulated ahead of time and discussed vigorously in cell meetings, but there is no questioning or criticism at the congress itself.

The congress, again technically, elects a central committee of seventy-one members and twenty-two alternates who include the hard-core leaders of the party and its ancillary organizations, especially the CGT. The central committee selects from its own members a fourteen-man Political Bureau, which deals with day-by-day affairs, and a six-man secretariat, headed by a secretary-general. Despite the elaborate paraphernalia of elections on which this structure appears to rest, the leaders, in practice, are self-chosen. And it is they, and in particular the Political Bureau, who give the orders that the whole party must follow.

A particularly important and distinctive feature of the Communist party organization is the power of the Political Bureau to give binding instructions to the Communists who sit in the National Assembly and the Senate. In Great Britain not even a party congress, in either the Labor or the Conservative party, can do more than issue recommendations calling upon the party's members in parliament to take certain kinds of action. It is even more unheard of for the executive committee of a party to issue a parliamentary mandate. But French newspapers regularly carry items to the effect that "the Political Bureau of the Communist party met and gave a mandate to its parliamentary group" to vote in a certain way or to pursue a certain policy. Leaders of the Communist party may also be deputies, but it is their role outside the

Assembly that is all-important. Thus the Communist deputies as a whole have been chiefly significant in the eyes of the party as instruments for their opportunist policies: appealing to or embarrassing the Socialists, attacking the Gaullists, and supporting or discrediting the Assembly, whichever suits their purposes at that moment.

The Political Clubs

A phenomenon of the Fifth Republic, rather more important in its early years than later, is the political clubs. These sprang up in response, for the most part, to the diminution of the role of political parties and of parliament, as compared to the role of the executive, and to the shifting realignments of political ideologies during and after the Algerian war. In all, there are or have been about 120 political clubs, with a membership of between 15,000 and 20,000. One type of political club has been concerned chiefly with discussion and political education, either among those who held relatively similar views, or among those who held a wider spectrum of political opinion. The other type of political club has envisaged action as the end result of discussion, and their members have been commonly hostile not only to Gaullism but to the parliamentarianism typical of the Fourth Republic.

Perhaps the greatest significance of the clubs is that they have furnished a political forum for young people. Most of their members have been under forty. They formed, particularly just after 1958, a new force or "new strata" that sought new ways to infuse vitality again into French politics. Most club members are intellectuals, a more clearly defined and respected group in France than in British or American society, and almost all have tended toward the non-Communist left. A few of the clubs—like the left-wing Christian Democratic *Groupes "Esprit,"* whose members have been meeting since 1932 to discuss articles in periodicals, and the more typical and more important *Club des Jacobins,* which was established in 1951 to reinvigorate the Radical left wing—predated the Fifth Republic, but most were founded in the dark days of 1958 when it was widely feared that the Republic might collapse in chaos.

Though most of their activities are private, there have been times, particularly in 1963 and 1964, when groups of clubs have sponsored public conferences to give publicity to wide-ranging discussions. These discussions have sought to aid new political relationships and policies and, in particular, to spur a closer association or even unity of the non-Gaullist parties. Deferre's candidacy for the presidency received an early boost from the clubs. Subsequently they provided Mitterrand with his most consistent support within the Federation of the Left. Thus they added a more specifically political role to their earlier contribution of keeping alive a questioning spirit during the Fifth Republic's period of political apathy.

Pressure Groups

Pressure groups are commonly discussed in conjunction with political parties. But, since French pressure groups, particularly under the Fifth Republic, have been more concerned either with direct action or influencing the administration, they are considered both in Chapter 1 and Chapter 6. Much of the most effective pressure by French special-interest groups is exercised quietly but fairly continuously on the bureaus of the ministries, a process aided by the fact that administrative officials and the top staff of technical, commercial, and industrial concerns often share common training and exchange positions.

As in Great Britain, interest groups were long considered in France to be either insignificant or slightly disgraceful, and de Gaulle himself distrusts and dislikes them. Nonetheless, as will become clear in the description of the French administration, a structure of advisory committees has long provided private interests with a built-in means of exerting political influence. As power shifted from the legislature to the executive and the administration under the Fifth Republic, the latter area inevitably became the focus for pressures. Not until the French political parties and legislature win again—if they ever do—a powerful role in the formulation, if not the execution, of governmental policy, will it be appropriate to analyze the activities of pressure groups in connection with party politics in France.

Conclusion

The party system of the Fifth Republic is in flux, affected by two contrasting trends: the one trend working toward a two-party confrontation within the non-Communist parties consisting of the Gaullists and their allies on the one hand and the non-Gaullist, non-Communist parties on the other; but the other trend developing an association among the parties of the left and left-center. The Gaullists have demonstrated a surprising ability to command electoral support in France, and the natural result has been to spur their opponents to find some way of working together that will afford them a chance to share political power, or at least to influence the way in which it is used. The revival of political concern, particularly during the presidential election of 1965, opened the way for the succeeding electoral battle for the Assembly. But continuing to confuse and frustrate the efforts of each part of the non-Communist, non-Gaullist political spectrum to organize cohesive support around itself are the self-seeking efforts of individual leaders and political groups, the tendency to split over philosophies or personalities, and the prevailing fear of the Communists.

The strength of the executive in the Fifth Republic has relegated the legislature to a subordinate position, with a concomitant lessening of the role of the political parties. Yet the very strength of the executive has come from its ability to count on an acquiescent parliamentary majority. There is no doubt, therefore, that a great increase in the parliamentary membership of the non-Gaullist, non-Communist parties, or of a stronger, more cohesive left-center, would result in a very different type of interaction between executive and legislature. It is in this perspective that party maneuvers in France must be evaluated.

3. ELECTIONS

The Electoral System for the National Assembly

The French have shown a dismaying enthusiasm for new electoral systems. No other country has tried so many different ones—five distinct types, and fifteen with noticeably different features, during the past hundred years—or has made electoral change so much of a habit. Only once in that period, between 1889 and 1919, have the French used an electoral system for more than two elections in succession. If, as Peter Campbell demonstrates in his careful study, *French Electoral Systems and Elections, 1789–1957,* French electoral systems were not to blame for governmental instability, neither were they able, during that period, to create stable regimes. Thus the perennial search continued for an electoral formula that would help to reduce the number of extremists at either end of the political spectrum, or lessen the number of splinter groups, or in some other way produce a cohesive majority.

Most electoral changes in France have attempted to further partisan ends. They have been designed to work to the advantage of dominant groups, as in 1945 when the MRP, the Socialists, and the Communists endorsed proportional representation in the well-justified expectation that they would gain more seats than under the two-ballot system of single-member districts, which favored those parties (at that time the Radicals) with strong local machines. Or else they have been designed to answer particular emergencies, as when the system of *apparentement* (electoral alliances) was introduced in 1951 to strengthen the center parties against the Communists and Gaullist RPF, or as when the single-member district and two-ballot system was revived in 1958 for the twin purposes of weakening the Communists and aiding the conservative parties. However justified the reason may have seemed at the time, the frequency of the changes and the obviousness of the purposes behind them have impaired the sense of legitimacy of both the electoral process and its results and thereby have seriously weakened public faith in the democratic system.

The two most important electoral systems used in France have been those of proportional representation with a list system and the single-member constituency with two ballots. The former was used in two different forms under the Fourth Republic; the latter was characteristic of the Third Republic, except between 1919 and 1927, and has been adopted by the Fifth Republic.

*Proportional Representation Systems
and Their Consequences*

The three elections held in 1945 and 1946 were based on strict proportional representation, under which each party received seats within a large electoral district (commonly the department) in accordance with the percentage of votes cast for it. In 1951, this system was replaced by a modified majority system in which all the seats in a department went to any previously announced alliance or coalition of parties that won more than half the votes. In case an alliance did not win a majority of the votes, the seats in a department were divided proportionately, as before, but the alliance secured the number of seats to which its percentage of votes entitled it and then divided them (as it did if it won all the seats in an electoral district) in proportion to the votes cast for the separate parties that formed the alliance.

Strict proportional representation gave a marked advantage to the parties with national strength. Since it tended to split the seats in each department between two or more parties, it penalized those regional parties that had previously been able to win all, or a majority, of the seats in a department in certain large sections of the country. A third, and perhaps more serious consequence, was that proportional representation with a list system provided strong control by party officials over the selection of candidates, since, unless more than half the voters insisted on a change, candidates secured seats in the order in which their names appeared on the ballot. Thus there was much less relationship between voter and candidate than in Great Britain, not only in the legislature but also at the time of the election.

The modified majority system opened the way for smaller parties to secure overrepresentation by uniting in alliances. Thus it worked—designedly—against the Communists and, in 1951, against the RPF. But of itself the modified majority system could do nothing to secure unity behind any given program. In 1951, the center parties in seventy-six districts formed alliances, none of them with the Communists but, because of local circumstances, thirteen of them with the RPF. In thirty-eight constituencies, an alliance won more than half the votes; in one constituency a single list did the same. But in 1956, the center parties formed competing coalitions, and in consequence only in eleven electoral districts did alliances win all the seats. In the absence of a general agreement among these middle-of-the-road groups to reduce their differences in the interest of excluding the non-democratic parties (the Communists and, in 1956, the Poujadists), the usefulness of the system was nullified.

The Electoral System of the Fifth Republic

The last Cabinets of the Fourth Republic and de Gaulle's Cabinet all revealed sharp differences of opinion over what electoral system should replace the discredited modified majority system. Since de Gaulle's government was specifically authorized to determine the electoral system while it still possessed full powers (though Parliament thereafter regained its customary right to revise the system or establish a new one), de Gaulle followed the majority view in support of the single-member district plus two-ballot system characteristic of the Third Republic, which also fitted his own desire for a system that could be easily understood by the voters. Election is for a five-year period unless there is a dissolution.

The Two-Ballot System

The two-ballot system provides that if no candidate should secure more than half the votes at the election, there will be a second election a week later, both held commonly on a Sunday. The week interval gives each party and voter an opportunity to decide whether to continue to support the same candidate as before or whether to support another candidate who has a better chance to succeed. Under the Third Republic, both left- and right-wing parties used to switch their votes to that candidate among their group who had the best chance to win. Moreover, new candidates could enter on the second ballot.

This latter practice was forbidden by the Fifth Republic, and any candidate receiving less than 10 percent of the vote (until November 1966, 5 percent) on the first ballot is not allowed to run on the second. These provisions operate deliberately to the advantage of those parties that have the largest base of support or that are prepared to combine behind the candidate most likely to win.

In 1958 the sharp division between the Communists and other left-wing parties effectively prevented them from yielding to each other on the second ballot except in a few instances where the Communists did not oppose persons who had voted "no" on the referendum. Since only thirty-nine candidates were elected on the first ballot in 1958, the second ballot was particularly significant. It was at that stage that the Communists suffered so greatly while the UNR gained its nation-wide victory. Fairly characteristic was the situation in the Goutte-d'Or district of Paris, where the wife of the secretary-general of the Communist party polled almost twice as many votes on the first ballot as the UNR candidate who came second, 11,455 to 6,786. But on the second ballot, when only the UNR and Socialists retained their candidates against her, she lost to the UNR candidate by 12,545 votes to 20,160 votes.

It was this kind of situation that led the Socialists and Communists to enter into the arrangement in 1962 for mutual withdrawals. As we have seen, this arrangement helped the Socialists to win thirty of their sixty-five seats and helped the Communists to win twenty-two of their forty-one seats. This temporary Marxist alignment frightened the conservatives into the arms of the Gaullists and led to the UNR virtually absorbing the right and right-center. Moreover, the arrangement between the Socialists and Communists threatened the former's fragile cohesion and alarmed the Radicals. Yet only a non-Gaullist, non-Communist centrist alignment or a left-center one including the Communists appeared capable of challenging the Gaullists in the next electoral contest for the legislature.

The Voter and the Candidate

Regardless of the changes in the electoral system, the conditions under which a person may vote and run as a candidate in France have remained approximately the same over the years. Candidates must be over twenty-three (voters over twenty-one), French by birth or naturalized for at least ten years (voters naturalized for five years), and free from any of the incapacities defined by law. These incapacities include such expected barriers as conviction for certain crimes. Since the days of General Boulanger, no one may run in more than one district. There is no positive residence qualification in France, but a negative provision exists under which prefects and members of the judiciary may not run in districts where they have served until after a designated time (between six months and three years, depending on the position) has elapsed.

The most significant innovation of the Fifth Republic is to require the nomination of a substitute who can fill a member's seat in the chamber should this member be chosen as a minister or accept an incompatible position— e.g., on the Constitutional Council or as a trade union official—or die. The position of the substitute is an anomalous one. He may or may not campaign, but if he does he has no financial responsibilities for the campaign. His name appears on the ballot along with that of the candidate, so that the voter is, in effect, selecting both; the voter's choice is complicated if he views the two candidates in a different light. And while the substitute assumes a parliamentary seat only if the member is unable to fulfill his own mandate, he is barred from opposing the member at the next election. The purpose of this provision is to keep ministers from moving in and out of the Assembly, but the character of Cabinets in the Fifth Republic has made it less important than was expected.

Candidates must announce their candidature at least twenty-one days before the first ballot, and, in a new effort to prevent frivolous nominations, each is required to deposit 1,000 new francs (approximately $200), which is not returnable unless the candidate receives at least 5 percent of the votes in either of the ballots.

Money in Elections

French political parties are under no obligation to publish the sources of their funds or their election expenditures. Moreover, no limit is set on spending in elections. In an effort to equalize the opportunities among candidates, the government reimburses everyone who retains his deposit for the expenses of certain types of publicity, including posters on official billboards and the printing and mailing of election addresses and cards. In theory, only this kind of propaganda is permitted; in practice, however, a good deal of unofficial material is circulated. With rare exceptions, French political parties and parliamentary candidates do not engage in the kind of splashy electoral advertising or gimmickry that often mark an American campaign. One candidate is reported to have spent the equivalent of $100,000 for spectacular self-advertising in the 1956 election, but the average total electoral expenditure for a national party is only two to four times this amount. Apart from unofficial contributions by trade union members to the Communists and the Socialists, most of the money contributed to electoral expenses comes from professional or from employers' groups, notably the CNPF (*Counseil National du Patronat Français*). These groups often support more than one party and may even contribute to a Socialist candidate if he seems likely to defeat a Communist.

Electoral Campaigns in the Fifth Republic

The 1958 Assembly Election

The 1958 electoral campaign was held in the shadow of the referendum two months before. Almost everyone, except the Communists, proclaimed his allegiance to de Gaulle. The UNR could claim most authentically, however, to be the Gaullist party, and it did so with the smooth techniques of modern publicity experts—with the added attraction of a series of well-known personalities who represented a variety of views.

Twelve parties or election coalitions presented the minimum of seventy-five candidates necessary to qualify for free radio and television time. The newest of the twelve were the UNR and the Union of Democratic Forces (UDF), which included the Mendès-France wing of the Radicals and François Mitterrand's wing of the UDSR. The political spectrum extended from Pierre Poujade's UDCA (Union for the Defense of Tradesmen and Craftsmen) to Maurice Thorez's Communist party. Noticeable were the splits in the Democratic Left between Guy Mollet's Socialist party and an Autonomous Socialist party made up of the dissident SFIO; among the Radicals, the Republican Center under André Morice, Felix Gaillard's Radical

Socialists, and the UDF; and between the democratic Catholics of Pierre Pflimlin's MRP and Georges Bidault's French Christian Democracy (DCF).

The Communists entered candidates in all districts on the first ballot and, despite their obvious isolation, optimistically avowed their intention of seeking a union of republican forces on the second ballot. The Socialists under Guy Mollet supported de Gaulle's policy in Algeria, the evolution of the Franco-African Community, economic expansion, and social progress. The UDF and Autonomous Socialist party called for negotiations with rebel and representative groups in Algeria and, on the home front, for more economic planning to secure full employment without inflation. Gaillard's Radical Socialists stuck to a more classic economic program but demanded a revolution in French education, particularly by making higher education more readily available to all, while André Morice's group supported a French Algeria. The MRP, badly shaken in morale, campaigned in support of de Gaulle's Algerian policy, European unity, and economic and social expansion. The Independents, in contrast to most other French parties, went all the way in support of the complete integration of Algeria and France, were skeptical about de Gaulle's policies toward the African territories, and favored an economic "liberalism" for France similar to West Germany's. The newly organized UNR took no precise stand on any issue and, despite the General's refusal to associate himself with any political party, stressed only its complete fidelity to him. Poujade sounded much more moderate than in 1956, though he assailed the Common Market. It was obvious, however, that his movement was at an end.

The Fourth Republic's adoption of the department as the electoral district had made campaigns less individualistic and elections no longer a matter of personality and camaraderie. But the return to the single-member district reintroduced most of the old campaign practices of the Third Republic. House-to-house canvasses replaced mass meetings in many places, though there were also a few well-publicized debates, notably between Mendès-France and his rightist and successful opponent, and between General Chassin of the Algerian ultras and the moderate

UNR Jacques Chaban-Delmas in Bordeaux. In general, however, the electoral campaign was less vigorous than were those of the Third Republic.

The 1962 Referendum and Assembly Election

The legislative election of 1962 followed so closely the referendum called to endorse direct election of the President that we must consider the two together. Despite widespread criticism and opposition from the older parties and, to a muted degree, from the constitutional bodies concerned, de Gaulle persisted in his determination to bypass the regular amendment process and refer the constitutional change to referendum. He so notified the chambers on October 2, 1962; the Assembly passed a motion of censure, bringing down the Pompidou government; de Gaulle dissolved the Assembly on October 6; and the fight was on.

THE REFERENDUM The campaign before the referendum on October 28 was marked by high political tension but little popular excitement. Both sides redoubled the assaults (now written rather than verbal) that had already been in process before the Assembly was dissolved. It was apparent that the opposition's arguments were almost entirely negative, that the executive was prepared to exploit to the full the government's monopoly of broadcasting (each of the six parties received ten minutes, while de Gaulle and the ministers spoke at will), and that de Gaulle was determined to make the referendum a personal vote of confidence in himself. On October 18, he declared:

> If you answer no, as all the old parties would like so as to restore their regime of disgrace, as well as all the plotters who want to promote subversion, or even if the majority of "yes" is weak, mediocre, risky, it is obvious that my role will be over, immediately and forever.

Many were torn between their unhappiness over this use of the referendum and their unwillingness to indicate lack of support for de Gaulle. The outcome indicated their uncertainty.

The tally showed the lowest proportion of "yes" votes yet received in a referendum by de Gaulle: 74.95 percent of the registered voters (who numbered 28,185,478) participated, but only 62.25 percent of the valid ballots (which amounted to 21,125,054) supported him. Thus the "yes" vote of 13,150,516 was only 46.66 percent of the registered voters. In fourteen out of ninety departments the "no" vote exceeded the "yes" vote, the first time this had happened in any department in a referendum in the Fifth Republic. Twelve of these fourteen departments formed an arc stretching from southwestern France to the Italian border (except for Alpes-Maritimes at the southeast corner). In these the opposition was most marked in the villages and small towns.

The areas of high "yes" votes formed a somewhat paradoxical combination. Two—those of western France (Brittany and Normandy), and of eastern France (Alsace and Lorraine)—coincided with traditionally conservative strongholds; but in the third, the large industrial area of northern France, the left had formerly been very strong. Interestingly, there was a marked coincidence between the areas of high positive votes and high birth rate.

In 1958, the Socialists, the MRP, the Independents, and, more reluctantly, the Radicals (as well as the UNR) had supported de Gaulle. The referendum indicated that when these four opposition parties opposed him, they lost more than half their votes. Only the Communists had voted strictly according to instructions, while one-third of the Socialist voters, half the Radical and Independent voters, and some 85 percent of the MRP voters had voted "yes." Though *Le Monde* wrote that there had been "no winners, no losers," de Gaulle had, in fact, got his way. The long-range impact, however, would be largely determined by the results of the legislative election to follow.

THE ASSEMBLY ELECTION In the campaign between the referendum and the election, the opposition showed itself as negative as ever and even more seriously divided. Since the constitutional factor was no longer at issue, it lost the support of certain professional groups and intellectuals. It found it difficult to answer the lofty Gaullist claim of representing order, efficiency, and rebuilding, and the charge that the old parties had brought France to stalemate and near-chaos. What may well have been deci-

Results of the Legislative Elections of November 23 and 30, 1958 [1]

	FIRST BALLOT		SECOND BALLOT	
	Votes	*Percent*	*Votes*	*Percent*
UNR or Gaullists	3,603,958	17.60	5,249,746	28.1
Communists	3,882,204	18.90	3,883,418	20.5
National Independents' Center	2,815,176	13.70	2,869,173	15.4
Socialists	3,167,354	15.50	2,574,606	13.8
Popular Republican Movement	1,858,380	9.10	1,370,246	7.3
Radicals	983,201	4.80	619,784	3.3
Moderates	1,277,424	6.20	570,775	3.1
Left Republican Rally	716,869	3.50	439,517	2.4
Republican Center	647,919	3.02	451,810	2.4
Christian Democrats	520,408	2.05	343,292	1.8
Extreme Right and Poujadists	669,518	3.03	172,361	1.0
Miscellaneous Left	347,298	1.04	146,046	0.8

[1] All percentages are based on the number of registered voters.

sive, however, was Guy Mollet's decision to form a negative electoral alliance between the Socialists and the Communists in which neither would compete with the other on the second ballot. This decision presented the right with a golden opportunity to flourish the Communist menace and further split the non-Communist opponents of Gaullism.

The first ballot, on November 18, had strange features. The total number of abstentions rose far above what it had been in any legislative election since World War II—31.25 percent. This may have been a mark of recognition that the Assembly had ceased to be the center of power. But the most important fact was that the UNR won 31.9 percent of the votes, a significant vic-

tory. The UNR, together with its affirmed allies, the dissident Independents, polled 5,847,403 votes, about two and a half million more than in 1958. These votes were won largely, though not exclusively, from the Independents and the MRP.

The extreme right virtually disappeared. In contrast, the Communist vote went up slightly, to 3,992,431—21.78 percent of the total cast. This was an increase from the 18.9 percent in 1958, but it was markedly less both in total and percentage than the more than five million votes and the 25 percent of those cast that were common under the Fourth Republic. The evident trend was toward the moderate right.

Out of the 435 seats for metropolitan France,

Results of the Legislative Elections of November 18 and 25, 1962 [1]

	FIRST BALLOT		SECOND BALLOT	
	Votes	*Percent*	*Votes*	*Percent*
UNR	5,847,403	31.9	6,165,929	40.5
Communists	3,992,431	21.8	3,243,041	21.3
Socialists	2,319,662	12.6	2,304,330	15.2
National Independents' Center	1,660,896	9.1	1,125,988	7.4
Popular Republican Movement	1,635,452	8.9	806,908	5.3
Independents	798,092	4.4	241,853	1.6
Left Center	705,186	3.8	432,389	2.8
Radicals	679,812	3.7	635,712	4.2
Extreme Left	449,743	2.4	183,844	1.2
Republican Center	81,627	0.5	51,164	0.4

[1] All percentages are based on the number of registered voters.

a second ballot was necessary in 369 districts. In 227 of these districts, the competition was narrowed by withdrawals to a contest between right and left: Gaullist on one side and Radical, Socialist, or Communist on the other. The second ballot results showed a decisive increase in Gaullist votes to 6,407,782, almost a million and a half more in these 369 districts than on the first ballot. The traditional left—Radicals, Socialists, and Communists—also increased their percentage slightly, with the Socialists securing the major advantage. Both the Independents and the MRP, on the other hand, lost substantially, a further indication that the UNR was benefiting at their expense. Finally, as we saw earlier, the UNR and its allies obtained 249 seats, a clear and unprecedented majority of the members in the Assembly. De Gaulle had succeeded in his objective of turning the legislative election into a second and even more successful affirmation of personal support.

Elections for the Senate

The Senate is a weak body, much less important than the Assembly. It is elected indirectly, mainly by local councilors. Of the 108,266 electors in 1959, 53 percent came from communes with fewer than 1,500 inhabitants, 25.5 percent from towns with 1,500 to 10,000 inhabitants, and only 21.5 percent from cities with over 10,000 inhabitants.

Of the 307 members of the Senate selected in 1959, 255 were from metropolitan France, 32 from Algeria, 2 from the Sahara, 7 from overseas departments, and 5 from overseas territories; 6 were chosen by French citizens living abroad. The 60 senators from the seven most populous departments of France were elected by proportional representation. Those from France, Algeria, the Sahara (Algeria and Sahara were eliminated from subsequent representation because of Algerian independence), and four of the overseas departments were selected in the double-ballot system by department-wide electoral colleges. These colleges consisted of the deputies for the department, the department councilors, all municipal councilors for towns with over 9,000 inhabitants (with an additional delegate for each thousand inhabitants over 30,000), and 1–15 delegates for towns

and villages under 9,000, depending on their size. Though there was a slight additional representation for the more populous towns, since under the Fourth Republic one additional delegate was allowed only for each 5,000 inhabitants over 45,000, the overrepresentation of the rural areas remained marked. Since, in addition, the elections were for nine-year terms (one-third chosen every three years), as in the Third Republic (in the Fourth Republic for six years), and many of the electors were bound to have been selected several years earlier, there is a serious danger that the second chamber is always out of touch with public opinion.

While the Assembly elections of 1958 brought many new members into the chamber, the Senate elections in 1959 returned a high proportion of former senators and deputies. Eighty-four percent of those senators offering themselves for reelection were successful. Of the 85 new senators, 34 were former deputies. Twenty-five of these included such former leaders as Mitterrand, Edgar Faure, and Duclos, who had failed to secure seats in the Assembly the November before. On the overall results, the Communists lost only two seats and the Socialists five, as compared with their representation in the Council of the Republic of the Fourth Republic, while the Radical-oriented center won three more seats, the MRP eight more, and the Independents five more. In light of the expectation that the Senate would act as a brake on the National Assembly, it was particularly striking that the UNR failed by two to secure even as many seats as had been held by the RPF.

The campaigning for the Senate was restricted to negotiations between departmental party organizations. The UNR and Independents tended to work together, but their overtures to the MRP and other central groups were largely unsuccessful. Communist discipline held when the MRP retired its candidates in favor of Socialist or Radical candidates in over twenty departments on the second ballot (necessitated by the lack of an absolute majority on the first ballot). Noticeable was the contrast between the party representation from particular departments in the Assembly and in the Senate. Thus the hoped-for difference in the political complexion of the two chambers was achieved, but it was not the difference that had been desired.

The rural elements, which were out of touch with the new industrialization, were once more entrenched in the Senate. At the same time, some of the ablest parliamentary leaders of the Fourth Republic had seats in that body, while the Assembly had a majority of untried and inexperienced members.

In 1964, a new act instituted majority voting for party lists of candidates in all cities of more than 30,000 inhabitants (158 cities) in place of the existing system of proportional representation. The system had already been in effect for the 37,808 municipalities having fewer than 30,000 inhabitants. If a list receives a majority of the vote, it gains all the seats; if not, there is a runoff election between parties receiving at least 5 percent of the vote. In that case a plurality secures all the seats.

The government expected that this new system would polarize voting and force voters who had supported the center parties, which had done so well in 1959, to vote for either the Gaullists or the Communists. No clear pattern emerged, however, in the municipal elections of March 1965. If anything, the Socialists and Communists, working in each other's interests, emerged with an advantage. Otherwise the UNR would have won a majority in the Paris city council. In fact, the abolition of the proportional representation system in the larger towns, far from working to the advantage of the UNR, worked against it. The UNR won no seats in Marseilles and Lyons, the second and third largest cities in France, and lost Grenoble, Le Mans, and other smaller towns. On balance, the UNR held its own but made no noticeable impact at the grass-roots level. Of the towns affected by the change, only twenty-four changed hands, mainly to the advantage of the Communists. In the municipal elections, at least, and by projection in the elections for the second chamber, the UNR lacks the strength it evidenced in the Assembly elections of 1958 and 1962.

Elections for the President

The most dramatic and far-reaching constitutional change made during the Fifth Republic has been the change from indirect to direct election of the President. Controversial as was the process for winning support for this change, there is no doubt that it has revivified French politics. In the total picture of elections under the Fifth Republic, the election for the President in December 1965 emerges as the most significant, largely because it was marked by a type of political campaigning previously unknown under this constitutional system. Moreover it provided the most serious test up to that time of de Gaulle's popularity and, possibly, furnished the best indication of future developments.

The President of the Fifth Republic was always intended to be the key representative of the nation as neither the President of the Third nor of the Fourth Republic was supposed to be. There was therefore no intention of leaving his election to the two chambers (as had been the practice in the earlier regimes), particularly in view of the debacle of December 1953, when it took thirteen ballots to elect Senator René Coty, a moderate right-wing conservative. On the other hand, there was still too much fear of direct election in 1958 to entrust the choice of a President to the electorate at large. The compromise was to use an electoral college only slightly modified in composition from that which chose the senators.

A major difference between the electoral college for the Senate and for the President was that the latter included for this one time among its 81,764 members 3,643 of the elected representatives from the member-states of the Community, of which the President of France was ex-officio president. Another slight difference was that the electors from communes in France with fewer than 9,000 inhabitants were not special delegates; rather, the mayor and a designated number of councilors served as delegates. This change reduced the representation of villages under 1,500 people to 51 percent and of towns with between 1,500 and 10,000 inhabitants to 20 percent, while it raised only to 20 percent the representation of cities with over 10,000 inhabitants. This gave the rural elements the strongest voice in two of the three elected institutions of France.

In the first presidential election of the Fifth Republic, de Gaulle clearly chose himself for an office he had designed, and he subsequently made full use of its potential powers, as we have seen. Nominated by thousands of electors (at least fifty were necessary) from all the non-Communist parties except Mendès-France's UDF (which nominated Albert Chatelet, Dean of the Faculty of Science at the University of Paris) and the Communists (who nominated Georges Marrane, Mayor of Ivry), de Gaulle received 62,394 out of 79,470 votes cast—78.5 percent of the vote. The votes were cast on December 21, 1958, in the capital of each department of France and in the capital of each of the territories overseas. There was no stalemate, but there was also none of the glamour of the former electoral gatherings at Versailles.

The President is elected for seven years and may be reelected indefinitely. There is no provision (as there was in the 1946 constitution) limiting his terms. Although most people expected that de Gaulle would succeed himself, they were not prepared for the dramatic events of 1962 in which his attempted assassination (on August 22) was followed by his introduction of successful plans to provide for the direct election of the next President.

The present system of presidential elections was set up by the constitutional revision of October 28, 1962 (approved by the controversial referendum), the organic law of November 6, 1962, and decrees of January 25 and March 14, 1964. These provisions established that the election should take place by direct vote not less than twenty nor more than thirty-five days from the expiration of the presidential term (or the permanent incapacity of the President). Thus elections were due between December 4 and 19, 1965. Once again the process of second ballot was established so that if no candidate received an absolute majority of the votes on the first round, a runoff election would be held two weeks later between the two candidates receiving the greatest number of votes.

A candidate could be nominated by petition of any hundred members of parliament, of the Economic and Social Council, of General (i.e., Departmental) Councils, or elective mayors so long as they were drawn from at least ten different departments or overseas territories. A deposit of 10,000 francs (about $2,000) was re-

quired from each candidate; if he did not receive at least 5 percent of the vote, he forfeited his deposit. In that case, however, he was to receive an equal amount toward his expenses. A National Electoral Campaign Control Commission, composed of five high civil servants, was to supervise the campaign regulations, which provided for equal opportunity to use radio, TV, propaganda posters, and so forth, but only during the official campaign period, which was limited to fifteen to seventeen days.

First in the field was Gaston Deferre, Socialist Mayor of Marseilles, who was launched by the national weekly newspaper, *L'Express,* in September 1963 and officially announced his candidature as early as December 1963. Chairman of the SFIO in the Assembly, he also controlled the largest Socialist departmental organization in the country. But if his lack of dogmatism on Socialist doctrine and clericalism made him acceptable to the center parties, his forthright anti-Communism led to opposition, not only from the Communists themselves but also from the Mollet wing of his own party. In January 1964 Deferre won a grudging endorsement from the Socialists (and subsequently from the Radicals) while keeping a free hand for his campaign. He then established committees with a wide membership spanning the Socialists, Radicals and UDSR, Christian Democratic and Socialist trade unions, political clubs, and university professors. Thereupon he undertook a number of provincial tours. But though he attracted attention, Deferre gained little support. Public opinion polls in late 1963 and 1964 showed a two to one preference for de Gaulle over Deferre, a gap that widened when the polls included other alternatives. Nor did the chances appear more promising for two other early candidates, Jean-Louis Tixier-Vignancour, a right-wing extremist, and André Cornu, from the Radical grouping. When Deferre withdrew in June 1965, the only serious contender left was de Gaulle himself.

All the more remarkable, therefore, was the liveliness of the final campaign. Of the six candidates at the end, only three were of significance: de Gaulle himself, who majestically waited until the last moment to announce that he was running; Jean Lecanuet, ex-President of

The Presidential Election
December 5 and 19, 1965

Votes obtained by	Number	Percent of valid votes	Percent of registered voters
FIRST BALLOT			
Charles de Gaulle	10,828,523	44.64	37.45
François Mitterrand	7,694,003	31.72	26.61
Jean Lecanuet	3,777,119	15.57	13.08
Jean-Louis Tixier-Vignancour	1,260,208	5.19	4.35
Pierre Marcilhacy	415,018	1.71	1.43
Marcel Barbu	279,683	1.15	0.96
SECOND BALLOT			
Charles de Gaulle	13,083,699	55.19	45.26
François Mitterrand	10,619,735	44.80	36.74

the MRP and the center candidate, who had been virtually unknown before the campaign but soared up on the public opinion polls from 3 percent to 20 percent in the last month of the campaign; and François Mitterrand, from a small Radical-associated group, the UDSR, who also secured both Socialist and Communist support. It was Lecanuet's brilliant TV performances and modern campaign, his youth (he was 45—de Gaulle was 75) and good looks, and his pro-Europeanism, that sparked the official campaign period and brought a new concern for politics into French life. It was Mitterrand's solid support from the Socialists, Communists, and Radicals that won him second place in the polls.

The supreme surprise of the election was that in the heaviest polling in France's electoral history, with a turnout of 85 percent of the enrolled voters, de Gaulle received just under 45 percent, forcing him into a runoff election in which he won just over 55 percent. Although he was returned to the presidency for another seven years, de Gaulle had lost the mystique and the widespread sense of his indispensability that had dominated French politics since 1958.

The Geography of Elections

We have already suggested, in the preceding sections, the geography of voting under the Fifth Republic. The maps opposite show the areas from which the two most widely and consistently supported political forces in contemporary France—Gaullism and Communism—draw their major support.

4. HOW WELL DOES THE FRENCH PARTY SYSTEM WORK?

Any attempt to evaluate the French party system raises the same questions that arose in connection with British parties. The answers, however, are quite different.

In one sense, French parties offer their members and the voters a more accurate spectrum of political views and of leaders than does the British system, simply because the choice is far greater. Although it is often the despair of those seeking a broad association of political interests, it is also a matter of pride that any fervently held political view can be—and often has been—reflected in a particular political party. If the extreme right has been eliminated, as the 1962 election returns suggest, it is because France's economic growth is solving the problems that gave rise to it.

In another sense, however, the choice provided by the French political spectrum is less meaningful than the simpler British one. The very fact of the multiplicity of French parties makes it extremely difficult—one no longer says impossible—for any party to win a majority of

Geography of the 1958 French Election

PERCENTAGE OF THE FIRST VOTE CAST FOR THE COMMUNISTS

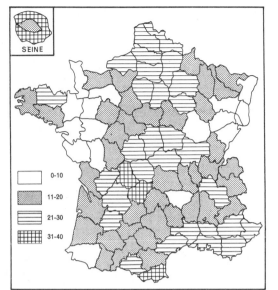

SEINE

- 0-10
- 11-20
- 21-30
- 31-40

PERCENTAGE OF THE FIRST VOTE CAST FOR THE U N R

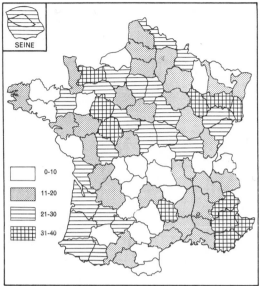

SEINE

- 0-10
- 11-20
- 21-30
- 31-40

Source: Adapted from *Le Monde,* November 25, 1958.

The Referendum of October 1962

The Elections of November 1962

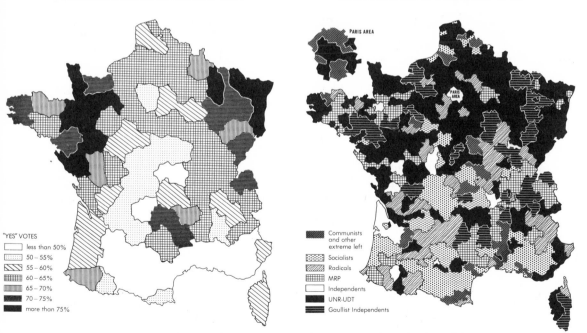

"YES" VOTES
- less than 50%
- 50 – 55%
- 55 – 60%
- 60 – 65%
- 65 – 70%
- 70 – 75%
- more than 75%

- Communists and other extreme left
- Socialists
- Radicals
- MRP
- Independents
- UNR-UDT
- Gaullist Independents

PARIS AREA

PARIS AREA

Source: Les Elections Législatives de 1962 (Paris, Imprimerie Nationale, 1963).

The Presidential Election December 5 and 19, 1965

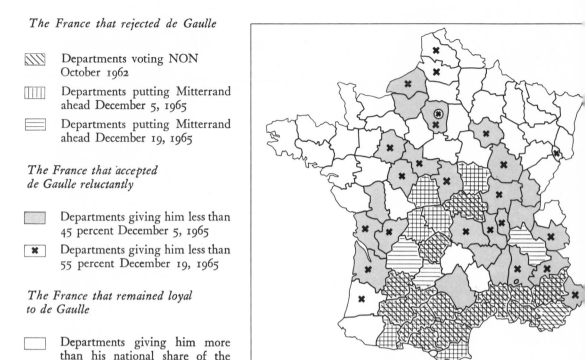

The France that rejected de Gaulle

▨ Departments voting NON
October 1962

▥ Departments putting Mitterrand
ahead December 5, 1965

▤ Departments putting Mitterrand
ahead December 19, 1965

*The France that accepted
de Gaulle reluctantly*

▦ Departments giving him less than
45 percent December 5, 1965

✗ Departments giving him less than
55 percent December 19, 1965

*The France that remained loyal
to de Gaulle*

☐ Departments giving him more
than his national share of the
votes in both rounds

Source: Manchester Guardian Weekly, December 30, 1965, p. 4.

the votes and legislative seats. It is even more difficult to envisage any regular alteration of a governing and an opposition party as in Great Britain and the United States.

A major difference between British and American parties, on the one hand, and French parties, on the other, has to do with the period at which the process of mutual concessions and compromise takes place—a process that is inevitable if groups holding different views and possessing different interests are to be persuaded to work together. In Great Britain and the United States, the parties, in appealing to the uncommitted voter in the middle, tend to moderate their stands and achieve compromise *before* the election. In France, such compromise has commonly occurred *after* the election, through jockeying inside and outside the chambers. Thus the process is less the result of appealing to the voters than of bargaining among political leaders. It is noticeable, however, that the introduction of the direct election of the

President led to a franker and more broadly gauged appeal to voters than has marked legislative elections in the past.

It is now misleading to say, as we once could, that the French, unlike the British and the Americans, have no direct way of passing upon the principles or the officials that are to guide the government. French voters indicated both in 1958 and in 1962 that they support General de Gaulle and those politicians who are prepared to support his policies. But this is still not to say that French voters can yet choose decisively *between* two sets of political alternatives. British and American voters can choose their leaders and, to some extent, their policies, because each country has a basically two-party system, and only in such a system is one party *or* the other certain to win a majority. Many Frenchmen have been asking themselves whether France should not have a two- or at most a three-party system, and whether such a system would not give the people a much better opportunity to participate in their government.

Any two- or three-party system that France might develop, however, would almost inevitably differ fundamentally from the two-party system in either Great Britain or the United States. In both the latter, the opposing parties accept certain common political assumptions and values; neither party feels that the country is irretrievably lost if the other triumphs in the elections; and each party knows that there will be another election and another chance to win. In France the existence and the electoral strength of the Communists threaten this assumption. If they should ever turn out to be the dominant party of the future, the result might be not an advance toward democracy but an advance toward civil war. The conservative parties detest the Communist party, and they have no confidence that if it won power it would ever again yield it.

The great hope for French democracy must be, therefore, that the non-Communist parties, in cohesive groupings, will maintain or increase their electoral strength and legislative representation. The non-Gaullist, non-Communist parties are groping toward alignments that with or without the Communists could offer substantial opposition to the Gaullists. But will they succeed? Still more important: Will the UNR remain a major party after de Gaulle leaves politics, or will it split between those alignments toward which its non-Communist opposition is moving? The future of the French party system depends on the answers to these questions.

The 1967 Election

The 1967 election for the National Assembly —held March 5 and 12—resulted in a much reduced majority for the Gaullists but an alignment that will enable them to maintain their control of the chamber. The election returns indicated a turning away from the center in favor of either the Gaullists or the non-Communist and Communist left and thus a more definite division between two great forces than had previously appeared in French politics. The results for the 486 seats (16 of them overseas) were: Gaullists (the UNR together with the Independent Republicans under Giscard d'Estaing), 244; the Federation of the Left (a fusion of Radicals, Socialists, and splinter parties of the left under François Mitterrand), 116; Communists, 73; Democratic Center (under Jean Lecanuet), 27; various moderates, 15; moderate left, 5; extreme left, 5. The Democratic Center can be expected ordinarily to support the Gaullists rather than the left.

In the first electoral round on March 5, when it was necessary to secure an absolute majority of the votes to be successful, the Gaullists appeared to be doing well. They polled 37.75 percent of the vote, approximately the same as in 1962. The 79 candidates elected at that time included M. Pompidou, the Premier, and 10 of the 26 members of the government who stood for election. The Communists also increased their share of the votes, from 21.84 to 22.46 percent, while the Federation of the Left and, even more, the Democratic Center suffered reductions on their percentage of the vote.

In the second and decisive balloting on March 12, a major factor in the striking increase in seats received by the non-Communist left and the Communists was their adherence to their political pact to unite behind the candidate of either group who was best placed to win. Of the 18.7 million valid votes cast in the 397 districts contested on March 12, the results were as follows: Gaullists, 7.8 million (42.6 percent); the Federation of the Left, 4.5 million (24.1 percent); Communists, almost 4 million (21.4 percent); Democratic Center, 1.3 million (7.1 percent). Thus the balance had tilted toward the left. It remained to be seen whether the non-Communist left and the Communists would continue in the Assembly the cooperation they exhibited in their election pact.

4. The French Parliament

1. THE CHARACTER OF THE NATIONAL ASSEMBLY

The Powers of the National Assembly

Nowhere do the constitution and the practice of the Fifth Republic differ more markedly from those of the Fourth Republic than in the transformation of the National Assembly. Formerly the dominant agency of the government, it is now a representative body that is limited in authority, and controlled by, far more than it controls, the executive. In the Fourth Republic, the National Assembly was the center of power, and between elections it spoke in the name of the people of France. Under the Fifth Republic, there has been a strong move toward executive rule and, indeed, toward personal rule by the President.

Nonetheless, and according to the theory of the constitution, the Fifth Republic is a parliamentary regime, just as the Third and Fourth Republics were. In presenting the constitution, Debré declared that "the parliamentary regime is the only one suitable for France." In form, and to a certain degree in practice, the basic principles of parliamentary government persist, and the government is still responsible to the National Assembly, although the censure procedure for overthrowing it is a novel one. The distinctive change in the character of the French political system under the Fifth Republic is the increased prerogative of the whole executive—within which the dominant power exercised by President de Gaulle arises from his personal position, not from a constitutional base—and the fact that for the first time in French parliamentary history the executive is supported by an organized majority, the UNR and its allies, that underwrites the wishes of the executive. Should new elections change this situation, the interaction between executive and parliament would also change decisively.

The Composition of the National Assembly

The election of 1962 provided the UNR–UDT with more seats than any French party had ever had before in the Assembly—229 altogether, only slightly less than an absolute majority. With the 20 dissident Independents who were elected at the same time as avowed allies of the UNR, the executive could count on a clear majority in the house, an unprecedented situation in French parliamentary history.

This majority of seats had not, of course, been reflected in so decisive a majority of the votes. Rather surprisingly, the use of single-member constituencies and the two-ballot system created distortions in 1962, as it had in 1958, that were greater than those created by proportional representation under the Fourth Republic. Specifically, the UNR received only 31.9 percent of the votes on the first ballot in 1962 but received 46 seats, while the Communists won only 9 seats with 21.79 percent. On the second ballot, the UNR won 183 seats—making up its total of 229 deputies—with 40.51 percent of the votes, while the Communists, who retained 21.31 percent of the votes, virtually the same as before, won only 32 seats—making their total in the Assembly 41. The Gaullist Independents, whose support provided the UNR with its absolute majority of seats in the Assembly, received only 4.36 percent of the votes but 12 seats on the first ballot, and an insignificant 1.6 percent of the votes but 8 seats on the second ballot. Thus together the UNR

The French National Assembly

AFTER 1946 ELECTIONS

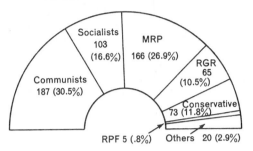

AFTER 1951 ELECTIONS

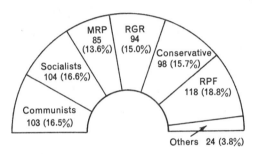

AFTER 1956 ELECTIONS

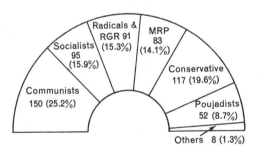

AFTER 1958 ELECTIONS

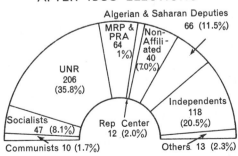

and Gaullist Independents totaled only 36.26 percent on the first ballot and 42.11 percent on the second and yet won 249 seats out of 464.

Interestingly enough, the 1962 election, like that in 1958 and in 1945, introduced many new faces to the National Assembly. In 1958 only 131 of the 552 members (including those from Algeria and the Sahara, which had become independent by 1962) had served in the previous Assembly, and only one-quarter of the deputies among the UNR, Independents, and MRP had had previous legislative experience. In 1962, 225 deputies were new to the Assembly, 121 of them Gaullist.

The Meeting Place

In contrast to the rectangular chamber of the House of Commons, the National Assembly meets in a semicircular amphitheater in the Palais Bourbon, which has close-packed benches rising sharply one above another. Members of the Ministry occupy special benches down front, where the representatives of committees may also sit when their topics are under consideration. In front of the auditorium is a high ornate desk, approached by a flight of stairs on either side. Here sits the President of the Assembly, flanked by secretaries at lower desks. Immediately in front of the President's desk is a rostrum, the "tribune," from which deputies may address the Assembly.

Parties are commonly grouped on the curved benches according to the shade of their political views. The left, of course, is the prized position, and almost any kind of maneuver will be made to secure some of its prestige. Despite the obviously conservative character of most of the UNR deputies, that party (which first favored the British system of seating the government

AFTER 1962 ELECTIONS

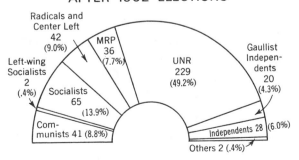

across from the opposition) refused in 1958 to sit on the extreme right (forcing the Independents to sit there) and was ultimately given a center position from which it overflowed into areas commonly occupied by parties more suitable to those positions. In 1962, the elimination of the extreme right, and a vast reduction in the strength of the Independents, forced the UNR into the section on the right of the chamber. (The diagrams on page 63 indicate the relative strength of the major political groups following the elections of November 1946, June 1951, January 1956, November 1958, and November 1962. The diagrams, however, do not attempt to reproduce exactly the complicated and shifting groups or seating arrangements in the Assembly.)

The spirit of such an assembly differs fundamentally from that of the House of Commons. Instead of the sharp division between government and opposition—which forces every member of Parliament to take his position clearly on one side or the other and which makes any deserting member extremely conspicuous—the French arrangement has been one of slight gradations from left to right. Parties blend into one another, and deputies could formerly shift from one party to another with ease. Under the weak party discipline of the Third Republic, and the changing party alignments, especially on the right, of the Fourth Republic, the instability of governments was sometimes attributed to the facility with which a member could shift to the left or the right and vote with his neighbors against his own party. Winston Churchill expressed a typically British reaction to this situation when he told the House of Commons in his famous speech of October 28, 1943, that

> ... the semi-circular assembly, which appeals to political theorists, enables every individual to move round the centre, adopting various shades of pink according as the weather changes. I am a convinced supporter of the party system in preference to the group system. .... The party system is much favored by the oblong form of Chamber. It is easy for an individual to move through those insensible gradations from Left to Right but the act of crossing the Floor is one which requires serious consideration. I am well informed on this matter, for I have accomplished that difficult process, not only once but twice.

A more important consequence of the arrangement is the type of parliamentary oratory it permits. The French deputy who wishes to address his colleagues does not rise in his place, as in Great Britain, and speak in casual and conversational tones with courteous references to the honorable gentlemen on his right and left. He mounts the tribune, and often he orates. The speeches in the National Assembly frequently are more polished and brilliant than their Anglo-Saxon counterparts, but it is doubtful that they contribute as much to serious discussion and compromise. There is a great temptation to elicit cheers and applause from the close-packed benches and to impress or electrify an audience composed of connoisseurs of eloquence. The temptation is almost as great to provoke the fury of the opposition by the vigor of one's attack and the sharpness of one's taunts. Noble sentiments from the left are met with ironic laughter on the right; a particularly nasty taunt or insinuation provokes shouts of protest, and, in extreme instances in the past, deputies on one side of the auditorium have hurled themselves on their opponents, while attendants hastily intervened and the presiding officer suspended the session.

To attribute such episodes to the fiery Gallic temperament is a great oversimplification. In reality they reflect two great handicaps from which the French political system has long suffered. First, some political differences are so deep as to make it extremely difficult for men of the extreme left and the right to treat each other with the courtesy and forbearance that are so fundamental to the British parliamentary tradition. Second, and even more important, is the fact that on the extreme left (and earlier, on the extreme right) there is little if any loyalty to the institutions of parliamentary democracy as such. In Great Britain the first loyalty of almost every member of Parliament is to the constitutional system; very few would be willing to discredit the system in order to win an advantage over a political opponent. In France members at a political extreme may actually profit by making parliament appear ridiculous; they realize that the mass of the French people would turn to either a Communist or a fascist dictatorship only if they were convinced of the unworkability of democratic institutions.

The Organization of the National Assembly

The President of the National Assembly

The presiding officer in the French Assembly has always had a less honored position than has the Speaker of the House of Commons. Under the Fourth Republic, the lack of discipline and orderliness among the deputies made his office an extremely difficult one. There has been a noticeable change under the Fifth Republic. Now his audience is much less unruly, and issues rarely rouse the kind of tension so prevalent in the Fourth Republic, simply because the Assembly now has so much less power. The only occasion on which the Palais Bourbon, the "House without Windows," regained its old passionate atmosphere was during the one successful motion of censure of the Fifth Republic, that of October 4, 1962, over de Gaulle's decision to use the referendum to test opinion on the direct election of the President. That motion brought down the Pompidou government, but, as we have seen, it failed to change the course of de Gaulle's policy.

The President of the Assembly has certain new functions that increase his prestige and are intended to help him control the Assembly if control becomes a problem. He is one of those consulted by the President of the Republic on the existence of an emergency. He chooses three of the nine members of the Constitutional Council. Moreover, he may submit to that body a private member's bill that he believes constitutional but that the government questions. Under the standing orders, he can call deputies to order and force the closure of debate. Both these powers are subject, however, to practice, which, in the National Assembly, has characteristically developed out of action rather than rules. Although the President of the Assembly ranks fourth in precedence in the country, the Assembly's current lack of power suggests that, in fact, he occupies a position less important than that of his predecessor in the Fourth Republic, who had to attempt to keep that all-powerful body in check through personal persuasion.

The Groups

Unlike the Speaker of the House of Commons, it is not the President of the Assembly who allocates time in more important debates to the representatives of different points of view and who arranges for sittings. Rather, it is the *Conférence des Présidents*—the heads of recognized groups. Instead of allowing any group with at least fourteen members (as at the beginning of the Fourth Republic, although the number was later expanded to twenty-eight) to set up a formal organization and choose as its spokesman a president who enjoys special debating privileges, the Fifth Republic requires the group to have thirty members. Although this provision denied the Communists this opportunity after the 1958 election, all six major parties qualified (the Independents had twenty-nine seats) in 1962. Each group draws up a political declaration for its members to sign, and this declaration and the list of members are filed with the Bureau.

The Bureau

The Bureau is made up of the President of the Assembly together with its other officers (six vice-presidents, fourteen secretaries, and three questors). It handles not only the debates, but also the counting of votes, the drafting of minutes, and general arrangements. As was true in the past, positions on the Bureau are distributed among the party groups in proportion to their strength. Through the questors, the Bureau also handles the Assembly's accounts. Perhaps its most discretionary function is to determine whether deputies' bills are admissible under the restrictions of Article 40 on financial legislation. Between sessions, the Bureau protects the immunities of the deputies.

2. THE NATIONAL ASSEMBLY IN ACTION

Constitutional provisions have combined to make the National Assembly of the Fifth Republic an even less effective body in practice than is the House of Commons. In relation to the traditional functions of a legislature—making and supporting a government, criticizing and controlling that government, and shaping the laws—the National Assembly has been placed at a great disadvantage: it can overthrow a Ministry but it cannot create one. Unlike the

House of Commons, the tradition of the National Assembly has been one of power, not of criticism; it is not well fitted, therefore, to assume the role of critic.

The National Assembly and the Ministry

It is still common in parliamentary countries to say that the first duty of a legislature is to make and to support a government. In Great Britain, this statement has lost much of its point, since in ordinary circumstances it is the voters rather than the members of Parliament who decide which party shall be in power, that is, which members of which party shall constitute the Cabinet. In France, the Fifth Republic has removed from the Assembly what used to be a key power: the approval of the choice of the Premier.

It is true that after the Premier has been nominated by the President of the Republic, he presents his program first to the Assembly and then, through a minister, to the Senate. At this time the Assembly, by simple majority, can reject the Premier. It can also defeat his government by voting against any statement of policy or legislative text on which he demands a vote of confidence. Further, as we have seen, the Assembly can introduce a motion of censure if one-tenth of its members have endorsed it, and the government must resign if the motion receives the support of an absolute majority of the deputies. These, however, are negative provisions. Where the National Assembly used to be preeminently the maker of Ministries, it can now only dismiss them—and the one experience of 1962 suggests that the advantage is slight, if it exists at all.

It could be argued that the National Assembly has always possessed only a negative power over Ministries and that the decisive difference between its position under the Fourth and the Fifth Republics is the presence in the latter of the large bloc of UNR deputies who support the Premier whom the President has chosen. It is true, of course, that if the Assembly were subdivided into many small parties, the Premier would find it more difficult to secure the necessary support. But there are other factors that vastly strengthen the government in its relations with the Assembly. The incompatibil-

ity rule, which makes it necessary for a deputy to resign his seat in the Assembly if he becomes a minister, takes the maneuvering about places in a Ministry out of the realm of the parliamentary parties. The revived power of dissolution means that a vote of censure may, and experience suggests will, lead to new elections, which few deputies relish. Moreover, and still more important, the government possesses defined powers over the budget and over a segment of rule-making, powers that thus reduce the authority of the Assembly in these spheres. In addition, sometimes in the background but sometimes very much in the foreground, are the reserve and even the emergency powers of the President.

According to the constitution, parliament meets for two ordinary sessions a year beginning on the last Tuesday in April and the first Tuesday in October, respectively, and lasting a maximum of three months and two and a half months, respectively. In addition, it can be called into a special session of at most twelve days for a specific purpose by either the Premier or a majority of the Assembly. In March, 1960, 286 deputies requested a special session of the Assembly to deal with farmers' grievances. Though 286 deputies formed a clear majority of the members of the Assembly, de Gaulle refused their request. He argued that the proposal for the special session had been inspired by a professional group, the Farmers' Association, and was therefore from outside the Assembly, although this is not an unusual source of legislative proposals elsewhere. He pointed out that there had already been two special sessions (both of which, however, had been called by the government). Beyond this he questioned whether the Assembly could prepare satisfactory legislation on agriculture in twelve days, declared that the government was working on the subject but had not yet completed its proposal, and pointed out that any measure the Assembly might suggest would involve either decreasing revenue or increasing expenditures, both of which were outside its province. Thus de Gaulle assumed the right to decide whether action under a provision of the constitution was justified or not, and decided that it was not. He impaired, if he did not destroy, one of the safety valves of the regime. In doing so, he further weakened the position of the Assembly.

The Assembly still retains the power, of course, to defeat legislation proposed by the government. The struggle over de Gaulle's plan for an independent French nuclear striking force demonstrated, however, that the ability to force a vote of confidence on the life of the government places the latter in a strong position to force the hand of the Assembly. Late in 1960, for example, Premier Debré twice answered strong criticism of the measure from the left and center as well as motions of censure with a demand for a vote of confidence. Although the deputies were frustrated and angry at being denied the chance to postpone or modify a measure with such far-reaching and possibly negative implications for France's European policy, they were unwilling to take the supreme step of overthrowing the Ministry. Thus, in much the same way as a British Prime Minister is able to force through the House of Commons a particular measure that the House would not support on a free vote, the French Premier under the Fifth Republic is able to control and dominate the once uncontrollable National Assembly.

In the debate on nuclear policy, however, the Ministry and Assembly engaged in the kind of interaction characteristic of the parliamentary system in its classical form. The Assembly retained its right to withhold confidence, and the Ministry forced the Assembly to declare for or against its continued life. But this classic expression of parliamentary action operates in a less traditional milieu in France than in Great Britain and thus handicaps the Assembly in maintaining executive responsibility under normal circumstances. On the one hand, the President of the Republic not only has the constitutional functions of supervision and arbitration between government and parliament; in practice, he has assumed the right to intervene to the disadvantage of the Assembly. On the other hand, because of French political history and the multiparty system, the parliamentary procedures that keep a powerful executive alert and responsive to the criticism of private members and the community have never been developed in France. Thus the Assembly fails to exercise as much influence as it might otherwise do, even in its circumscribed role, as we will see in considering its work as a critic.

The Assembly as Critic

There are two particular ways in which deputies can criticize the government and check on its actions: through a vote of censure and through questions. Limits have been placed on both these techniques, however, to prevent them from being used to weaken the Ministry or to obstruct government business. Behind these limits lies the general conception, characteristic also of Great Britain, that the government should not be defeated on anything less than an issue of confidence. Unlike Great Britain, however, the tendency in France under the Fifth Republic has been to be chiefly concerned with numerical majorities (which the British party system almost always places at the disposal of a Ministry) rather than with the pertinence of the implied or explicit criticism.

The Vote of Censure

Votes of censure operate in two ways. If initiated by the deputies, each vote must have the signature of at least 10 percent of them to be brought to a vote; to succeed, it must receive an absolute majority of all the deputies. Moreover if the motion is lost, the deputies who signed the original motion lose their right to sign another motion of censure in the same session. These restrictions do not hold when the government attempts to force through a bill (to establish an independent nuclear striking force, for instance) by making passage a matter of confidence, since such a measure is automatically accepted by the Assembly twenty-four hours after the announcement if no motion of censure has been introduced in the meantime. Even if the motion of censure is introduced, it requires an absolute majority, and thus in effect the overthrow of the government, to defeat the measure.

Questions

The French have never used the parliamentary question with the same effect as the British do, partly, at least, because under the Fourth Republic the question had little political significance. In contrast, the *interpellation,* which was a request to a minister for an explanation of his actions, had a great deal of political significance, since it always carried the threat that it might be followed by a condemnation of the minister and thus of the Cabinet of which he was a member. By eliminating the interpellation and retaining only the parliamentary question, the Fifth Republic has drawn the sting from this procedure.

The British House of Commons sets aside the first period of its formal session for questions that may range over the whole gamut of administration and policy, but only Friday afternoon is reserved for questions under the Fifth Republic. A deputy may wish his question to be either "with debate" or "without debate," but the Conference of Presidents has the decisive word on how it shall be treated and may even decree a written rather than a spoken answer. After the answer to a question without debate, a deputy has five minutes in which to comment, after which the minister may reply. A question with debate is elaborated by the deputy in a fifteen- to thirty-minute speech; the minister may answer immediately or announce his intention to have a full debate within two days. If the minister replies immediately, a debate follows in which the time for expressing different points of view is organized by the President of the Assembly.

Written and oral questions remain largely what they were under the Fourth Republic: means of eliciting information, securing the interpretation of a decree, questioning an abuse of law, and, less often, raising issues of policy. Written questions have long been popular and might be still if ministers were more punctilious about answering them. They are published in the official record of the Assembly, and the reply is supposed to appear within a month; ministers may ignore questions, however, or declare that the public interest prevents them from replying. The postwar innovation of oral questions, a deliberate attempt to copy British practice, has not yet been molded to serve Assembly purposes of executive supervision.

The Assembly as Legislator

One of the sharpest innovations of the Fifth Republic is to restrict the legislature to certain fields of rule-making, while the rest are assigned to the executive. In the past the government has exercised wide powers through decrees, special

powers, and other instances of delegated legislation, but parliament remained the final judge of their extent and duration and parliament had the ultimate right of ratification. Under the Fifth Republic the legislature may make *rules* governing certain enumerated subjects—notably personal rights and civil status, electoral laws, creation of nationalized industries, the penal code, liability to taxation and national defense, amnesty, and declaration of war—and lay down general principles governing another list of subjects—education, labor, trade unions, social security, local government, national defense, property and commercial rights, finance (under conditions defined in an organic law), and long-term social and economic projects. The list is long, but it gives rise to as many, if not more, questions than it answers. How, in particular, is the line to be drawn between a legislative decision on general principles and its application, which is in the exclusive field of the executive?

In drawing the line between legislative and executive competence, use is made of a unique and impressive French institution, the Council of State (*Conseil d'Etat*) (which will be considered in more detail in Chapter 6), as well as of the Constitutional Council. In regard to all laws passed *before* the constitution of the Fifth Republic came into force, the Council of State determines whether or not they now come within executive competence; if they do, they may be modified by decree. The Constitutional Council makes the decision on the boundary between the two jurisdictions if the law was passed *after* the constitution came into force. But while the government can challenge the competence of the Assembly to deal by legislation with a particular subject, there are no comparable means by which the Assembly can question the government's use of the decree power.

As in so many other places, this strengthening of the hand of the executive in rule-making and the consequent curbing of the legislature may well have gone too far for the healthy interaction of the two. It is apparent that the legislature attempted to do far too much in the Fourth Republic and also that modern social and economic problems demand prompt handling by executive agencies rather than piecemeal treatment by a large and inexpert body.

Nonetheless the pendulum seems to have swung very far.

French practice in the making of legislation is to give the text to the President of the Assembly, who announces its receipt, has it printed, and, in contrast to British procedure (according to which the critical "second reading debate" precedes the sending of the bill to committee) but like American practice, assigns it to the appropriate committee.

The Committees

Major changes between the Fourth and Fifth Republics in the role and importance of committees mark yet another lessening of the influence of the deputies. In the Fourth Republic, nineteen specialized committees (or *commissions,* as the French call them) of forty-four members each, chosen according to the strength of party groups and with more or less permanent assignments, dominated the legislative work of the National Assembly and played a controlling role in both finance and administration. Under the Fifth Republic, there are only six standing committees. They have large memberships and shift their attention to whatever subjects the Assembly wishes them to consider. They were deliberately made rather unwieldy bodies in an effort to reduce their political importance. The change also enhances the importance of the *ad hoc* committees (which have no fixed membership and are elected by a majority of the Assembly), which are designed for use on particularly important questions or on matters that require speedy action.

Parliamentary groups—that is, those with at least thirty members—are allocated seats on the standing committees proportionate to their representation in the Assembly; debate is unrestricted; ministers may be questioned if they are willing (and they usually are) to appear; and decisions are taken by majority vote. Committee chairmen, who are chosen by agreement between the leaders of the major parliamentary groups, do not play the dominant role they do in the United States but have considerable responsibilities in guiding and even limiting the discussion of such large bodies.

The finance committee has more prestige than the others, although it enjoys nothing approaching its former power of investigating the budget of every department and interpreting finance as related to every aspect of policy. Under the allocation of responsibilities laid down in the constitution, the Assembly is not to reduce revenues or to increase expenditures. But by wily proposals balancing the two, the Assembly, on one occasion, managed to persuade the government to restore ex-servicemen's pensions and increase family allowances. Thus it demonstrated that constitutional provisions cannot necessarily withstand pressures exerted on representatives who are ultimately dependent on popular support for their election.

The final and conclusive factor reducing the importance of committees in French legislative procedure is that the ensuing debate on a government bill (*projêt de loi*) is not on the text of the measure that the committee has accepted but on the government text. Moreover, the Assembly may be required to vote on the whole of this text, or the text with such amendments as the government has accepted, or on specific clauses. Thus the sparkling and often dramatic role of the committee *rapporteur,* who used to open, and often dominate, the debate on a measure, is a thing of the past.

Apart from these major changes, the consideration of a bill is much the same after the committee stage as it used to be. Safeguards have been instituted, however, against dilatory motions that used to be so prominent in the past. Moving the "preliminary question"—that is, moving that the matter not be considered at all—can be done only once in the course of a measure; similarly there can be only one effort to prove the measure is incompatible with the constitution. Amendments can be made only to specific clauses of the bill. Thus speedy action on government legislation has become relatively common.

In sum, the Assembly lacks any decisive independent legislative power. A deputy may introduce a *proposition de loi,* but it must first secure the approval of the Bureau of the Assembly on its constitutional acceptability, then of the Bureau of the Finance Committee, and then of the government. Moreover, should a law be passed, the Assembly would still have no means of forcing the government to take action to implement it unless the government wished to do so.

Voting

Although the Assembly now has an electronic system of voting, installed in 1959, the traditional ways of recording opinion are still used first: a show of hands or, in case of doubt, a rising vote. Should an ordinary record vote be required, it can be done electronically from the seats of the deputies. If the machinery is not working, the time-consuming older process of the open ballot (*scrutin public ordinaire*) is still used, with ushers passing urns into which deputies put their personal cards: white in favor; blue opposed; red abstention. In the more formal record vote at the tribune, voting may be either electronic or by card.

The Fifth Republic has tried to introduce personal voting to replace the Fourth Republic's vote by proxy, under which, at times, one deputy (known as the "postman") would cast the votes for his whole party. But though there is now more restraint, the rule of personal voting seems honored in the breach rather than in reality. Thus do old habits persist despite new forms.

One further and unpopular innovation of the Fifth Republic is to provide an attendance bonus that is withheld if deputies do not attend and vote regularly. Absence without valid excuse (valid has been interpreted liberally) from three consecutive sessions of a committee means temporary loss of membership and of one-third of attendance pay; absence from more than one-third of the record votes in any one month entails loss of one-third of that month's attendance pay; absence from one-half the votes means loss of two-thirds of the month's pay. But Frenchmen are past masters at circumventing distasteful provisions, and it has yet to be demonstrated that this attempt to secure more regular participation has had a particularly useful effect.

3. THE SENATE

The Fifth Republic renamed the second chamber the Senate and provided it with power in legislation coordinate to that of the As-

sembly. A smaller body whose members have a longer term of office than do those of the Assembly—nine years to five—the Senate might seem, therefore, to be a potential rival to the lower chamber, as it was at times during the Third Republic. Its indirect mode of election has always been designed to act as a counterweight to the base of universal suffrage of the Assembly. Yet within the generally weakened position of the legislature, the Senate plays a vastly subordinate role. Even so, de Gaulle has long talked of abolishing the Senate and replacing it with an upper chamber composed of representatives of economic groups.

As elsewhere, the deciding factor in any disagreement between the Assembly and the Senate is the executive. The Assembly can no longer override the Senate on legislation as it did under the Fourth Republic, and, unless the government intervenes, a disputed bill can go back and forth indefinitely—in what is called "the shuttle" (*la navette*). In effect, then, the Senate can block legislation in which the government is not interested. But if the government so desires, it can promote procedures, either passive or active, that bring the measure to a vote. In the first instance, it can require the two houses to establish a fourteen-member commission, half from each chamber, to seek agreement on the bill, which is then brought to a vote, though only with such amendments as the government approves. Failing agreement, the measure may be dropped. But if the government is actively concerned with the bill, it can request each chamber to give the measure a further reading and then instruct the Assembly to vote either on the commission's draft or its own, and either with or without the Senate's amendments. In this latter case a simple majority vote by the Assembly is all that is needed to override the Senate.

A significant illustration of how the Senate's power in legislation can be nullified by the government and by an acquiescent Assembly was provided by the Senate's efforts to prevent the change from proportional representation to majority voting in the larger cities, as described in Chapter 3. Drawing its own electors from those selected by local elections, the Senate sought to preserve the system that had returned so many senators from the center parties.

The government hoped (as it turned out, vainly) that changing the system in the larger cities would benefit the UNR. The Assembly passed the measure on May 21, 1964; two weeks later, the Senate voted a bill that differed at key points from the government measure; the joint conference committee reached a stalemate. The government then moved to secure passage of its bill. On the second reading in the Assembly it cut off debate by calling for a "blocked vote," which requires the deputies to vote for the measure as introduced. The same procedure was required in the Senate, but there the bill was defeated. The measure was then returned to the Assembly, where it was reaffirmed in its original form at third reading. With the President's signature, the process was at an end. The Senate had failed to affect the character of a bill that changed the form of voting for its own electors.

But if the Senate cannot do more than suggest alternatives and temporarily delay the passage of a measure the government wants—thus performing the classic role of a second chamber —why does de Gaulle wish to abolish it and establish an economic upper house in its place? There are both personal and theoretical reasons. De Gaulle reacted bitterly to the sharp criticism he received from members of the Senate and, in particular, from its presiding officer, Gaston Monnerville, an able and popular Negro from French Guiana, on his use of the referendum rather than a constitutional amendment to test opinion regarding the process of direct election for the President. De Gaulle even refused henceforth to receive Monnerville at the Elysée Palace or to let a senior member of the Cabinet go to the Senate. But under the constitution the President of the Senate acts as President of France if the incumbent is ever incapacitated. By transforming the upper chamber from a body that reflects local opinion to a super economic and social council (see Chapter 6), de Gaulle could serve two of his purposes: eliminate a body within which the opposition parties remain dominant, and establish a new kind of succession.

Beyond this largely personal objective, however, de Gaulle envisages a type of functional representation that would go well with his notions of technocracy. After his reelection as President, he began to speak of replacing the Senate with a purely consultative body that would draw its representatives not only from the municipalities and departments but also from the new regional assemblies and from economic organs. Such a body would fit his view that what France needs is to have its divisions—which he sees reflected in the political parties—overbridged by organs that stand for national unity. The Presidency is such an organ, and to make parliament more acquiescent he now proposes a consultative and composite body to replace the one part of governmental machinery that is still dominated by his critics.

5. The French Executive

The most striking feature of the Fifth Republic is the power and prestige of the President of the Republic and the unmistakable stamp of de Gaulle's personality on all domestic and international affairs. This is not only the dominant characteristic of the new regime; it also marks its sharpest contrast to the past.

The power of the executive has been a subject of perennial controversy in French politics. Generally speaking, the parties of the left have looked upon a powerful executive as a threat to democratic institutions, while the parties of the right have seen in a strong executive the only hope for political order and authority. The constitution of the Fourth Republic represented a clear victory for the parties of the left, with authority concentrated in the National Assembly. The constitution of the Fifth Republic is as strongly oriented toward a powerful executive.

In France the executive includes both the President, who like that of the United States is *not* responsible to the legislature, and the Premier and Ministry which, as in the United Kingdom, *are* responsible to the legislature. Whatever balance the constitution of the Fifth Republic intended, or suggested, between these two sources of executive power, there can be no doubt that the President has become dominant in every sphere of political activity. With a guaranteed term of seven years, a centralized administration and no federal division of powers, an acquiescent Premier and Ministry, and a curbed legislature, President de Gaulle possesses political powers that an American President might envy and that a British Prime Minister, regardless of the size of his majority, would never dream of using.

Contrast with the Past

This far-reaching and pervasive authority of President de Gaulle contrasts sharply with the situation prior to 1958. Under the Third Republic the President of France had acted as something of a nonhereditary constitutional monarch. He was a dignified head of state who could preside on ceremonial occasions, who stood above party, and who did not engage in partisan political activity. The rebuke given to Marshal MacMahon in 1877 and the forced resignation of President Millerand in 1924 for similar partisanship were warnings enough against making independent decisions.

Seldom have such rebukes been necessary. After the sad experience with Napoleon III, republicans were careful to see that no President should enjoy the prestige of popular election; and after the MacMahon crisis they took care to choose men who were colorless, reliably republican, and possessed of little popular appeal. Clemenceau's advice to Frenchmen to "Vote for the most stupid" may have overstated the matter, but of all the Presidents of the Third Republic only Poincaré could be considered a statesman of the first rank. Men of the prominence and ability of Clemenceau and Briand were regularly rejected.

As a result, the prestige of the French President stood much lower than that of the British monarch. He excited none of the reverence attached to the descendant of generations of Kings, and his personal abilities commanded little respect. Much of his work was purely ceremonial. He presided at official functions, received ambassadors, and represented the nation at dip-

72

lomatic affairs and at ceremonies of all sorts throughout the country. Like the King of Great Britain, he was expected to lay cornerstones, open exhibitions, inspect hospitals, schools, and housing projects, attend peasant festivals, and tour the French empire as a symbol of the interest of the nation in its overseas possessions. At all times, he was expected to be good-humored, kindly, affable, gracious, and patient.

Though the makers of the constitution of the Fourth Republic deliberately tried to reduce the power of the presidency, the office actually gained more power than it had had before and provided the President with considerably more opportunity to exert influence than has the British monarch. Whereas the British King ceased to attend Cabinet meetings more than two centuries ago, the President presided over the meetings of the Council of Ministers and had the right to participate in discussions (although he could not vote). This role was of some importance, since in practice the Council of Ministers discussed certain issues of policy instead of restricting itself to formal action, as it had under the Third Republic. Moreover, when for the first time records were made of these meetings, the President of the Republic became their custodian. The President also had access to all important diplomatic papers, as was not always the case with his Third Republic predecessors.

1. THE WORK OF THE PRESIDENT

Under the Fifth Republic, however, all these possibilities for exercising influence have been turned into positive sources of activity and power. The many formal offices the President holds have provided him with unparalleled opportunities for keeping himself informed on the course of policy in all public spheres and for directing it when he wishes to do so—as increasingly he has.

The most important of these formal functions is to preside over the Council of Ministers, which has been turned into a forum for substantive debate on policy. In the first few years after de Gaulle succeeded to office in 1958, the Council of Ministers continued to act largely as a ratifying body for decisions reached jointly by the President and the Premier. By bringing policy discussions into the Council, however, as de Gaulle did after Pompidou replaced Debré as Premier, he has established direct and continuing relations with the ministers themselves and has made its sessions more nearly like those of a Cabinet, but of the American rather than the British type.

Other official duties of the President include presiding over the Superior Council of National Defense (a little-publicized, consultative body in an area in which de Gaulle takes particular interest and assumes particular responsibilities) and, rather more surprising, over the High Council of the Judiciary. In addition, he presided over the Executive Council of the Community (see Chapter 9) in the short period during which it functioned.

Unlike American presidential nominations of top administrative personnel, which must be ratified by the Senate, the French President's power of appointment is very wide and needs no formal ratification. While all French Presidents have had a role in proposing Premiers, de Gaulle is the only one who has determined who the Premier shall be. The acquiescence of the chambers in the leadership of Michel Debré, himself a parliamentarian and a believer in a "reformed" but functioning parliamentary system, is not surprising, particularly in the tense period succeeding 1958. But the measure of their docility has been their acceptance of Pompidou, who had never been in parliament or even a member of a political party, and who was obviously de Gaulle's lieutenant rather than a Premier in his own right.

The President also makes appointments to all state civilian and military posts, although the sheer magnitude of this task means that he must depend heavily on advice from the Premier and the Council of Ministers. The constitution specifically provides that the President appoint the members of the Superior Council of the Judiciary, a role shared under the Fourth Republic with the National Assembly (see Chapter 7). The President also has the right of pardon, although a pardon is supposed to have the countersignature of the Minister of Justice.

The role most congenial to de Gaulle is his position as commander in chief of the armed forces. The President is also empowered to conduct international negotiations and to shape and sign treaties, other roles into which de Gaulle has entered with satisfaction and vigor and without, so far as can be seen, being restrained by the constitutional requirement that his actions be countersigned by the Premier.

All decrees passed by the Council of Ministers must be signed by the President to become valid; so must all laws, within fifteen days after they have been passed. It is conceivable that the President might refuse to sign a law, thereby exercising a "pocket veto," but until the legislature reestablishes a separate authority of its own there will be no need for such tactics. Indeed, the President's use of his power to dissolve the legislature has already demonstrated that he will use his whip hand in case of a confrontation.

In the end, however, the power of the President, like that of any other chief executive in a nondictatorial state, rests on his ability to convince his country, or at least a voting majority, that he is acting in their best interests. The President's selection of the Premier, his leadership of the Council of Ministers, his ability to use the referendum (constitutionally, or even, as we have seen, unconstitutionally) to appeal to the people over the head of the legislature, and his right under Article 16 to declare a state of emergency for whatever period of time he deems necessary and for its duration to exercise ultimate power, have vested de Gaulle with the widest measure of individual power and discretion since the days of the Napoleons. France's continued trust in him suggests that, despite rumblings of protest from time to time, public confidence is still widespread. It is questionable, however, whether any other President could command the same measure of support or would be allowed to exercise the same degree of power.

The Staff of the President

The effectiveness of all executive work is determined in large measure by the efficiency of the organization and the personnel that underpin the making and the execution of decisions. De Gaulle's military background and experience, coupled with his wide-ranging concern for all aspects of public policy, domestic as well as foreign, have led to a dramatic expansion of the presidential staff. Indeed, there has developed an administrative structure operating on behalf of the President that is parallel to and has sometimes been competitive with that of the civil service. Americans familiar with the White House setup find it similar in many ways to what has evolved under President de Gaulle.

The expansion of the presidential staff amply documents the revolution that has taken place in the presidential role. President Auriol's Elysée staff in 1953 included only two political counselors—one prepared his papers for the relatively infrequent meetings of the Council of Ministers, and the other handled relations with the press—and twenty-one officers of professional rank. The moment de Gaulle assumed office in 1958, he appointed seventeen political counselors, of whom four were assigned to Community affairs. This latter group, which had been enlarged by 1964 and had moved to offices outside the Elysée Palace, concentrated on France's relations with the former French African territories. By 1964 the other counselors had grown in number to twenty, and the total presidential staff, excluding secretaries and minor administrative personnel, to fifty-two.

De Gaulle's dislike of detailed administrative work means that his staff is responsible for summarizing reports and policy proposals coming from the Premier's office, or from ministers, for watching progress of policy matters in which the President is particularly interested, and for developing position papers on pressing policy issues and on matters on which de Gaulle finds ministerial action too slow. Two different approaches to reforming secondary education, for example, were produced by the Ministry of Education and by the education specialists on the presidential staff. Only after much publicity and considerable "in-fighting" of the type with which Washington is so familiar—and in which Whitehall engages only infrequently and discretely—did de Gaulle endorse the ministry's plans.

The potential, and occasionally real, clash between presidential staff and high civil servants was neutralized, and then virtually eliminated, by de Gaulle's practice of drawing his presidential aides from among the civil servants themselves, either on a temporary or permanent basis. Only ten out of the seventeen political counselors in 1958 were high civil servants; three were long-term Gaullists who had been put in charge of relations with parliament, political parties, and the press. By 1964, seventeen of the twenty top aides were high civil servants, and the other three were professors with special responsibilities for education and research. De Gaulle had retained no generalists or political figures in these roles.

The change reveals the enlarged focus of the President's activities. So long as the Algerian war dominated de Gaulle's concerns, he paid relatively little attention to domestic policies. But once that war was over, his impatience with what he called a "flabby" state machinery and his dominance of the working relationship between himself and Premier Pompidou—which contrasts sharply with Debré's partnership view of Premier-President relations—led to his increasing involvement in the everyday affairs of government.

The presidential staff has expanded not only in numbers but in influence. At the same time it has become more closely intermeshed in attitudes and personnel with the higher civil service of the ministries. The end result has been to lessen administrative rivalries but, at the same time, to make and keep the presidency the dominant force throughout the administration.

2. THE PREMIER [1]

From being the creature of the National Assembly of the Fourth Republic, subject to instant dismissal through the withdrawal of essential votes, the Premier in France seems to have become the creature of the President of the Fifth Republic. This was certainly not the intention of the framer of the constitution of the Fifth Republic, Michel Debré, who became the Republic's first Premier. Debré managed to combine an impressive loyalty to de Gaulle with

[1] According to strict terminology, under the Fifth Republic the Premier is Prime Minister; the older term *Premier* has been retained, however, to avoid confusion with the British Prime Minister.

an insistence on the rights (however circumscribed) of parliament and of himself as Premier. He also fulfilled the more traditional role of the French Premier, cajoling, threatening, and ultimately driving his program through the chambers. It is a mark of the new day in French politics that what overthrew Debré was not the withdrawal of support from within the Assembly but his dismissal by de Gaulle. Pompidou's self-effacing role vis-à-vis the President put an end to any attempt to maintain a dual executive on relatively equal terms.

It is not new for the role of the French Premier to be determined by the system within which he is working. Under the Third Republic, if anyone challenged the Premier's status as *primus inter pares* (first among equals), it was to insist that he was not even *primus*. His Cabinet was likely to include several men not only of equal but of greater political stature, including the heads of other political parties and former Premiers. Moreover, there was nothing to correspond to the British Cabinet's loyalty to a party leader, and the Premier lacked the prestige that an American President and a British Prime Minister enjoy because, in reality, they have been elected by the people and enjoy something of a popular mandate.

Those who drafted the constitution of the Fourth Republic intended to make the Premier a real leader on the pattern of the British Prime Minister—an innovation indeed. Formerly, the ministers had sent their bills directly to the Assembly; now they had to be signed by the Premier before they could be presented. Under the Third Republic ministers might call votes of confidence on their own initiative; now such votes could be called only by the Premier, after full Cabinet discussion. But while the drafters of the constitution of the Fourth Republic clearly hoped that these powers would give the Premier genuine authority and prestige, the fact that they were exercised jointly with others (that is, with the appropriate minister or, in the case of high appointments, with the President), combined with the existence of the multiparty system, largely undercut this hope. Thus, except in the rare case of Mendès-France, it was the conciliators like Henri Queuille, René Pleven, and Antoine Pinay who were the most successful Premiers, rather than dynamic individuals with programs of their own.

But some may well feel that the Premier of the Fifth Republic has the most difficult task of all. He does not have to contend with individuals within his Ministry, who outshine him nor is his term of office so insecure. But no other Premier has had to work with a President who is far more powerful than himself. Thus, though his position in relation to the Assembly is relatively strong, he is far less independent as an executive than a reading of the constitution would suggest.

According to the constitution, the Premier chooses his own ministers, formulates governmental policy in conjunction with them, presents it to the Assembly, or, in case the response is slow, carries it out through the government's independent powers (especially over organic laws and finance policy). In practice, however, his activity has been limited to a joint formulation of policy with the President (in which the Premier has played an increasingly subordinate role) and to managing the legislature so that it will accept the government's program.

The Premier and the Cabinet

The role of the Premier under Debré differed from that under Pompidou for many reasons. The two men held different attitudes regarding their relations to the President, the ministers, and the Assembly. In addition, there was a sharp dividing line in the operation of the executive after the end of the Algerian war in mid-1962. De Gaulle was then left free to expand his concerns into all aspects of government, a role that he may not consciously have sought but was drawn into by the very interrelatedness of governmental activities and decisions.

Debré, strongly attracted by the role of the British Prime Minister, insisted on being the intermediary between his ministers and the President as well as the chief figure in dealing with the Assembly. Pompidou, in contrast, has not resisted de Gaulle's increasingly direct contact with individual ministers, holds infrequent Cabinet meetings, and uses interministerial committee meetings not as final decision-making sessions but in an attempt to secure agreement before taking matters to the Council of Ministers. Nor does Pompidou seem to have resented de Gaulle's highhanded actions in amending the constitution to provide for the direct election of the President.

The position of the ministers has been strengthened by their immunity from parliamentary criticism, their long periods of office, their civil service orientation (most of them were civil servants and continue to concentrate on administration), and their increasingly close contact with the source of ultimate power, de Gaulle. Since, however, de Gaulle does not interfere with the details of policy so long as he is satisfied that the general lines are satisfactory and the activity sufficiently energetic, the ministers possess a great deal of responsibility. They and their staffs deal with the interest groups that, more effectively than the political parties, represent the dynamic forces at work within the country. By thus acting as the coordinator of policies rather than the driver of a unified political and administrative machine, Pompidou is probably contributing to the general effectiveness of policy rather than reducing it.

The Premier and the President

Though he acquiesces fully in de Gaulle's leadership, Pompidou feels that his particular responsibility is to reduce de Gaulle's work load. Thus, where Debré sought to share executive responsibilities and decisions and, indeed, virtually controlled all except foreign policy decisions, Pompidou, in the succeeding period of unified domestic and foreign policies under presidential leadership, has tried to simplify and focus those choices that are to be made at the highest level. As Premier he still performs the role of personal chief of staff for de Gaulle that he took over in 1958. At the more official level on which he now performs, he channels the business of government so that de Gaulle makes all final decisions in all fields, but in most cases only de Gaulle's acceptance or rejection is necessary. Only where agreement at lower levels cannot be secured is de Gaulle forced to concern himself with the arguments on both sides.

Despite Pompidou's self-effacement and self-restraint in his relations with the President, the constitutional provisions for the office of Premier invest it with some of the characteristics of the office of Vice President of the United States. As Premier, Pompidou makes important statements on policy to the Assembly and often to the press. Occasionally he has replaced the President at ceremonial functions. It is not surprising that some people have suggested that de Gaulle is grooming Pompidou to be his heir. Yet the very qualities that make Pompidou so admirable a chief of staff for a de Gaulle would be quite inappropriate for a de Gaulle-type President.

The Ministers

The Fifth Republic, in one of its most decisive breaks with the past, provided that members of parliament must resign their seats if they wish to accept ministerial office. In the past in France, with rare exceptions, and always in the United Kingdom and the older Commonwealth countries, ministers have been required to hold seats in parliament. The constant interchanges between ministers and backbenchers, and the ability of the backbenchers through questions or interpellations to keep the government constantly alert and responsive, have been among the most characteristic and most valued features of these parliamentary systems. By forcibly separating the legislature and executive through the incompatibility rule, General de Gaulle (on whose insistence it was introduced into the constitution) moved the Fifth Republic toward executive leadership of the American type.

A further similarity between current French and American practices is the lack of importance ascribed to the party experience and party identification of ministers. British Cabinet ministers, as we have seen, often choose themselves, in the sense that they are too important within the party to be overlooked by even an imperious Prime Minister. American Presidents, in contrast, choose members of their Cabinet from either party—Secretary of Defense Robert McNamara, for example, is a Republican—and from private as well as public life.

Yet the American Cabinet has never included any substantial number of civil servants, as have the Cabinets under the Fifth Republic. In the first Ministry of 1958, seven ministers were

civil servants. The practice thereafter has been to draw about one-third of the members of the government from the civil service, including the holders of such "political" posts as those of Finance, Defense, Foreign Affairs, and Interior. This significant role of high civil servants may, indeed, be a still more distinctive characteristic of de Gaulle's Republic than the incompatibility rule, which prevents ministers from holding seats in the legislature.

Whether France will continue both the incompatibility rule and the dominant role of high civil servants in the government once the de Gaulle era is over is open to question. De Gaulle's personality and prestige need no enhancement from either his Premier or his ministers. The chambers and the parties, as we have seen, react to President de Gaulle rather than to the Premier. But a lesser man in the presidency might well make necessary more colorful, more dynamic, and more representative figures in the Ministry if its interaction with the Assembly is not again to plunge into frustration and stalemate.

The Council of Ministers and Council of the Cabinet

The French government has always met in two different ways: as the Council of Ministers, and as the Council of the Cabinet. The former meets under the chairmanship of the President; the latter, under the chairmanship of the Premier, without the President. There have been major differences, however, in the role played by the two in the earlier Republics and in the present one. Under the Third Republic, the Council of the Cabinet, which was created to prepare for the meetings of the Council of Ministers, became the real policy-making organ, and the Council of Ministers merely a ratifying body. The same was largely true under the Fourth Republic, although in certain respects the Council of Ministers became more significant. Under the Fifth Republic, however, the significance of the Council of the Cabinet has been greatly reduced, and the Council of Ministers has become the decision-making body. Indeed, only fifteen meetings of the Council of the Cabinet were held in 1959–60, a time when de Gaulle was absorbed by the Algerian crisis, while there were a hundred sessions of the Council of Ministers. With de Gaulle's release from Algerian affairs, and with Pompidou's premiership, the Council of Ministers has become even more dominant.

The Government Secretariat

Until the Fourth Republic, informality and *ad hoc* decisions and organization were characteristic of the operations of the Council of Ministers and the Cabinet. Under the Fourth Republic, minutes of Council meetings began to be taken, and the embryonic secretariat established in 1935 was extended. Under de Gaulle, a still more extensive expansion has taken place. The Secretary General of the Government, who has been the head of the secretariat since 1947, and his staff prepare and circulate the agenda of the Council of Ministers, check the preparation of bills and administrative regulations, prepare the minutes for the President, and report on decisions and their implementation.

Like so much else under the Fifth Republic, the Secretariat General, which was previously of particular importance to the Premier and is still associated officially with that office, now also performs manifold coordinating tasks for the President, particularly in connection with the changed role of the Council of Ministers. Although the Premier has his own *cabinet,* or private secretariat, like other ministers, the Secretary General of the Government has long directed a considerable part of the Premier's staff and still provides the major preparation for his relations with parliament.

The Secretariat General also performs something of a general coordinating role. The Planning Commissariat, the Atomic Energy Commissariat, and the offices of the Delegates General for scientific research and the development of the Paris region are associated, though somewhat indirectly, with the Secretary General. Also attached, but with its own Director General, is the division responsible for the management of the civil service. The School of National Administration (*École Nationale d'Administration*) and the Center for Advanced Administrative Study (*Centre des hautes études administratives*) are also linked to the Secretariat, but the connection is tenuous. In the end, even the efforts of the de Gaulle Republic to secure executive supervision and coordination of the administration have not been outstandingly successful.

The Premier and the Assembly

However diminished the importance of the Premier vis-à-vis the President, and even vis-à-vis the ministers, there is no doubt that the Premier and his government have become a great deal stronger than ever before in their relations with the Assembly. The constitution of the Fifth Republic strongly tilted the balance of power away from the chambers and in favor of the government.

Among the new rights accorded to the government by the Fifth Republic are the right to the priority of government bills in the parliamentary timetable, the right to propose amendments to bills, and the right to open a general debate on a measure in either chamber. Thus deputies now hear the government's case on a bill before the *rapporteur* of the relevant committee can present his criticisms, and the debate takes place on the government's text, not on the text that emerges from committee. Moreover, the government has the right to reject amendments proposed from the floor after the committee stage, and also to force the chamber to vote either on particular clauses of the bill or on the bill as a whole. As we have seen, the government can also spur a decision on a bill over which there is disagreement between the Senate and the Assembly. What the government cannot do, however, is to secure the passage of a bill (unless it is on finance) that the Assembly refuses to approve.

In finance, the government has been given special powers to avoid a not uncommon situation of the past, i.e., having the deadline for the budget go by before it was voted. The constitution has provided a time limit for budgetary debates at the end of which the government can impose the budget by decree power if the Assembly has not voted it. The Fifth Republic also attempts to enforce more effectively the provision (which also existed under the Fourth Republic) that deputies cannot propose measures involving increases in expenditures.

But more significant than the constitutional procedures that have strengthened the hands of the government is the fact that the government has enjoyed majority support in the Assembly for its crucial policies—except over the direct election of the President, where the opposition clearly misread the temper of the public.

So long as the Gaullists secure a majority of the seats in the Assembly and/or so long as the parties of the opposition fail to present a unified front that offers a credible alternative, the Premier and his ministers will have little difficulty ensuring the acceptance of the President's policies.

6. The French Administration: National and Local

1. THE CHARACTER OF THE FRENCH ADMINISTRATION

Changeable though the French political system has been, Frenchmen know that behind its vagaries and instabilities stands, and has stood since Napoleonic days, a centralized administration that deals efficiently, and usually justly, with the manifold problems of public concern. Far more of a technocracy than is the British and even more the American administrative structure, the French administration is often regarded outside as well as inside France as a model of its kind. What some call its impressive self-confidence and self-reliance, however, seems to others authoritarianism.

The tasks placed upon the French administration, both traditionally and now, have a collectivist flavor that helps to explain its pervasiveness. The state-wide administrative institutions that Napoleon consolidated have always undertaken certain social and economic activities aimed at national development. Some parts of the Third Republic, and much more of the Fourth, accepted the concept of the welfare state, with its correlative expansion of public responsibilities. Still more distinctive than its welfare programs have been the extent and success of French national planning since World War II.

Under the Fifth Republic the increased freedom of the executive from legislative supervision and control has given the civil service additional scope for action. While at times under the Third and Fourth Republics the civil service was the major, even the only, operating part of

government in the hiatus between Ministries, it always had to devote a good part of its energies to persuading politicians to support administrative projects. With the administration now so firmly rooted in the Cabinet itself and in the President's staff, it can often replace persuasion with action. There is thus some reason for calling the Fifth Republic a "civil service" or "administrative" state.

This is not to say, however, that France is being governed without reference to interest and pressure groups. Under the Third and Fourth Republics the establishment of numerous consultative committees was aimed at providing effective channels of influence for representative groups seeking special privileges and opportunities. So long as political parties were major factors in determining policy, interest groups divided their attention between these parties and the administration. As political parties and parliament became less important under the Fifth Republic for determining the character of policy—they have rarely determined its details—the interaction of pressure groups and the administration has become the more powerful determinant of public action. Groups within the administrative service itself have also sought to win recognition not only as representative bargaining agents, as in the Whitley Council system, but also as advisers on the form and occasionally the substance of public policy.

Such efforts to influence governmental action hardly contribute genuinely to the public interest. Nor does the pressure exercised directly by particular groups on administrative bureaus without having gone through the filter of a nationally organized political party. The tendency seems to be to pit special groups—farmers, railway workers, even postal employees—against an administration that believes less in compromise of the British type than in the existence of a "right answer" for every problem if only sufficient technical skill and know-how are available. In an expanding and prosperous economy, potential conflict—evidenced by angry protests, slow-downs, and strikes—tends to be neutralized, although post-Algerian France has had many such outbursts. More straitened circumstances, however, might provoke the very instability that the strengthening of the executive has sought to prevent.

The Public Sector

The French national government has always played a role in the economy, and this role has steadily increased. Nonetheless, neither the division between public and private activities, nor their association in "mixed" corporations, is clear-cut or logical. France, like some other Continental countries, has a number of long-established state monopolies: for example, the manufacture and sale of tobacco and matches. The state controls the production and distribution of fuel and power—electricity, gas, coal, and atomic energy—and has substantial interests in oil. The national government is dominant in transportation—railways, airlines, and two shipping companies—but private interests compete both in air and sea transportation and control most of the road transport. The state also engages in manufacturing; it controls most of the aircraft industry (a Popular Front development), about a third of the motor industry (which was nationalized because of the Renault plant's collaborationist activities with the Nazis), naval shipyards, some subsidiary production of refrigerators, tractors, and motorcycles, and the production of most fertilizers. Most surprising is the state control of insurance companies.

Much of this control developed by spurts rather than systematically. Under the Third Republic, state intervention was usually prompted by the economic difficulties of private enterprise. The persistent deficits of the railways, for ex-

ample, led finally to their being merged into a single government company in 1938 under a *mixed corporation*—that is, one whose board represents both public and private stockholders, and where public money indirectly subsidizes private activity. Broadcasting began in 1922 as a public enterprise, but private stations appeared later on. The manufacture of planes for maritime aviation was placed under a mixed corporation in 1933; in 1936 it was merged with the production for civil aviation under semi-autonomous mixed companies.

The postwar extensions of nationalization, though comprehensive, followed no planned program in France, as they did in Great Britain. True, the National Council of Resistance, leftist in orientation, formulated a program that looked to the day when the nation would take over "the fundamental methods of exchange and of production" and when the working class would share "in the conduct of the nation's economy." This program reflected a mistrust of private enterprise, a desire for better working conditions, and an awareness of the need for rapid reconstruction. But the Council had no clear plans for nationalization, and de Gaulle was unenthusiastic about such a development. Nonetheless, when he was succeeded in January 1946 by Felix Gouin, a Socialist, the rather tentative nationalization program of the first year of Liberation was extended and then brought to an end.

The Extent of Nationalization

Five nationalization projects were undertaken from December 1944 to December 1945: the coal mines in the north of France, comprising about two-thirds of those in the country; the Renault automobile works; the Gnôme et Rhône Airplane Motor Company; the principal airlines; and, most important of all, the greater part of banking and credit. In 1946 came the full nationalization of the coal mines (with minor exceptions), of the producers of gas and electricity (except for the natural gas industry and small gasworks and electrical companies), and of the thirty-four largest insurance companies, representing about 68 percent of the premiums paid in France. Further, the rules governing the Bank of France were extended to the Bank of Algeria. The assets and property of newspapers that had appeared during the Occupation were transferred to a national company. In all, about 20 percent of France's industrial capacity was nationalized, probably the highest percentage in any democratic country.

The French program of nationalization had certain marked similarities to that in Great Britain, but also significant differences. It was more empirical than the British and also more varied. Though the British went further in nationalizing inland transport, they have nothing comparable to France's partial nationalization of credit and insurance. On the other hand, British public ownership is more monolithic than is the French—that is, in Great Britain nationalization commonly extends throughout a particular field, whereas in France it tends to be limited, except in coal mining, to the largest companies in that field. A further difference is that the punitive motive for nationalization, which led the state to take over the Renault plants, the Gnôme et Rhône Airplane Motor Company, and newspapers issued during the Occupation because of their collaborationist activities, did not exist at all in Great Britain. Finally, nationalization ceased in France after the airlines, the two largest maritime shipping companies, and the Paris transport system were brought under public control early in 1948. The bill to nationalize the steel industry was never brought to a vote. Thus the French drive for nationalization came to an end earlier, but with more pervasive effect, than did the comparable drive in Great Britain.

Economic Planning

Although nationalization played a role in the recovery of France, the more decisive and long-range state contribution toward overcoming France's prewar stagnation and relatively low industrial capacity has come through France's own particular type of economic planning. Unlike the coercive and highly directive planning of the Soviet Union, French state planning operates by stimulating different segments of the economy toward accepted short-range goals. Thus it is commonly called *indicative* rather than *dirigisme*—that is, it indicates and stimulates lines of development rather than forcing them.

Characteristic of French planning have been its flexibility, its dependence on financial incentives, its emphasis on increasing the quantity of production, and its relevance to selected needs and goals. The emphasis of the first three Plans—1946–53, 1954–57, 1958–61—was on modernization and equipment. The first Plan concentrated on a few basic industries: coal, electricity, transport, steel, cement, and agricultural machinery. The second and third Plans concentrated on adjusting the economy to participation in the Common Market and on increasing exports and raising domestic living standards. The fourth and fifth Plans—1962–65 and 1966–70—have been more concerned with social and general economic development, the latter particularly in backward regions.

No one would claim that planning should receive the full, or even major, credit for France's current prosperity. Indeed there was considerable debate over whether the fifth Plan was even needed. There seems general agreement, however, that if government stimulus is no longer vital, except in stagnant areas, stabilization may be aided by the overall view of the economy that French planners try to provide.

2. THE ORGANIZATION OF THE PUBLIC ADMINISTRATION

In contrast to the relative independence of local government in Great Britain, and its self-assertiveness in the United States, the public administration of France is distinguished by its unity. French ministries occupy a position of dominance that has not been affected by the decentralizing (*decentralisation*) of particular functions to local bodies and public enterprises. Although these bodies and enterprises generally possess financial and administrative autonomy, they do not have the semi-independence of local government or public corporations in Great Britain. The French view the establishment of separate bodies in France as a delegation of state functions that does not impair the unity of all public services.

In general, the expansion of services in France

has led to the enlargement of the domain of the ministries. The nineteenth-century British theory of limited governmental responsibilities —laissez faire, or the public order state—never operated in France, nor has the British concentration of ministries in the capital city. In response to the monarchical and Napoleonic notion that government agencies operate their own services and are broadly responsible for the economic and social welfare of the community, French ministries have always maintained a network of regional and local branches and many functional agencies that keep the ministries in continuous and intimate contact with communities throughout the country.

The breadth of the functions of the ministries and the wide dispersal of their offices and staffs have made the problem of executive supervision particularly difficult, much more so than in Great Britain. Many of France's best civil servants, in fact, operate in supervisory roles. There is also a network of personal secretariats (*cabinets*) of ministers, inspectorates, and advisory committees undertaking supervisory work. In a very real sense, therefore, there are two levels of national administration: the active level (consisting of the ministries), and the supervisory. Each plays an essential role in the functioning of the French public administration.

The Active Central Administration:
The Ministries

Contrary to what we might expect, the structure of ministries in France is far less coherent and uniform than in Great Britain. Ministries tend to be collections of units or services tied together very loosely under a single minister. Many of these units have long enjoyed considerable administrative autonomy and prestige of their own and have no intention of being dominated or submerged. Moreover, until the recent reorganization of regions, the external services of different ministries were not even planned according to uniform divisions. Thus any accurate description of the French national administration would have to be undertaken ministry by ministry.

Certain distinctive differences from the British administrative structure are, however, ap-

parent. First, the British depend much more on semiautonomous local agencies and officials for the execution of national policies. In France, only a small proportion—less than 5 percent— of the central administration works in Paris; the rest are engaged in direct administration in the provinces. The direct external services provided by ministries are termed *deconcentration* as distinguished from decentralization, since the former involve field offices rather than separate local or corporate bodies. This practice of extensive field offices has always been characteristic of French ministries, whereas in Great Britain the practice was not introduced until after World War I and has never been extensive.

Second, technical personnel, in the broad sense of specialists, who are found in advisory roles in the British national administration, play a much more important role in France both in policy-making and in day-to-day administration. Indeed there is in France no class of general administrator in the British sense, since all French administrators receive specialized training. Because administrative law is so highly developed and important in France, legal training of a broad character is part of the preparation of almost all administrators. It is also true, however, that many specialists in more technical fields become general administrators at later stages of their careers. It is in this sense of "government by experts" that the term *technocracy* is used for the French administration.

Third, British ministries are more stable than French ministries. While both countries provide relatively permanent structures for foreign affairs, armed forces, interior, labor, agriculture, and the like, there is a great deal more reshuffling in France of particular services from minister to minister—a process even more evident under the Fifth than under the Fourth Republic —than there is in Great Britain. Moreover, some French ministries have short lives—as had the Ministry of Information and the Ministry of Repatriation—or else their functions are transferred to the Premier's office and then come under administrative agencies rather than ministers. This process is rather bewildering to the outsider, but it provides a great deal of flexibility and perhaps scope for useful experimentation.

Fourth, French ministries only rarely are headed by an official comparable to the British permanent secretary of a department. The chiefs of *directions,* units roughly comparable to British departmental divisions, are directly responsible to the minister, a practice incompatible with a coordinating civil service head. Moreover, the very variety of functions within single ministries makes such coordination difficult. (The only two ministries with a Secretary-General—that is, the French equivalent of a permanent secretary—are those with a clear unity of purpose: Foreign Affairs and Telegraphs.) Finally, ministers in the days of unstable Cabinets were reluctant to delegate coordinating authority to a permanent civil servant, preferring to entrust it instead to their own *cabinet* of personal aides.

The Supervisory Administration

The highly important and diversified supervisory administration in France has no obvious parallel in Great Britain, largely because the need that gave rise to it in France is satisfied by a different kind of structure in Great Britain. In France, the supervisory administration consists of a personal secretariat, known as the *cabinet,* attached to each minister, the inspectorates and advisory councils. Among the latter, the administrative section of the *Conseil d'Etat* is particularly important.

The Cabinet

A particularly sensitive and significant role is played in France, as in many Continental countries, by the minister's personal secretariat, or *cabinet.* Often called the minister's "eyes and ears," the members of his *cabinet* must share his political aims and yet also act as the administrative coordinators of his ministry. Originally, most *cabinets* were composed of political appointees, but increasingly they are staffed by technically competent high civil servants. One member, at least, usually concentrates on the minister's behind-the-scenes parliamentary business (there is no French equivalent of the British parliamentary secretary who can speak for the minister on the floor of the house) and may therefore be drawn from outside the service. The technical and coordinating functions of the *cabinet,* however, have made it advisable to draw most of the members from those whom the civil service will most respect—namely, the higher civil service itself.

Cabinets are limited to ten members (except for those of the Premier and the Ministers of Foreign Affairs, the Interior, and Finance) and are regarded as civil servants to whom most though not all the rules of the service pertain. Although their term of office in a ministry is commonly only that of a particular minister, members of a *cabinet* perform many of the functions of a permanent secretary, act as a brain trust, and speed along the minister's policy. Thus the overall working of the administration depends to a considerable degree on their tact and skill.

The Inspectorates

Inspectorates exist side by side with public services and expand with their growth. They may be concerned with all activities in a ministry, or they may concentrate on a particular activity. They exist within virtually all the ministries, except those of Foreign Affairs and Justice. They are flexible instruments of supervision, composed entirely of civil servants, and their members provide a pool of experience at the disposal of ministers for special administrative or advisory functions.

The most important inspectorate is that of finance. Together with the Court of Accounts (*Cour des Comptes*), a judicial body with powers and responsibilities roughly equivalent to those of the Comptroller and Auditor General in Great Britain, the Inspectorate of Finance audits all accounts on behalf of the Ministry of Finance. Its members possess wide powers of investigation, which extend to any matter affecting public funds.

In addition to this function, the *Inspection des Finances* comprises a special élite corps of the best graduates of the *École Nationale d'Administration,* the gateway to the higher civil service. Complaints are often heard that this inspectorate possesses a near monopoly of the best positions throughout the administration, particularly in financial and economic fields. This may be looked on as recompense for the fact that the most brilliant graduates are responsible for auditing, one of the most mundane though most essential tasks in the administration.

Advisory Bodies

Advisory bodies belong to two distinct groups: those composed wholly of civil servants, of which the *Conseil d'Etat* is the most famous and influential; and those of a representative character. The selection and composition of the latter vary widely, but most have a mixed membership of officials and representatives of interest groups. Eight out of nineteen ministries in 1959 had advisory councils concerned with all aspects of their work. Several ministries have a number of such councils. The Ministry of Health and Population, for example, has national councils for public health, public assistance, social work, and hospitals, as well as for doctors, dentists, midwives, nurses, pharmacists, and opticians.

The apex of the representative structure is the quasi-parliamentary Economic and Social Council (*Conseil Economique et Social*), a somewhat modified successor of the Economic Council of the Fourth Republic, which seems to be consulted somewhat more seriously in technical matters than was its predecessor. Composed of representatives of various organizations, persons of eminence in cultural, social, and economic fields, and with a strong official element, the Council gives advice both early and late in the formulation of the Plan. It has fifteen specialized sections to which nearly a hundred experts are co-opted, mainly from private enterprise, and it includes many of the same members as the somewhat less effective Planning Council.

How influential are the wealth of advisory bodies of various types that associate representatives of interest groups with the active administration is difficult to evaluate. Rarely do these bodies have powers of decision, although projects must sometimes be referred to them for comment. The effectiveness of their advice depends not on sanctions but on the weight of the arguments they put forward and often on the degree to which the minister is in sympathy with what they propose. Nonetheless, they provide a useful exchange of information that helps keep civil servants aware of currents of opinion in the country.

Although the advisory councils give interest and pressure groups formal access to the French administrative system, they find less formal channels even more effective, particularly under the Fifth Republic. It is often said that the prime stimulus of governmental action, outside that provided by de Gaulle, comes from the interaction of the representatives of pressure groups and members of the administration. And it is true that the natural role of political parties in focusing and cushioning the activities of pressure groups was greatly diminished in the early years of the Fifth Republic by the shift of power from the legislative to the executive and administrative branches. What the future holds depends on whether or not the political parties manage to return to the center of the stage. Whatever happens, however, is unlikely to diminish the importance of the most important general advisory body in France: the *Conseil d'Etat,* or Council of State.

The Council of State

Though technically the Council of State does not have direct responsibilities for administrative coordination and control, it is a body of confidential and trusted advisers that gives technical advice to ministries on the drafting of legislation (which in consequence is unusually polished) and also aids the executive in planning and preparing its legislative program. It has been traditionally responsible for checking the form and character of governmental decrees, and its role in this regard has been spelled out under the Fifth Republic. Article 38 of the constitution, which legalizes "special powers" under which the government can issue *décrets-lois* in matters normally within the sphere of legislation, also specifies that these ordinances must be examined by the Council of State.

By any standard the Council of State is a most remarkable institution, without parallel in Great Britain or the United States. Set up originally by Napoleon, its chief duties have always been those of planning, advising the executive, and resolving whatever difficulties may arise in the administrative field. Perhaps the most striking aspect of the Council of State is that it is composed of interrelated parts: an administrative body, which has the most intimate knowledge of the legislative program of the Cabinet, and a judicial body, which forms the supreme administrative tribunal of the country, as described in Chapter 7. The prestige and authority of the Council of State rest on its extraordinary independence in both its advisory and its judicial capacities.

The senior members of the Council of State are organized into five sections: four small administrative sections (of seven members each in 1962) that handle matters concerned with finance, interior, public works, and social affairs, respectively (they may meet together on matters of concern to several ministries), and a fifth, much larger (twenty-eight members) judicial section. The junior members of the Council, known as *auditeurs* (first and second class) and *maîtres des requêtes,* prepare reports for the consideration of the 58 *Conseillers d'Etat.* Promotion is from one grade to the next, and the total number of members of the Council in 1959 was 169, roughly equal in each of the three major groups. Particularly since 1963, the organizational division between the Council's administrative and judicial work has been overbridged as much as possible, to enable each to have insight into the problems and policies of the other. Thus every *auditeur* and *maître des requêtes* serves both in the judicial section and in one administrative section; *conseillers* may move from one to the other; and some members of each are always members of the other. Thus the two roles are intermingled and at the same time are kept rigidly separate in decision-making.

The legislative work of the Council of State has been more important under the Fifth Republic than ever before. The restriction on the legislature's power to amend government bills puts a heavy responsibility on the Council to give these bills their correct legal form and to alert the Cabinet to unintended consequences or potential illegalities. The Council of State is also expected to guard against the impetuous use of decree powers and to restrain the executive from unconstitutional procedures. Its position in the latter regard was weakened, and the constitutional standing of the regime impaired, by de Gaulle's disregard for the Council's strong majority opinion against using the referendum to amend the constitution to provide for the direct election of the President, and by his disregard also for the sizable minority opposition to the change on the ground that it distorted the balance between executive and legislature. Nonetheless, the Council remains the chief administrative restraint on executive action and is considerably more effective than the Constitutional Council (see Chapter 2). Unlike the United States Supreme Court, the Council of State exercises its restraint before, rather than after, the fact.

On all regulations of public administration— that is, the measures necessary to carry out a law—the Council of State must be consulted by the Premier, in whom resides the rule-making power in the Fifth Republic. Only in certain technical matters is the government forced to follow the advice of the Council of State, but in practice its advice is always influential. So too is the advice it tenders to ministries, on their request, concerning decrees, policy, and coordination. Although most of its work is necessarily unpublicized, the Council of State clearly enjoys general confidence and respect. It is the most distinctive and one of the most useful of French institutions.

The Organization for Nationalized Enterprises ("Établissement Public")

Nationalization in France is broad in scope and involves novel forms of representation. The mixed corporation, in which stock is held by private interests as well as by the state, has been used for the railways, the airlines, and two major maritime shipping companies. The French agencies are financially autonomous, as are British and American public corporations. Similarly, they are independent legal entities capable of suing and being sued; they are liable to taxation; and their employees are not subject to civil service rules, although they may enjoy comparable conditions of service. But the French nationalized enterprises are distinctive in two respects: they are looked on as part of a unitary state machinery, and they make wide use of the representation of special interests on their boards of directors (a device with which British and American public corporations have never experimented).

Under the formula of "industrialized nationalization" proposed by the *Confédération Gén-*

érale du Travail as early as 1918, most nationalized enterprises possess boards of directors composed of representatives of the state, the workers, and the consumers. This is known as tripartite representation. It provides for unsalaried boards (except for the chairman) in which the representatives of workers and consumers often predominate, in place of the British salaried boards whose members are appointed by the government. One further, though not surprising difference, however, is that the French boards of nationalized industries are at best advisory and supervisory rather than management agencies. They are particularly weak in influencing decisions when the chief executives of public enterprises work in close liaison with supervising ministries.

The chief difference between public enterprise in Great Britain and in France is that in France the officials in both the relevant ministries and the public enterprises tend to look on themselves as part of a single system. Although the directors of nationalized enterprises function with considerable independence, they have no more independence than does the chief of a division within a ministry. Since the crucial decisions—for example, on wages, prices, and investment—are made by the government, since the top personnel is appointed by the government and often drawn from the civil service, and since board decisions are subject to ministerial review, the issue of control, which is often so vexing in Great Britain, hardly arises in France.

It is true that the French have also experimented with other techniques for controlling public enterprises. Under the Fourth Republic both the National Assembly and the Senate had special committees to examine the records of public enterprises. These committees had far wider powers than their British counterparts or, indeed, than other French committees. There are no such committees, however, under the Fifth Republic. Public enterprises have advisory committees representing various interests, as well as the tripartite representation, on their boards. The Electricity and Gas Council, for example, has representatives from the legislature, ministries, local authorities, private and industrial consumers, the corporations themselves, and, perhaps most surprising, their own

staffs. But though this Council is supposed to be consulted on all measures concerning gas and electricity, this is not always done, its recommendations are not made public, and its quasi-judicial functions in case of disputes between corporations and local authorities are virtually ignored. Thus while there is a remarkable degree of formal representation of special interests throughout the system, there is no evidence that it challenges the ultimate unity and central control of the administration.

The Organization for Economic Planning

The great difference between French and Soviet planning is well illustrated by the contrast between the small, flexible staff of the French Planning Commissariat and the pervasive planning machinery of the Soviet state. Fewer than a hundred people form the Planning Commissariat, and many of these are clerical. Its dynamism comes from a relatively small group of very intelligent and, on the average, very young civil servants of varied backgrounds and skills who work through the ministries rather than trying to supersede them, and also through a large number of specialized committees representing special interests and special experience.

At the heart of the Planning Commissariat's imaginative drive has been a remarkable series of Planning Commissioners. The first of them, Jean Monnet, has a legendary reputation. Unlike most administrators, the Planning Commissioner is not responsible to any single minister. Rather, he is considered to be on the same level as a minister and even attends Cabinet meetings when appropriate. Indeed, Jean Monnet might be called the first nonpolitical minister, a forerunner of those so common under the Fifth Republic.

Although the Planning Commissioner has relatively little formal power, he has wide influence, partly through the network of agencies with which his staff is concerned, partly through his membership in key agencies like the National Credit Council, and partly through the widespread effects of the Plan. The Commissioner also participates in the work of various European and international organizations. It is not surprising that both Monnet and his successor, M. Hirsch (formerly Monnet's deputy), should have moved from the Planning Commissariat to direct the European Coal and Steel Community and subsequently Euratom, the European Atomic Energy Commission (see Chapter 9).

Each Plan specifies the segments of the economy to be stimulated by injections of public funds and the goals for increased production. The spadework for the Plan is done through specialized committees, which are set up afresh for each Plan. There were twenty-seven of these committees for the fourth Plan, twenty-two of them concerned with particular sections of the economy, such as steel, agriculture, and building schools and hospitals, and the other five with finance, productivity, employment, regional development, and scientific research. Almost a thousand persons, drawn from the administration, private industry, labor, and other specialized groups, served on these committees, and many of them were recognized leaders in their fields. The committees themselves divide into study groups, which include many more people with particular technical skills. This unusually broad and representative base has done much to bring a sense of democratic participation into the planning process.

The Planning Commissariat is particularly active during the earliest and later stages of the preparation of the Plan. At the start, it works with the economic research unit of the Treasury and with the Economic and Social Council to develop assumptions about the rate of economic growth and the desired direction of economic development. Once these are agreed upon, the specialized committees are called into existence and set to work. When the committees conclude their work, the Planning Commissariat takes their material, coordinates and refines it, refers a provisional draft of the Plan to the Economic and Social Council and the Planning Council (which is also representative of relevant interests but is less important than the Economic and Social Council), and presents it to the Cabinet for final retouching and approval.

Parliamentary consideration of the Plan has been relatively slight until recently. The first and third Plans were not presented to Parliament at all, and the second was presented only during its third year of operation. The fourth Plan consisted of a nine-line bill with five hundred and eighty pages of appendices: the kind of document that inevitably stultifies and makes worthless any general discussion. The fifth Plan received quite searching parliamentary consideration.

Despite the small legislative role in the preparation of the Plans, their ultimate form is the result of a broadly democratic process. Moreover, this process involves a systematic overview of the problems and prospects of the economy undertaken for the purpose of proposing governmental action. The public support accorded the Plans has come almost as much from the wide participation in the preparation of the detailed material on which they are based as from their obviously rewarding results. French postwar planning is the most distinctive and visible evidence of the constructive interaction of the public administration with private interest groups acting in the national interest. It reflects the far-reaching implications of state responsibility for the social and economic well being of the French people. It embodies an important dimension of the postwar trend in the French administration toward technocracy.

3. LOCAL GOVERNMENT

Local government is more important in France than in Great Britain or the United States, because it is an integral part of a hierarchy of national planning and operations. The most significant recent development in French local government—the administrative division of France into twenty-one economic regions, each under its own regional or "super" prefect—arose directly out of the need for units better related to economic realities and ministerial responsibilities than are the ninety-five (formerly ninety) departments. Indeed, if logic had been pressed to the full, France would have been divided into only nine economic regions, since there are only nine thriving commercial centers outside Paris around which to organize them. The decision to establish twenty-one regions may have been motivated by the fear that if there were fewer regions there might be a demand for popular assemblies in each, patterned on the council system in local government. Such assemblies might have won more authority than the local councils now possess and thus have established local centers of power that would have been anathema to the French theory and practice of centralized and integrated public administration.

Local government in France has a different meaning from what it has in Great Britain or the United States. In those countries, local government is prized because it encourages local participation in public affairs, roots many local decisions in local bodies with their own source of funds, and thus, so the theory runs, forms an important (some would say invaluable) counterbalance to the national government's control of so many aspects of life. Both in Great Britain and the United States many local services—including education, medical care, and public utilities—were first provided at the local level and were only subsequently integrated into a national system.

In France, however, both the process and the assumptions run the other way. The French have always taken a broad view, as we have seen, of the scope of national responsibilities. Since the days of Napoleon I, local representation and local responsibilities have been intermeshed with the integrated, national structure of administration.

French local government has alternated in practice between local control, prefectural control, and a balance between the two. The National Assemblies established a democratic and decentralized system of local government in 1789 and 1790. They set up elected councils in the *departments,*[1] the largest local subdivisions, and also in the *communes*[2] (including cities,

towns, and villages), and placed extensive powers in the hands of locally selected executives. Napoleon completely overthrew this system, however, and replaced it with a highly centralized administrative hierarchy, headed in each department by a *prefect* who controlled the communes in the area as well as the department at large and was merely "advised" by nominated local bodies and officers. Thereafter, continued efforts were made to increase local participation in deciding local affairs. Both the departments and the communes ultimately won back the right to elect their own councils. Moreover, each communal council achieved the right to choose its own executive officer, the mayor, who was vested with considerable power. The characteristic feature of a French department, therefore, is the cooperative relationship between the prefect and the locally elected bodies. Since national politics, and national politicians, often have their base in the local sphere, the interaction between the prefect on the one hand, and the mayor or even the chairman of the departmental council on the other, is not so one-sided as the unity of the French administrative structure might lead one to expect.

Scope and Resources of Local Administration

The administration of local services is chiefly through the field services of the ministries and the prefect. Purely local services are restricted to fields that the national government has not entered. In the nineteenth century local communities were forbidden even to establish local services such as gas, water, and garbage disposal in competition with private enterprise. Gradually, however, this rule was relaxed, and French towns now provide a range of local services that in some respects exceed those of British and American municipalities.

The major field in which local units provide supplementary services is that of relief and public welfare. Departments and communes have some mandatory responsibilities here—for ex-

[1] The basic units of French local administration are the ninety-five *departments,* of which the original eighty-three were established in 1790 by the Constituent Assembly, the rest resulting from subsequent additions to French territory. They bear no relationship to earlier historical divisions (as do many English counties), since they were deliberately designed to stamp out local particularism. Each department was kept small enough so that any person could make the round trip from his home to its governing seat in the course of a single day. A surprising feature to a foreigner is that the departments have included not only areas in Continental France but also in overseas territories. The administrative subdivisions of Algeria long formed three of the departments. In 1946 Martinique, Guiana, Réunion, and Guadeloupe became departments as a mark of close assimilation, indeed "oneness," with metropolitan France.

[2] The *commune* is the unit of local administration with the soundest basis in history and local sentiment and the greatest degree of self-government. Communes vary vastly in

size, however, and may be urban or rural. All cities, including Paris, are communes, but so are small rural districts, including sometimes only a score of houses.

There are two other units, the *arrondissement* and the *canton,* but they inspire little popular sentiment and lack important governmental functions.

ample, they *must* establish institutions for orphans, the insane and feeble-minded, and young delinquents, as well as schools for the deaf, blind, dumb, and subnormal. But they *may* also establish health and welfare clinics, and playground and sports facilities. Special aid for large needy families and expectant mothers is characteristic of the relief measures that local units extend on their own initiative. Public employment services are a postwar addition to local powers. More surprising is the provision by many towns of nursery schools and institutions for training in architecture, art, and technical fields.

Most French towns of any size now have municipal warehouses, markets, public baths, stadiums, botanical gardens, and libraries. More surprising to Americans, they also operate or finance municipal theaters, opera houses, and conservatories of music. The departments have no developments of this kind; their purely local activities are restricted to looking after their own public buildings and property.

The greatest weakness of French local government is its inadequate revenue. By law the independent income of French local units is limited to a variety of small taxes, a small fraction of some national taxes, the income on public property, and profits from municipal enterprises. Thus they have no single substantial source of funds comparable to the property taxes or rates collected by American or English local governments.

By far the greatest proportion of local expenditures are obligatory under national law, either as contributions toward national services or as outlay for mandatory local services. In return, the national government extends grants-in-aid of local services, which amount to about 20 percent of total local expenditures. But general financial arrangements have proved highly unsatisfactory and have all too often encouraged irresponsibility or curbed local initiative.

Organs and Officers

In England, as we have seen, there is only one main organ of local government in each unit, the council. But in the two most important local units in France, the department and the commune, there are three centers of authority:

the prefect, the locally elected council, and the council's own elected executive: president in a department, mayor in a commune. The mayor has a relatively strong position in his commune, but the president of the council in no way challenges the dominance of the prefect in the department.

The prefect is the titular head of the department and acts as such whenever the state is represented in its corporate capacity. In situations of disorder or danger, he has independent powers to act. His major functions, however, are administrative, and his supervision extends to any matter of national concern. In relation to the departmental council, the prefect possesses a power known as *tutelle administrative* (administrative guardianship), which he exercises mainly by reviewing decisions or insisting on the performance of required functions (for example, providing for mandatory expenditures). Still more important, however, is the reinforcement through a decree in 1964 of the prefect's position as director of all state activities in his department, except those specifically retained by the central administration (namely, armed forces, judiciary, education, finance, and the labor inspectorate).

The position of the prefect had been challenged by increasingly independent decisions made by the external services of the ministries. National deputies, who were also members of departmental councils (they have numbered at times between two hundred and three hundred), and members of the highly important "mayors' bloc" in the chambers who wanted particular types of policies or decisions, had found it easier to get concessions from ministries than from the prefect. But the 1964 reform has greatly strengthened the position of the prefect and his staff as coordinator of all national services in local areas of the regional, or "super," prefect in each region. The need to plan economic activity regionally, rather than departmentally, had been apparent since World War II. As early as 1950, private groups organized what they called Regional Economic Expansion Committees. In 1954 these committees were recognized by the government. In 1959–60, metropolitan France was divided into twenty regions, plus Paris (see accompanying map), and the capital of the largest department

The New Regions

in each of the twenty regions became the seat of an Interdepartmental Administrative Conference. The capstone of this development came in 1964 with the establishment of regional prefects assisted by small general staffs and by advisory committees of special interests. These advisory committees have been called regional versions of the Economic and Social Council.

The purpose of the regional organization is to coordinate the external services of the ministries at the regional level. Local jealousies have already shown themselves, and the present boundaries for regional action may not turn out to be satisfactory in the long run. What is particularly important, however, is that France's traditional administrative units at the local level

are not being allowed to hinder imaginative national economic planning. It is possible, also, that the kind of coordination being sought at the departmental and regional levels will have an impact on Paris and will produce more organizational integration both within the ministries and among them.

4. THE PUBLIC SERVICE

The quality of public service, like the quality of a private service, depends on the training, experience, character, and sense of devotion of its members. The French public service has certain distinctive qualities that arise out of the milieu from which its members are drawn, the type of responsibilities it carries, its traditions, its structural organization, and its career possibilities. In virtually all these respects there are noticeable differences between the public service in France and those in Great Britain and the United States.

We have already emphasized the pervasiveness and stability of the French public service and the degree to which it has been regarded as the stable element in French government. Despite the variety of regimes through which France has passed, the public service has always retained a strong sense of its own positive mission to provide administrative continuity under all circumstances, and to stimulate and even direct economic advance. Its impulse is not in any sense toward socialist or revolutionary goals (despite the syndicalist sympathies within its lower ranks) but rather toward capitalistic and national advance. It is largely due to the national public service that the foundations of France's present prosperity were so well established under the Fourth Republic.

Much more than the British, the French public service enlists recruits from all classes and from all regions of the country. The very pervasiveness of the national public service—so much greater than in Great Britain, where many tasks are performed by local officials (1,300,000 in the local government services in Great Britain, compared to 400,000 in France)—makes it both visible and attractive. As a result, there is keen competition to qualify for public service, particularly through the university-level technical schools which lead to the higher civil service. To graduate from one of these *grandes écoles* is to gain distinction useful in any walk of life, including business and commerce, and often leads to a career in business after the stated period of service to the state has been performed. An important by-product is that whereas in Great Britain the managers and directors of big business firms have their natural contacts with members of the Conservative party, those in France are more likely to share common interests and assumptions with high civil servants.

But if the *grandes écoles* produce graduates with certain common standards, they also foster particularism. Each of these schools has tended, especially in the past, to lead to a particular part of the public service. The general civil service code, passed in 1946, was intended to unify the whole service by providing uniform conditions for its management and organization under a single body. This code, somewhat modified by practice and regulation, has done a good deal to blur the distinctions among different sections of the public service, but it has done little or nothing to bridge the sharpest division in the French public service, that between the members of the *grands corps,* who hold the highest posts, and the rest of the civil administrators. The former hold positions of power and prestige both within the service and within France itself. They are rarely, if ever, rivaled by their opposite numbers in Great Britain, and even less in the United States.

Organizing the Civil Service

Until the civil service code of 1946 was passed, the administration itself, and many individual ministries, defined their own conditions of service. The code is now assumed to apply to all except the judiciary, the military, and services or public corporations of an industrial or commercial character. Even within the public corporations, however, the code applies to those on salary; those who are paid hourly wages have comparable advantages to those of the civil service which are spelled out in special codes.

Modeled on the organization of the British civil services, three other reforms were introduced following World War II. A civil service division (*Direction générale de la fonction publique*), placed directly under the Premier, was created in 1945 to provide a hoped-for but not wholly successful unity of direction. A school of administration (*École Nationale d'Administration*) was set up the same year to recruit for the administrative class (executive and clerical staffs are still recruited by the department) and to develop post-entry training programs. And an overall structure established four general classes—A, B, C, and D—roughly equivalent to the British administrative, executive, clerical, and typist classes.

Despite these efforts to enforce uniformity throughout the civil service, the *grands corps* continue to maintain their distinctive position. Although in principle the highest posts are open to civil administrators (in particular from the specially created nonspecialized corps), in practice they tend to remain the preserve of the members of the *grands corps.* These are looked on as a pool of talent, and they may be moved to any section of the administration in which they are needed. They provide a sort of personalized unity, because of their common training, but not the overall organizational unity aimed at by the reforms of 1944–46.

Recruiting and Training the Higher Civil Service

Training is an integral part of the recruitment of higher civil servants in France. In Great Britain, as we have seen, the aim is to choose men of high intelligence and character for the administrative branch and to let them learn on the job. In the American service, recruitment is based either on academic capacity, tested by special examinations, or on experience. In France, however, stiff competitive examinations must be taken for entrance to a course of training. The *École Nationale d'Administration* (ENA) is the most important training school for higher civil servants, but certain ministries—Finance, Industry, Public Works and Transport, and the Armed Forces—continue to operate their own technical schools.

The French insist on impartiality in the selection of those who are admitted to the ENA. The *Conseil d'Etat,* ever vigilant for the rights of individuals, polices this rule and has refused to allow the government to reject candidates on grounds of political affiliation, since, in practice, this restriction would refer only to a connection with the Communist party. Neither religion, sex, nor residence can be taken into account. There has even been some reluctance to interview candidates, for fear personal bias might enter in. The impossibility of otherwise testing character, however, has led to the introduction of oral tests for entry to the ENA.

Since the major objectives in establishing the ENA were to draw the high civil service from a broader social base and to make it possible to abolish the separate examinations for the *grands corps,* one common examination was established. Moreover, half the places in the ENA were to be reserved for candidates already in the executive class (commonly recruited by de-partmental competitive examinations and with training only on the job). Since the examination must be taken by age thirty, the latter provision produced a smaller number of applicants than was expected (in 1959, 99 civil servants applied, compared to 326 university graduates; only 14 civil servants were accepted, as compared with 46 university graduates). In any case, a proportionately high percentage of the civil service applicants turned out to be unsuccessful university candidates seeking a second try. The end result is that the French higher civil service, like the British, is still drawn predominantly from the middle and upper-middle classes, although there is now a sprinkling from the lower-middle class and the working class. Over 65 percent of the university graduates and 35 percent of the civil servants admitted to the school in 1959 came from the families of high civil servants or of men holding professional or managerial positions.

Examinations determine both whether an applicant will be admitted and what his future prospects will be. More than three-quarters of the common written and oral examinations test such subject matter as law, history, and economic geography. For the rest the candidate chooses one of the four main branches of administration: foreign service, general administration, or social or economic administration. The three-year training courses have many features in common and include both practical experience in a government department or a provincial prefecture and academic training. The decisive point for the student's future career comes at the end of the second year, when a final examination determines where he or she will be assigned: the fortunate few to the *grands corps (Conseil d'Etat,* Court of Accounts, finance inspectorate, or prefectoral corps), and the rest to the general corps of civil administrators. Once the die has been cast, specialized experience and training are provided in the section to which the students have been assigned.

Nothing in Great Britain or the United States parallels the rigorous training and controlled experience provided by the ENA. The internship during the first year enables the student to experience responsibility and authority in a significant situation where there is direct contact with citizens. Moreover, it is designed to provide "a new look" at life. Thus those from country districts serve in a city; those from the south serve in the north. Following the final examination, students acquire experience in private industry that will help them understand the problems of industrial management. Although the French have not been able to eliminate caste from their higher civil service, at least they provide their top administrators with well-rounded practical experience and theoretical training that any country can envy.

Conditions of Service

French civil servants enjoy far greater mobility both inside and outside the service than do their opposite numbers in Great Britain and the United States. They can move from one administrative section to another, and they may do so to secure promotion. They may take a post in a public corporation, a local authority, or an international organization without losing any of their rights, including their pension rights. More surprising, they may take leave and enter private employment without resigning, and they retain both their seniority and pension rights as of the moment of the change. Most startling of all, and in direct opposition to the situation in Great Britain, a civil servant may go into politics either as a member of parliament or as a minister. Indeed, as we have seen, one-third of all the ministers in most Cabinets under the Fifth Republic have been civil servants. Since there is no need for them to sever their connection with the service, the sharp distinction between politician and civil servant that the British maintain so carefully is blurred if not eliminated. This ability to move from public to private employment and back again, and from administrative to political roles and back again, reinforces and explains the key position of the higher civil service in France.

Every French civil servant is formally responsible under the law for carrying out the duties of his particular office; he must obey the orders issued by his superiors; and he must adhere strictly to all laws and executive orders. The responsibility of maintaining strict professional discretion is also emphasized.

Side by side with the duties for which a French civil servant is legally responsible stand the rights that he is assured. Among legal rights is protection by the government against suits for libel or attacks resulting from the performance of his duty and the long-existing right of a civil servant to take legal action over any violation of the personnel rules by a superior official, or over an administrative decision that might harm the collective interests of civil servants. Among economic rights is the right to receive a salary that is at least 120 percent of "the vital minimum," which is an officially endorsed subsistence wage. Among social rights are family allowances and other social security benefits of generous character. Most important in the view of many civil servants are the rights of association and representation, including the right to form and join staff associations, or *syndicats*,[3] and the right to have staff members on all administrative and technical commissions concerned with conditions of service.

Unions and Strikes in the Public Service

The most troublesome issue included in the definition of the status of civil servants is that of membership in *syndicats*, or civil service unions. The syndicats are the outgrowth of early staff organizations that fought for better conditions of employment. Strongly influenced by syndicalist doctrine, which proposed workers' control of all concerns, these staff associations sometimes aimed at controlling the work of their particular ministries (e.g., "The Post Office should be run by the postmen" was one slogan). In time the larger staff syndicats federated nationally into four major organizations —the General Federation of Civil Servants, the Postal Federation, the Teachers' Federation (primary and secondary), and the Federation of Public Utility Workers—which were more moderate than some of the earlier syndicats.

[3] The French make a distinction between *le droit syndical*, which is the right to trade union organization for the defense of common economic interests, and *le droit d'association*, which is a less far-reaching right to form an association with other persons for a common purpose. French civil servants have had the right of association for many years but although *syndicats* of civil servants have long existed *de facto*, the right to organize into trade unions was not officially recognized until the Law on the Status of Civil Servants of October 1946.

Nevertheless, the militant efforts and concerted pressures of the syndicats, coupled with their political agitation, roused fears that they might use their combined strength for purposes opposed to those of the government. For this reason, the right to affiliate with organizations such as the CGT has not yet been resolved *de jure,* though there has long been *de facto* affiliation.

Even more tension has centered about the use of the strike as a means of staff pressure. According to syndicalist doctrine, organized workers should use sabotage and the general strike as steps toward the overthrow of the capitalist order. In a modified form this ideology has been popular among the members of government unions, although strikes have been usually of restricted scope. A few serious incidents, however, have strongly affected opinion. In particular, the memory of the postal and railway strikes of 1909 and 1910 (the latter crushed by calling the strikers into the army and setting them to break their own strike) has persisted ominously on both sides.

Although the right to strike has not been defined, civil service strikes are not uncommon. When such issues have been referred to the *Conseil d'Etat,* it has generally opposed penalties for strikes. It has declared, however, that prefects, public prosecutors, the police, and higher civil servants cannot go on strike and that the services of key government departments and nationalized industries must be maintained at all times. A 1963 law provides that five days' notice of a strike must be given by all employees of central and local government and of public enterprises providing public service. To circumvent this minor restraint, however, dissatisfied unions, in particular that of the broadcasting service, took to delivering daily notices just in case!

Commissions Paritaires

The rank and file of the civil service have equal representation (*paritaire*) with their employers on the administrative and technical committees (*commissions paritaires*) that supervise the organization and functioning of the whole civil service. Although this machinery is not unlike that of the British Whitley Councils, the French system appears to give more weight to employee representatives.

The administrative committees, to which staff members are elected by their colleagues, consider recruitment, promotion, discipline, transfers, and other personnel questions. The technical committees, whose staff members are designated by the most representative of the unions, are concerned with practical problems of organization, efficiency, and reform that may be referred to them by the minister or by a union.

At the top of the system is the National Civil Service Council (*Conseil Supérieur de la Fonction Publique*), with twenty-eight members (fourteen from each side) chaired by the Premier himself. It hears appeals from the administrative committees, coordinates the work of the technical committees, and advises the Premier on administrative organization. Since 1959, each section has been able to meet separately. The Council meets only if the two do not agree; decisions are then taken by majority vote, with the Premier holding the deciding vote.

Neat as the system of consultation appears, neither side has been particularly helpful in making it work. Higher civil servants have tended to be uncommunicative about the reasons for their decisions, and the unions are sometimes intransigent on their objectives. At least, however, consultation has become the normal practice.

The Status of Employees in Nationalized Enterprises

In general, labor in nationalized enterprises occupies a position midway between the civil service and workers in private industry: it has a more effective share in management than the latter, and less limited union activity than the former. Most frequently, the rules governing recruitment, dismissal, and remuneration remain the same under nationalization as before. But special guarantees for union activity are provided by agreement (e.g., the union is guaranteed all material facilities, such as meeting halls, which it needs for pursuing its objects by legal means), and there is an absolute prohibition, embodied in law, against discrimination toward an employee because of union activity.

In addition, there are particular rules governing conditions of work and conciliation machinery for each of the nationalized enterprises. For example, the Miners' Charter (which takes the place of the collective agreement in private industry), includes provisions regarding pay, holidays, hours of work, social security, and so forth. Moreover, it establishes joint disciplinary and conciliation committees at the local, district, regional, and national levels. The first two levels of committees are particularly concerned with the enforcement of the Charter, but all may examine complaints and attempt to settle individual and collective disputes.

Local Government Officials

Because national supervision of their activities is so extensive and so detailed, local officials in France have somewhat less influence than in England. Nonetheless, the quality of local administration depends on their ability, and the general standards maintained throughout the local services compare favorably with those in England.

Since 1930 the national government has insisted that each local unit must either have its own merit system or accept the civil service rules designed for local administration by the Council of State. With the exception of a few executives at the top and the ordinary laborers at the bottom, all local officials are now selected by open competitive examination. These tests stress general educational qualifications and, in consequence, there is less differentiation between officials in the higher ranks and those in the lower than is true in English local government. Some observers believe that the emphasis on general educational qualifications rather than on specialized knowledge makes the chief official in the permanent service, the *secrétaire de la ville,* a more useful coordinator of local activities than is his opposite number in England, the town clerk. The effective coordination that exists is also due, however, to the unified control of the prefect over all departmental services.

The rules governing positions in local services are designed to provide security rather than to foster initiative or efficiency. Promotions and salary increases are too rigidly regulated to permit outstanding employees to advance quickly, but at least favoritism is no longer a factor. Strong staff organizations have instituted many other safeguards for the local employees, particularly in cases of disciplinary action, which must be considered by regularly constituted councils that can impose only a carefully specified series of penalties.

How Satisfactory Is the French Civil Service?

The French civil service has long been the underlying element of stability in the French governmental system. The rapidly changing Ministries of the past threw upon it not only heavy burdens but also a wide measure of power. By instituting a stable regime with centralized executive authority, the Fifth Republic has provided the civil service with long-needed coordination and control from above. This is particularly the case in regard to services demanding long-range planning and interrelation with other aspects of government.

The civil service has responded to this coordination more readily because the present Council of Ministers is oriented away from politics and toward the civil service's own interpretation of how the country should be run. If the regime is not strictly speaking a technocracy, it has certain elements of one. The most important ministries are headed by men who are themselves higher civil servants. General de Gaulle clearly favors continuing the practice of drawing the holders of these positions from this source.

Does this mean, then, that the civil service is less responsive to public purposes than before? Not necessarily. The group defining public purposes is now less subject to party pressures and maneuvering than before, but this development has freed it, as the British executive is free, to consider public purposes from a broader perspective. The situation is not without danger, since too much freedom from party control can lead to irresponsibility. But this danger is in the sphere of the executive, not of the civil service.

7. French Law and Courts

1. FRENCH CIVIL LAW

Much of the world has done French law the honor of imitation. English common law spread only to those countries colonized by the British, but French civil law became the pattern for many Continental European and Latin American countries. Even countries such as Iran, when they decide to supersede local customs by a unified national body of law, turn to the codes of French civil law, which are the product of a similar need.

The legislators of the revolutionary period in France expressed their common goal of national unity by creating an integrated, uniform system of laws. The mosaic of national, regional, and local laws existing in prerevolutionary France had led to utter confusion. In the south, the principles of Roman imperial legislation still prevailed in 1789, while in the north there were many systems of customary law embodying feudal and Frankish principles. Voltaire declared in the middle of the eighteenth century that a traveler crossing France had to change laws more often than he changed horses. A common national system of law seemed essential to bind France into a unified state.

The legislators of the revolutionary period had a further, equally imperative reason for restating legal rules and principles: they were carrying out a great social and economic revolution. The antiquated land laws, the privileged position of the Church, the hunting rights of the nobility had been swept away in an early outburst of democratic fervor. But the traditional criminal procedures, the penal code, and the rules governing the relations among individuals that remained were far from conforming to the statement of individual rights embodied in the Declaration of the Rights of Man and of the Citizen. Thus a drastic overhauling of legal rules and principles was imperative.

Overhauling and systematizing the legal rules affecting every aspect of life was a monumental task, however, and the legislators of the revolutionary period were able to make only a beginning. In 1791 they drafted a penal code; in 1795, a code of criminal procedures. They began work on a civil code, but by 1800 they had produced only three incomplete drafts.

The vast enterprise of consolidating all French law was continued by French jurists, however, often under the personal direction of Napoleon, whose administrative genius and, less fortunately, authoritarian views contributed to the final form of the codes. In 1804 the Civil Code appeared; in 1806, the Code of Civil Procedure; in 1807, the Commercial Code; in 1808, the Code of Criminal Procedure; and in 1810, the Penal Code. Together, they formed the *Code Napoléon,* a comprehensive, systematized body of laws covering all cases likely to be brought to the courts. As revised, supplemented, and enlarged in response to changing conditions, the Napoleonic codes constitute the law of France today.

Code Law

The characteristic feature of French law is its codified form. The requirements of the new society ushered in by revolution led to many new and advanced legal rules. But the principle of codification was not new. It had been embodied for centuries in the codes of Roman law, which were themselves the result of the work of generations of Roman jurists who transformed the ancient tribal laws of the city of Rome into a great unified body of laws, shaped by Stoic and Christian conceptions of justice as well as by the needs of a great empire. Roman law, which had been extended to France after the Roman Conquest, survived in the southern part of the country (as it did not in England) after the breakdown of Rome's political authority. French kings later found those parts of the Roman law that exalted the authority of the state and the ruler a useful weapon in their struggle to reduce the power of the Pope within France and to bring their own powerful vassals under control. And though the French Kings never succeeded in their efforts to establish a national law, they managed to enforce a number of royal ordinances throughout the country and to get most of the regional customs codified in the sixteenth century. It is not surprising, therefore, that when national law was established, it should have been presented in codified form on the pattern of Roman law.

Influence of Roman Law

Roman law influenced the substance as well as the form of the Napoleonic codes. Its emphasis on centralized authority rather than on the interests of the individual fitted the new French nationalism, though it might seem to conflict with French individualism. The paternalism so evident in Roman law was reflected in many of the provisions of the codes. The greatest influence, however, was the practice of relating the rules on particular subjects to general principles of justice. The judges who developed the English common law cited specific precedents rather than abstract principles of right as the basis for their decisions, however much they might privately be influenced by the latter. The jurists who prepared the French codes, like those who had prepared the great Roman codes, often prefaced the legal rules on a given subject by a statement of the basic principles on which they rested.

The Character of the Codes

The codes reduced and consolidated the laws to relatively small compass. The Civil Code, for example, deals with civil status, marriage and divorce, ownership, domicile, guardianship, contracts, wills, torts (such as trespass, slander, deceit, assault), and so forth. It comprises 2,281 separate articles, each framed with a precision of language and clarity of expression so remarkable that one of France's greatest writers, Stendhal, is said to have read a few articles of the code every day as a lesson in style.

The articles of the codes provide the basis for judicial decisions: they are the fundamental source of reference for judges making a decision in any given case. This practice marks the fundamental distinction between "code law" and "case law." Even in interpreting a statute, the judges in Great Britain and the United States refer to earlier decisions of other judges in similar cases. In France, however, judges acting under code law are supposed to base their decisions on the code. But just as Anglo-American judges sometimes interpret earlier cases in a way that supports their own concept of justice, so French judges often are influenced by earlier decisions in their application of principles.

The codes cannot, of course, cover all eventualities. Conditions change, and new laws must be passed to bring the rules governing community action into line with community needs. Thus while the codes remain the basic statement of law in a particular field, a new statute must be given full weight as the most recent statement of law by parliament. A judicial decision will take into account, therefore, all the statutes in a given field, whether or not they are embodied in the code. Some of the advantages of code law disappear when there are many isolated statutes that must be taken into account in addition to the original codified statement of rules. As a result, trained jurists must sometimes undertake a rather extensive recodification, which is then passed by parliament in the form of a statute. The Code of Criminal Procedure, the Penal Code, and the bankruptcy provisions of the Commercial Code had to be reworked as early as 1832. Public standards changed markedly during the nineteenth century, particularly in these fields, and two more revisions of the criminal and the penal law were necessary before the end of the century. In March 1959, a new Code of Criminal Procedure came into operation that integrated many useful changes into the existing system.

The Civil Code was reworked and reissued in revised and extended form in 1904, on the hundredth anniversary of the original code. It is now somewhat dated, however, being better adapted to an agricultural than an industrial society. In particular it puts an exaggerated emphasis on the value of real estate as compared to other modern forms of wealth. The law of marriage settlements was reformed in 1961. Otherwise, no major reconsideration has been given recently to the Civil Code.

The Role of Jurists in Making Law

Code law appears to do away with the influence of judges in making law, because, apart from the interpretation of particular points of law made by the Court of Cassation (which in practice is accepted as binding), the decisions made by judges in particular cases lack the influence they have in Great Britain on the decisions of other judges. But since the most highly trained French jurists do the work of preparing and revising codes, France, in this sense, has jurist-made law.

The codes are laws, but even more than most laws they must be drafted with the greatest care. They are a distillation of the essence of the laws on a particular subject. They acquire the force of binding rules through the authority of the legislature and the executive, but they acquire their wording and emphasis from the jurists who prepare them.

The Advantages of Code Law

Code law has two obvious advantages: easy accessibility and uniformity. English and American common law must be sought in hundreds of volumes of law records and digests. French civil law is embodied in a comparatively small number of books. When the Shah of Iran telegraphed Paris to ask for the codes, a selection of commentaries, and a commission of French jurists, he was asking for all that was needed to establish a new system of national law for his country.

This does not mean that the ordinary citizen can apply the rules of the French codes as easily as a judge. The French have always maintained that only professionals should interpret legal rules; they have no group comparable to the unpaid and untrained English justices of the peace. The existence of the codes does mean, however, that it is not necessary to spend a lifetime studying earlier cases in order to become a judge. The English judiciary must be drawn from the comparatively restricted profession of barristers, because case law must be learned through long experience. Code law is so much more accessible that anyone with legal training can make use of it. This fact has a direct influence on the size and character of the French judiciary, which includes about 3,500 members, with ages ranging from twenty-five to seventy-five (in contrast, the English judiciary—apart from the justices of the peace and magistrates —numbers only about a hundred, all of mature age). The large size of the French judiciary means that French justice can be decentralized to a degree that contrasts sharply with the centralization of the English court structure in London.

The Disadvantages of Code Law

Code law does, however, have certain disadvantages. Most important is a certain lack of flexibility. The codes lay down rights, rules, and principles that should be applied under all circumstances. Case law, in contrast, modifies the judgment of parliament (which must deal with broad principles and rules) by the judgment of the jurist, who is dealing with cases that arise from day to day. The judge in the English legal system works from the particular toward the general; the judge in the French system works from the general to the particular.

Each approach has advantages for special types of cases. There are certain fields, such as contracts, promissory notes, and wills, in which written documents predominate. Here general and comparatively rigid rules can be applied over and over again without working an injustice. But in questions of personal relations and human conduct, flexibility, rather than exactitude, contributes to justice. To such fields the long, slow process of constant change characteristic of case law seems especially suited.

French and English law are not so different, however, as these comparisons might suggest. Both England and the United States have codified the law in particular fields, and they may extend the practice. And the regular French courts make use of precedents, though not to the extent of English judges, who observe the rule of *stare decisis* (that is, the binding force of precedent) much more rigidly than does the American bench.

Legal Systems as a Product of History

Both the English and the French systems arose historically and in response to particular conditions, not in response to abstract conceptions. England developed a structure of national law centuries before France. The English common law system was considered complete—that is, it could handle any kind of case—by the middle of the thirteenth century. The contributions of equity and statutory law were additions made as need arose, and they were woven into a system of laws that was unified despite its different strands. Since England already had a national legal system, there was no need to construct one in modern times.

France, however, lacked a national system of laws at a time when national self-consciousness coincided with revolutionary changes in economic and social standards. It had to create quickly what the English had built up gradually over hundreds of years. In this task the example of the Roman law was a signal help. By adapting its forms to their needs, France and other countries have built up the second of the great modern legal systems.

2. THE JUDICIARY

The English and the French judicial systems differ most sharply in their methods of selecting the judiciary and the relationship of the judiciary to its administrative officials. English judges are drawn from the legal profession, and only from that section of it that has been "called to the bar," the barristers—a fact that makes for close harmony between lawyers and judges. But in France a young man decides at the beginning of his career whether he will be a lawyer or a member of the judiciary, and in all likelihood he will remain in the role he has chosen.

To become a judge, a law graduate must pass the competitive examination for entry to the training school set up in 1958 for the judicial profession, the *Centre National d'Etudes Judiciaires,* and satisfactorily complete its three-year course. As soon as students enter the school, they become civil servants and are paid a salary; this is in an effort to raise the standards for recruitment and open the service to all, regardless of economic status. They spend the first year in some part of the judiciary; the second, in academic studies. Examinations at the end of the second year determine the type of court to which each will be assigned, and in the third year they concentrate on training for that particular work.

In England and the United States judges serve only on the bench, but in France members of the judiciary fall into two main categories: those who judge cases, known as *magistrats du siège* (that is, judges who sit on the bench); and the state prosecutors, who form the *paquet* or *magistrature debout* (that is, standing magistrates). The latter (and not the police, as in England) act on behalf of the state in criminal cases; they do not have the same independence as the judges on the bench, since prosecutors can be given orders and are ultimately under the authority of the Minister of Justice. Judges have security of tenure and cannot be disciplined by the government.

Since the judiciary is a career service, promotion has been a matter of concern. Under the Fourth Republic, promotion was determined by a body not under the influence of the Minister of Justice, the *Conseil Supérieur de la Magistrature* (*magistrature* means the collective body of the judiciary). Six of the *Conseil's* members were elected by the National Assembly (not from among its own members) and four by the judiciary itself. The Ministry of Justice never became reconciled to this system, however, and the eleven members of the High Council set up in 1958 are all chosen by the President from lists submitted by the judiciary; the President himself and the Minister of Justice are *ex officio* members. Moreover, under the Fifth Republic the High Council does not prepare the promotion list as it did under the Fourth Republic. Instead, it merely gives its advisory opinion on a list compiled by a special committee made up of seven members of France's highest court, the Court of Cassation, and six officials of the Ministry of Justice. Since the number of classes in the service was sharply reduced in 1958, from ten to two, and since salary increases have become virtually automatic, there is now less strain than there used to be over promotion and shifting within the service. Though the High Court now has less influence on promotions, it retains its control over the disciplining of judges, an important factor in their independence.

3. THE REGULAR COURTS

The French believed that justice is a service that should be provided conveniently and cheaply for everyone, much of the pattern of such services as the postal or the insurance service. Thus French law is administered by a network of centrally organized local courts that make justice easily available to every citizen.

Yet, though the French courts are organized under the Ministry of Justice, they are not simply another part of the administration. On the contrary, the most distinctive feature of the French court system is its division into regular and administrative courts; this distinction arises precisely from the fact that the French distinguish so sharply between the administration and the judiciary.

Because they were fearful that the courts would try to interfere with the social and economic changes they were introducing, the National Assemblies of the early revolutionary period specifically forbade the judiciary to limit or encroach upon the sphere of the administration. The constitutions of the subsequent Republics have included no similar prohibition. Nonetheless the courts in France have never adopted the practice of judicial review so significant in the United States, a fact that leads the French themselves to say that France has a truer separation of powers than has the United States.

Though there has never been pressure in France in favor of judicial review, French leaders recognized soon after the Revolution that the absence of a judicial check upon the actions of the administration was potentially dangerous. They met this danger not by expanding the powers of the ordinary courts but by developing a separate structure of courts, the administrative

courts. In France, therefore, any case that affects an administrative official or in which the state is a party (with the sole exception of criminal cases) comes before an administrative court. By excluding such cases from the regular court system, the French leave the latter free to devote their full attention to disputes between individuals (civil cases) and those in which an individual is accused of a breach of public order (criminal cases).

The Hierarchy of the Regular Courts

In 1958 the Fifth Republic reorganized the system of regular, or "ordinary," courts. The major casualties of the change were the three thousand professional *juges de paix* (so different from the unpaid, slightly trained English justices of the peace), who used to be found in almost every small canton and who concentrated on conciliation and minor civil cases. Modern transportation made such highly decentralized and numerous courts seem unnecessary, and the revised system reduced the total number by four-fifths.

The basic structure now consists of a lower court in each arrondisement and a higher one in each department. If a department is densely populated, more courts are provided—172 in all for 95 departments. The reorganization has made more judges available to serve in the higher courts.

The court structure is divided all the way to the appeal court level between courts concerned with civil cases and courts concerned with criminal cases. There is considerable difference in procedure between the two. But the appearance of separation in the court system masks a good deal of connection. Both civil and criminal courts at the arrondisement and at the department levels are staffed by the same judges and they use the same courthouse. Moreover, the twenty-five courts of appeal, and the Court of Cassation at the apex of the system, hear appeals from both civil and criminal cases.

The French facilitate the right of appeal but at the same time limit and structure it. Unless a case involves very minor sums, there is always a right of appeal except from the assize courts. Only one appeal can ever be made on matters of fact, however, and such appeals always go to

REGULAR COURT SYSTEM OF FRANCE

Elective or Appointive Lines
Channel of Appeal

Court of Cassation: Supreme Court of Appeal (*Cour de cassation*)

83 judges who work through five Sections: two civil (personal and family status, and property)
of fifteen members each; one commercial; one social; and one criminal
7 judges to a case (15 if a principle involved, and all members if a second appeal)

Reviews interpretations of *law* in civil and criminal cases.
If the *Cour de cassation* quashes judgment, it sends case to another court at same level as that from which case was originally referred. On second appeal gives authoritative interpretation that must be followed by lower court.

Appeal Courts (*Cours d'appel*)
Several sections including one on social laws
3 to 5 judges

Takes appeals on matters of *fact* from civil and criminal courts and retries case.
Prepares indictments for Assize Courts.

| CIVIL CASES | HIGHER COURTS | CRIMINAL CASES |

CIVIL CASES

HIGHER COURTS

CRIMINAL CASES

Assize Courts (*Cours d'assises*)

95 (one in each department)
3 judges and jury of nine (verdict of guilty requires a majority of eight votes).

Original jurisdiction for most serious crimes, like manslaughter.

Civil Courts—Superior
(*Tribunaux de grande instance*)

172
3 or more judges

Cases involving substantial sums, personal or family status, or real property.
Unlimited jurisdiction (that is, can try any case no matter how serious).

Criminal Courts (*Tribunaux correctionnels*)
172
several judges

More serious offences. Can impose prison sentences from two months to five years and levy fines from two hundred francs up.

LOCAL COURTS

Courts of First Instance
(*Tribunaux d'instance*)

455 (one for each arrondisement)
1 judge

Minor civil cases.
Conciliation functions.
Settle election disputes.
Judge also presides over police court, family and guardianship councils.

Police Courts
(*Tribunaux de police*)

455

Minor offenses. May impose penalties of one day to two months in prison and small fines.

Commercial Tribunals
(*Tribunaux de commerce*)

Members elected for two years by local businessmen.
Act in certain commercial cases defined by law; appeal only if considerable sum involved.

Industrial Disputes Councils
(*Conseils de prud'hommes*)

Equal number of worker and employee representatives.
Chosen for six years (one-half retiring every three years).
Arbitrate disputes arising out of industrial contracts. Appeal only in more serious cases.

SPECIAL COURTS Appeal, when allowed, to Appeal Courts.	
Children's Courts (*Tribunal pour enfants*) One judge chosen from court panel for three-year term. At each seat of Superior Court.	**Courts of Farm Leases** (*Tribunaux paritaires de baux ruraux*) At each seat of Court of First Instance. To settle lawsuits between lenders and borrowers of rural funds.
Social Security Commissions (*Commissions de sécurité sociale*) One judge of Court of First Instance plus two representatives of interested parties.	**Court of State Security** (*Cour de sureté de l'Etat*) *5 members: 3 judges and 2 senior officers appointed by Council of Ministers* Crimes and indictable offenses against state security.

the appeal courts regardless of whether they come from the arrondisement- or department-level civil or criminal courts. If the appeal involves an issue of law, it goes to the Court of Cassation.

The Court of Cassation, which ordinarily acts through one of its five sections, does not retry the case, as do the courts of appeal. If it disapproves of the interpretation of law, it sends the case back to another court on the same level on which it was tried before. In the exceptional case of a second appeal, the Court of Cassation meets as a whole and delivers a mandatory judgment on the point of law that must be accepted by the third court at the original level to which it is then referred. This power of the Court of Cassation (defined in a law of 1837) is limited in theory to the particular case and the particular court. Obviously, however, it has wide influence, despite the French principle that precedent is not binding from one court to the next. A noteworthy example of this influence was a decision in 1896 that extended employer liability for industrial injuries far beyond the intention of the Civil Code.

The higher the place in the hierarchy of courts, the larger the number of judges assigned to a case. At the lowest (arrondisement) level, cases in the *tribunaux d'instance* (civil) and the *tribunaux de police* (criminal) are heard by a single judge, although there are several judges at each center to ensure that

cases are dealt with promptly. At the second (department) level of the *tribunaux de grande instance* (civil) and the *tribunaux correctionnels* (criminal), each case is considered by a bench of three judges. The appeal courts, which are divided into sections, have five judges to a case. The Court of Cassation, at the apex, has five sections of fifteen judges each, and seven must hear a case on first appeal. In the unusual situation of a second appeal, all seventy-five judges compose the bench.

In only one place—the assize court, which provides original jurisdiction in cases of serious crime—is a jury used in the French court system. The assize courts are held quarterly in every department (and almost continuously in Paris). The verdicts in the assize courts, as we have seen, are not subject to appeal, making the one exception to the general rule.

Special Courts

Two long-established special courts that operate wherever local interests ask for them are the industrial and the commercial courts. Both concentrate on conciliation; the industrial courts between employers and employees on such issues as disputed dismissals, and the commercial courts between merchants on disputes over sales or bankruptcy. By holding formalities to a minimum, by giving those concerned the right to elect their own judges from among their own members, and by being cheap and quick, these courts are justifiably popular and perform useful functions that are reflected in their place in the regular court structure. Appeals from their verdicts can be taken to the courts of appeal or the Court of Cassation. This possibility reflects the fact that industrial and commercial courts deal with subject matters that are handled in their absence by the ordinary courts.

Two other special courts, added after World War II, deal respectively with social security legislation and with disputes between tenants and landowners over rents. These courts differ from those described above in that each has a professional judge, commonly assisted by two elected judges, one representing each side.

The most controversial special court was designed to deal with threats to the security of the state. Following the attempted Algerian coup in 1961, General de Gaulle used his emergency powers to set up a special court to judge those concerned. This court was subsequently abolished, and his effort to establish a second, comparable court was quashed by the *Conseil d'Etat* as being outside his bounds of power. Finally, in January 1963, parliament established a permanent Court of State Security.

How Satisfactory Is the French Court System?

The structure of the French court system provides many advantages that are lacking in England. The fact that not only the courts of first instance but also the appeal courts are decentralized brings justice within the reach of everyone. Further, convenience, speed, and cheapness are enhanced by permitting only one appeal, instead of two or even three as is possible in England. Finally, the uniformity of the system means that the inhabitants of a southwestern city have exactly the same kind of courts of original jurisdiction and appeal as the inhabitants of Paris. In England, in contrast, not only are the appeal courts centralized in London, but the county courts, despite their concurrent jurisdiction in lesser cases with the divisions of the High Court of Justice, hardly rank on a plane of equality with the High Court in personnel.

A general evaluation of the French court system, however, requires consideration of the same questions that were raised in regard to the court system in England. What is the atmosphere of the courts? Do they provide an opportunity for all aspects of a situation to be explored? Do the courts give private persons adequate protection in criminal cases in which the resources of the government are behind the prosecution? Do they provide speedy, effective means of settling disputes? And is justice, in practice, open to all on equal terms?

The Atmosphere of the Courts

The sessions of a French court are likely to seem sober and even dull to an American, for there is much less use of oral evidence in a French court than in an English or American court. Witnesses are often questioned prior to court sessions and their information presented in writing, thus providing the same amount of information as in the Anglo-Saxon court system but in a less dramatic way. Moreover, while eloquence in an American or English court is often for the benefit of the jury rather than the judge, there is little chance for the French *avocat* to practice this kind of persuasion, since juries, as noted, are used in only one court in France, the Court of Assize.

Is All the Evidence Brought Out?

But at the same time, to a much greater degree than English judges, French judges take upon themselves the responsibility for seeing that all the evidence is brought out in a case. The judge in an English court looks on himself as an umpire before whom two parties argue out their case. French judges, even in civil cases, examine witnesses (often outside of court), question lawyers, and press proceedings in whatever direction they feel necessary to elucidate the facts.

Is Adequate Protection Afforded the Defendant?

It is partly this active role of the judges in a French court that makes Anglo-Saxon observers feel that defendants in a criminal case do not always have an adequate opportunity to defend themselves. Procedure in English criminal law emphasizes every possible safeguard for the accused, and judges are sometimes placed under considerable strain by their desire to provide fair play and at the same time prevent an obvious criminal from escaping the verdict he deserves. French judges labor under no such inhibitions. But the French themselves have been chiefly dissatisfied with the way in which their jury system has operated and with the manner in which the police conduct the unofficial inquiries that precede those of the *juge d'instruction*.

Under the belief that juries were afraid to convict lest judges award too severe penalties, judges and jury were associated in 1932 in determining the sentence. In 1941, the three judges and seven jurors were joined into a single body that determines both guilt or innocence, and the penalty. Under the Code of Criminal Procedure of 1959, the number of jurors is raised to nine, and there must be at least eight votes (thus at least five jurors) before a verdict of guilty is pronounced. The role of jurors has thus been transformed from what it is in England into that of lay assessors, partly at least because French magistrates, lacking the experience of the skilled barristers who become judges in England, were so much less adept than the latter either at guiding cross examinations or at giving oral presentations.

A more serious problem for French justice has been the preliminary investigation on which the state's case rests. Before a person accused of serious crime is even brought before the Court of Assize (there is no *habeas corpus* act in France), a careful and often long investigation under full safeguards has been conducted by a court official, the *juge d'instruction,* who has become convinced of the accused's guilt. What has disturbed French liberals is not this investigation but the unofficial inquiries made by the police prior to handing over the suspected criminal to the *juge d'instruction*. The police, who are known as *police judiciaire,* are considered to be outside the jurisdiction of the Council of State, which has authority over the administrative system, so no check is possible from that source. The 1959 Code attempts to prevent certain police abuses committed in the past by officially acknowledging, and then attempting to regulate, their *enquête préliminaire*. Detention is supposed to be limited to twenty-four hours, strict records of the inquiry are to be kept, and the detained person has a right, of which he must be notified, to medical examination. Unfortunately, the period of detention has been greatly lengthened in certain cases, especially those related to Algerian rebel activity in France, thereby largely nullifying a useful reform.

It is not true, as is so often said, that in France a person accused of a crime is considered guilty unless he can prove himself innocent. But because of the long preliminary interrogations, there is a presumption of guilt that is evident in the attitude of the presiding judges. English and American criminal procedures are mainly motivated by fear lest an innocent person be convicted, French criminal procedures by fear lest a guilty person escape.

Do the Courts Provide Prompt and Inexpensive Remedies?

The French court system, with its decentralization and its limitation to one appeal, provides justice noted for cheapness and speediness—except for occasional long delays in the Court of Cassation. The costs of a review by the Court of Cassation, however, are borne by the state. Local lawyers are used more often than in England, partly because the uniformity of the courts and the relative simplicity of the codes mean that the skill and training of the lawyers are not quite so important as in that country, and partly because no single place in France is such a center for the legal profession as London is in England. Moreover, though there is no statutory limit on the costs of legal aid, agreement on this subject is generally reached between lawyer and client before the case begins. On the other hand, this system is far from being so helpful to those in need as the legal aid now provided in Great Britain.

To Sum Up

The French court system provides justice in a convenient, inexpensive, and equalitarian way that cannot be rivaled by the English or American systems. While it is true that French magistrates are not so learned as English judges, this shortcoming is not serious, since their task of basing decisions on the codes is less difficult than the work of English judges in interpreting case law.

The major criticism to be made of the French judicial system is that the independence of judges is not safeguarded as well as it is in England. According to the constitution (Article 64), the President of the Republic is "the guarantor of the independence of the judicial authority." While this conception may well fit de Gaulle's view of his office as supreme arbiter between all other branches of government, it is anomalous to entrust judicial independence to an executive officer.

Apart from this fact, and French concern about arbitrary action by the police, the French are well satisfied with their judicial system. It is noticeable, in fact, that in certain ways the English system is moving closer to the French, notably in becoming more equalitarian in the sense of drawing judges from a wider social group, and also of bringing justice within the financial reach of persons of moderate means.

4. THE ADMINISTRATIVE COURTS

Side by side with the hierarchy of the regular courts in France exists a second hierarchy, the administrative courts, which operate to keep the agents of the state within their grants of power, and to give individual Frenchmen a remedy against arbitrary administrative decisions. Nothing exactly like the French administrative court system exists in England or the United States, though in both countries there is an increasing amount of administrative adjudication. Most Englishmen and Americans still feel that the best safeguard of justice is to have one law for everyone, rather than to have separate courts for examining the acts of officials. But the vast increase in the functions and powers of the administration in every modern state increasingly raises the question of whether the highly flexible, inexpensive, and all-encompassing jurisdiction of the French administrative courts does

not, in fact, provide a better protection of individuals from administrative arbitrariness than the much more cumbersome practice in England or the United States of bringing suit against officials through the regular courts.

Administrative courts (which are concerned only with civil cases) exist on both the local and national level in France. Centered in twenty-three regions and in Paris are the twenty-four *Tribunaux Administratifs* which, since 1953, have not only considered cases arising out of charges and claims against local administrations but also almost all the first-instance work transacted up to then by the Council of State (*Conseil d'Etat*). At the national level, the French administrative court system is headed by the *Conseil d'Etat,* which we have already considered in its role as an advisory organ and administrative agency, and which is one of France's most remarkable institutions.

The French administrative courts annul decisions or rulings that they decide are outside the grant of power or are otherwise invalid, but they do not substitute their own decisions or rulings. In other words, they act as a check on the administration's use of its authority, but they do not direct the administration along any specific lines. Moreover, the damages awarded by the administrative courts are paid by the government, not by the erring official. An individual could institute a case against a public officer in the ordinary civil or criminal courts, but it would be rather more difficult to secure damages than in Great Britain or the United States, where the doctrine of personal liability for abuse of power is much more strongly entrenched than in France.

The general distinction between cases that go to the regular courts and those that go to the administrative courts is drawn from the type and manner of activities, rather than the legal status of the body involved. Thus where public agencies act like private undertakings—for example, nationalized industries—disputes go to the regular courts. Where semiprivate committees have power to regulate industries, however, and impose penalties for violation of their decisions—that is, where they have powers that private bodies do not have—their actions are subject to review by the administrative courts.

Any controversy about whether a case belongs in the ordinary courts or in the administrative courts is settled by the *Tribunal des Conflits* (Court of Conflicts), which is composed of four members of the *Conseil d'Etat* and four of the Court of Cassation. In case of deadlock (which has occurred only ten times since 1872), the Minister of Justice casts the deciding vote. Thus the line of demarcation between the ordinary courts and the administrative courts is decided by a body equally representative of the highest body in each hierarchy. In practice, its decisions have not lessened the jurisdiction of the administrative courts.

Lower Administrative Courts

The *Tribunaux Administratifs* form the basic structure of general administrative courts. Since 1953, when jurisdiction over many overdue cases was transferred from the *Conseil d'Etat,* they have almost invariably acted as courts of first instance in cases dealing with official misuse or abuse of power—for example, an order that cattle be destroyed made on the incorrect assumption that they had foot-and-mouth disease, or a regulation for which there is no legal basis of power, or which is not being used for the purpose originally designated. (The latter goes beyond the powers of British courts.) The Administrative Tribunals also continue to deal with appeals over local tax assessments, claims for breach of contract by local public bodies, and cases involving public works, sale of government property, and even local elections.

An Administrative Tribunal has five members, a president and four councilors. They are recruited by competitive examinations, or from experienced members of the administration who possess law degrees. Their personnel thus combines wide practical administrative experience with rigorous intellectual training.

The procedure in the Administrative Tribunal is simple and straightforward. Appeals may be mailed and need include only a small fee, an official form on which the complaint is described, and the necessary supporting documents. While petitioners may be represented by counsel in public session, this is not necessary. The court (unlike a regular court) makes the investigation itself, rather like the Ombudsman and his staff in Scandinavian countries, whose role has so much interested the British.

In addition to the *general* administrative tribunals, there are some forty different types of *specialized* administrative courts. The most important of these is the Court of Accounts, the supreme audit agency, but there are also many special courts. Sometimes, as in the field of public assistance (now known as social aid), these have their own network of lower and upper courts that reflect the wide scope of public intervention in and responsibility for the life of the individual.

All the specialized administrative courts as well as the general administrative tribunals come under the *Conseil d'Etat* as far as interpretation of law is concerned. Thus the *Conseil* occupies within the administrative court system the same place as does the *Cour de Cassation* in the regular court system.

The Council of State ("Conseil d'Etat")

The Council of State is by far the most important organ in the administrative court system. Moreover it has a high reputation both in France and abroad. In fact, of all French institutions, the Council of State, acting in its judicial capacity, is perhaps the only one that English and American observers feel might usefully be transplanted to their own countries. This is partly, as we have already suggested, because the particular problem on which the Council of State concentrates—administrative abuse or misuse of power—is increasingly significant in the modern welfare state, but also because the Council has proved itself in practice to be fearless, penetrating, and just in its operations.

To have administrative officials check other administrative officials might seem to make administrators judges in their own cases and so destroy the safeguards that the system is intended to provide. But the French believe that the more knowledge the members dealing with judicial matters have of administrative problems, the sounder their decisions will be. Thus deliberate efforts were made in 1963 to bring the administrative and judicial sides of the *Conseil d'Etat* still closer together. Members can move from one section to another, as we have seen, either through promotion or desire; nine members of the judicial section participate in the work of the full advisory body that counsels the government on bills and decrees; two judicial members are on the standing committee that gives advice on urgent bills and regulations; and, conversely, the administrative sections elect several of their members to sit on the judicial section. Thus the judicial section (*section du contentieux*), which has twenty-eight members, half the total membership of the *Conseil,* has an awareness and an understanding of current developments in the political and administrative spheres that no member of the judiciary in Britain or the United States can match.

The procedures of the *Conseil d'Etat* are similar to those of the Administrative Tribunals; indeed, they are very like those followed by such independent regulatory commissions in the United States as the Federal Trade Commission. The practice may be compared to that of a criminal court, except that the roles are reversed: the government official or agency is on trial on a charge made by a private citizen. At the level of the *Conseil d'Etat* the investigation is made by the nonjudicial members, the *auditeurs* and *maîtres des requêtes,* who are serving their apprenticeships and can expect at about the age of fifty to become judges. When presenting the issues of the case, following detailed investigation, the *maître des requêtes* is known as the *commissaire du gouvernement,* but he is an impartial examiner and his conclusions, usually though not always accepted, often condemn officials or agencies.

A well-known case in which individual rights were protected against a state ruling arose out of an appeal by five young men who charged that they had been excluded from the examinations for the *Ecole Nationale d'Administration,* the training center for the higher civil service, on grounds of political opinion—that is, that they were believed to be members of or associated with the Communist party. Meeting in plenary session on May 28, 1954, the *Conseil d'Etat* upheld the applicants and declared that the Secretary of State acting for the Premier (who by law had sole and unlimited authority to determine the lists of candidates) had no

right to keep them from sitting for the examination, a decision whose broad implications have governed admission to these examinations ever since.

In a more recent case in which the Council of State acted in opposition to executive policy, it quashed the special court set up by President de Gaulle under his emergency powers and thereby forced the government to use parliamentary procedures to establish the Court of State Security.

A major criticism of the procedures of the Council of State used to be that, though introducing a case was simple and inexpensive, it often took years before the case came to trial. Decentralizing most cases to the Administrative Tribunals has made it possible for the *Conseil d'Etat* to concentrate on appeals, and in 1956 its number of subsections was increased. Cases are now commonly decided within a year or two.

How Satisfactory Are the Administrative Courts?

Experience demonstrates that the Council of State acts as guardian both of public interests and of individual rights. The justice it dispenses can be secured with relatively little trouble and at almost no expense. If a plaintiff's claim is upheld, he pays no costs; if it is denied, he pays only a nominal amount. Although a claim for money damages may make special court and registration fees necessary, the total cost of proceedings is too small to deter anyone who has a reasonable claim.

Moreover, as we have seen, the Council of State does not hesitate to hold high administrative officials to the strict letter of the law and to make them produce full evidence that the facts on which their action is based are exactly as the officials state them to be.

Beyond this, the Council is generous in awarding damages to be paid by the government to injured individuals. If it finds that a civil servant has been wrongly dismissed, it may order his reinstatement and also provide that he be paid a suitable indemnity for the prejudice and loss he has suffered. More unusual from an

English or American view is a case in which a man was awarded damages for injuries caused by a shot fired by a policeman at a mad bull. In another, a municipality paid damages to a man injured in a duck-shooting competition organized by the mayor, despite the fact that the mayor had been held personally liable by an ordinary court. In a third case, the Air Ministry was held liable for damages caused by the crash of a military plane.

It is thus apparent that the administrative courts are not in any way prejudiced in favor of the administration, either when considering the unexpected results of administrative action or when considering an issue concerning administrative discretion. On the contrary, the intimate knowledge of the inside working of administration seems to make the Council of State particularly sensitive to any abuse of power and alert to check it.

Do French administrative courts afford more satisfactory checks on the arbitrary action of officials and better safeguards of the interests of individuals than do the English and American judicial systems, with their practice of depending largely on the ordinary courts for redress?

There can be no question that a Frenchman can more easily secure redress for the unintended consequences of an official act than can an Englishman or an American. But it is also true that neither the English nor the Americans face such a serious problem in connection with official liability as do the French, since both in England and the United States administration is far more decentralized than in France, and in both countries local units of government have long been liable for damages in many instances where the central government was not. Moreover, both the American federal government and the British government now permit suit against the state in torts, so that in most cases the Anglo-Saxon can now secure relatively the same pecuniary redress for the results of official mistakes as can the Frenchman. Under present conditions, the main difference between the Anglo-Saxon and Continental systems in matters of financial redress is that in Great Britain and the United States the unexpected consequences to someone else of an act in line of duty are not usually indemnified by the government as they are in France (for example, bystanders injured by bullets fired by a policeman pursuing a murderer are not recompensed by the state in the United States or Great Britain but they are in France).

Advocates of the Anglo-Saxon system maintain that while the French system provides greater protection against pecuniary loss by individuals, the Anglo-Saxon system provides a stricter adherence to law. They believe that the very fact that the ordinary courts deal with cases affecting the administration side by side with other cases means that government officials are kept aware of the necessity of adhering to the regular laws of the land. They point out too that the Anglo-Saxon notion of personal liability for abuse of power, regardless of whether the act is committed under orders or not, places the weight of personal responsibility directly on every official and prevents him from "passing the buck" to his superior.

Yet no one who has followed the Crichel Downs case can feel very confident that the ordinary processes for checking administrative action in the Anglo-Saxon system are as satisfactory as they have been assumed to be. There is perhaps no public service in the world with standards as high as the British, yet unjustifiable official arbitrariness occurred in that case for which there was no obvious remedy. Only the most determined and lengthy efforts on the part of the former owners of Crichel Downs disclosed the inequities of that particular situation. In France, in striking contrast, the five applicants to the ENA could file a simple petition with the Council of State and have it result almost automatically in a searching examination of the reasons why the Secretary of State, acting for the Premier, had taken the course he did.

It has been the proud boast of the Anglo-Saxon system that the nation-wide tradition that every person, whether government official or not, is subject to the common rules of the law of the land, preserves liberty under the law in a way which no other system can match. With the all-pervasiveness of the modern administrative bureaucracy, it seems open to question, however, whether some special instrumentalities are not needed in Great Britain and the

United States to buttress their present systems by providing formal, inexpensive, and speedy investigations into charges of official arbitrariness or abuse of power. It is obvious that it is not the administrative court system as such, but the high standards of integrity and independence of the French Council of State, that have made it such an effective guardian of the public interest and of individual liberties. It seems not too much to anticipate, however, that if Great Britain or the United States were to set up an administrative body patterned on the Council of State, that body would operate under the same high standards by which the Council of State acts to check the French administration from abuse or excess of power.

8. French Society in Change

Paralleling the political changes that have transformed France's governmental institutions have been the economic developments that are creating a modern, industrialized, and increasingly affluent society. Economic modernization, new techniques in industry and agriculture, new concentration on the needs of backward regions, the impact of the Development Plans, and France's participation in European integration and the European Economic Community have all contributed to a more vigorous and more developed economy. Inevitably, economic progress has led to demands for wider educational and social opportunities. The French have not yet responded so effectively as the British to these demands, but they are experimenting with new programs, particularly in education. Twenty percent of the national budget for 1966 was allocated to education, where the pressures of numbers, particularly in secondary schools, have outstripped facilities. Thus France is wrestling with the problems of change in every sphere of life.

1. EDUCATION

The aim for French education is to develop a unified and democratic program through which all qualified students can move from the lowest to the highest level. In the past the different kinds of education received by the children of different social classes made the distinction between those who could continue to higher training and those who could not dependent on wealth and position rather than on ability. Higher education remains, in practice, the preserve of the upper and middle classes, but most of the barriers have now been removed at lower educational levels.

Lower Education

In the past, the bourgeoisie and the working class customarily sent their children to different schools. Working-class children attended the free municipal nurseries and then the primary schools (similar to American grade schools) until compulsory education ended at the age of fourteen. The bourgeoisie, on the other hand, had nearly always sent their children to the kindergarten and junior departments of the secondary schools, which were more like American private day schools. The junior departments of the secondary schools concentrated on preparing their students for the competitive examinations (taken at age eleven) that all candidates for the secondary schools had to take, while primary education was largely vocational. Thus, though it was always possible for an unusually able student of working-class parents to make the transition to the secondary schools, it was far more difficult than for those who prepared in the junior departments of the secondary schools.

This early educational segregation, and the consequent difficulty that the children of the poorer classes had in passing the competitive examinations for the secondary schools, were reflected in the relatively small number of students who continued with education at that level, even though France abolished fees for secondary education in 1933 (well before Great Britain).

The great importance of secondary education, apart from its mental discipline, is as the sole route to the *baccalauréat*. This examination must be passed to qualify for many white-collar jobs or for entry to higher education required for professional positions.

The *baccalauréat* used to consist of a highly specialized series of written tests, given in two sections, a year apart. The program and format were changed no less than six times, however, between 1959 and 1966, sometimes quite drastically, in response to the pressure of numbers in the secondary schools and the demands of parents. Less stress is being laid on Latin and more on the sciences and the social studies, though not yet on economics, a subject still treated too theoretically and reserved at the university level for the law schools. In June 1966, for the first time, the *baccalauréat* was given as a single examination. These changes have had an unsettling effect on secondary-school children and have resulted in lower standards for access to higher education. A permanent form for the *baccalauréat* was promised for 1968. The growing democratization of French education to meet the needs of an increasingly complex industrial society is not without its problems, both in maintaining standards and in adjusting the curriculum to new social and economic needs.

Higher Education

Higher education in France is professional in character (as is the practice in Continental countries, in contrast to the more general education in English and American colleges) and is rarely completed before age twenty-three. It is provided not only in universities but also in a series of high-prestige, nonuniversity institutions, notably the *grandes écoles,* which are advanced professional institutes in which the best brains of the country are trained for careers in administration, education, industry and commerce, the armed forces, and so on.

In response to the vastly increased number of students now acquiring university entrance, the number of universities in France has expanded to twenty, plus a growing number of university colleges. The new institutions are in provincial towns and are becoming more popular because of their specialization in particular fields and because of the crowded conditions and high cost of living in Paris. Nonetheless, the University of Paris still possesses the highest prestige, particularly for a doctoral degree, and thirty percent of all French students—100,000 out of 300,000—still concentrate in the Paris area, even though facilities there are scarcely adequate for one-tenth that number. Despite the effort to encourage work in the faculties of sciences, their 129,000 students in 1964–65 were outnumbered by the 137,000 in the faculties of letters (two-thirds of the latter students were women).

A further problem for French universities is the overcentralization resulting from unified state control. Little can be done, and even less initiated, without official sanction, and the most vigorous young teacher-administrators spend much of their time and energy attempting to persuade officials at the Ministry of National Education of the need for new buildings and curricula.

Apart from a few nominal fees, French higher education is free. Nonetheless, some 65 percent of all university students in 1964–65 came from professional and executive families. The ingrained prejudice among the working class and farmers against higher education, coupled with poorer schooling in rural areas and the high cost of living in the cities, continues to perpetuate class distinctions and to prevent talent from being fully used. Within the universities, however, there is a spirit of friendship that produces strong bonds among students regardless of their backgrounds.

The cream of French talent, including some 4,100 students in 1966, is trained in the *grandes écoles.* The coveted entrance to these relatively independent establishments requires at least two years of training after the *baccalauréat* and success in stiff competitive examinations. The *grandes écoles* used to be looked on as potential threats to the Republic because their professional exclusiveness was combined with strong upper-class feeling. It was even said that their graduates constituted a "state within a state" because of their virtual monopoly before World War II of influential positions in education, diplomacy, the Council of State, and other government agencies. The graduates of the *grandes écoles* still occupy the highest position throughout France, both in public and private life. But their students are now fully supported by the state while they are training, thereby opening these opportunities far more widely to all classes in the community. *L'École Nationale d'Administration,* which has trained higher civil servants since World War II, as we have seen, is a good example of the reformed arrangements for the *grandes écoles.*

The New Educational Program

The pressure for admission to higher education—twice as many students now enter universities as in Great Britain—is the result of the reorganization of primary and secondary school curricula that, despite confusion and controversy, is developing a unified system. Primary teaching has become more democratic, and there is easier access for those of moderate means into secondary education. Apart from Sweden, France now has more children continuing from primary to secondary schools than any other European country.

In 1967 compulsory education was extended from age fourteen to sixteen. In 1900 there were 70,000 children in secondary schools; in 1970 there will be three million.

The 1960 reform aimed to give each child an education suited to his or her aptitude. The expectation is that children can be divided into three categories: those capable of abstract and theoretical studies, who should go through higher education; those who should have only a minimum of abstract and theoretical work but are capable of fairly extended education; and those who are unsuited to academic work and should concentrate early on practical training. Following a common elementary curriculum, there are two cycles of education, the first from age eleven to fifteen, and the second from fifteen to eighteen. During the first cycle, there are opportunities to move from one section to another according to demonstrated aptitude and accomplishments. The second cycle either ends with a certificate after two years or leads to the *baccalauréat.*

No phase of French education is yet settled permanently. Plans are under way for further changes in secondary and higher education. The excessive rigidities of the older system have been broken and the way opened to meet the needs of a dynamic economy.

The Catholic Church and Education

The sharpest controversy in French education has been over the influence of and, more recently, state support of private schools, a high proportion of which are parochial, or Catholic. Roughly speaking, one child in six attends a private primary school, and one in three a private secondary school. Since state facilities at both levels are already badly overtaxed, the facilities of the denominational schools are indispensable, particularly in the west of France. But long-standing hostility to religious influence in education has not yet abated, although one of the achievements of the Fifth Republic has been at last to provide badly needed state support for impoverished private schools.

This controversy has been one of the great divisive influences in French political life. It dates from the time when the Catholic Church was generally suspected of hostility to the Republic and when the republican government felt it necessary to restrict the Catholic teaching orders and to develop a system of free, public, lay education on the primary level. Fundamentally, the struggle was for the minds of the children. Republican statesmen were convinced that children educated by the Church would grow up to be supporters of the clerical and antirepublican groups and that only a school system that was republican politically and "neutral" theologically could create a generation of citizens devoted to the Republic. To the leaders of the Church, however, the "godless" schools of the Republic seemed anything but neutral, and every effort had to be made to restrict their influence.

During the late nineteenth and early twentieth centuries, when the Republic was struggling for its life, many of the public school teachers conceived of themselves as warriors in its defense. Often they looked upon the Church as the enemy of education and enlightenment, and, particularly after World War I, they were often socialist and pacifist in their outlook. In thousands of villages throughout France the opposition between left and right, between the Republic and the Church, came to be personified in the antagonism between schoolmaster and priest.

The poverty of the private denominational

schools forced the issue of state support on both the Fourth and the Fifth Republics. This issue had become the more controversial because Pétain's wartime regime extended financial aid to the parochial schools—an action that seemed to many staunch republicans new proof of the antidemocratic character of the Church. Despite the reluctance of the MRP, these subsidies were withdrawn when the Fourth Republic was established. However, despite prolonged and acrimonious debate, legislation following the 1951 election provided minimal aid for the denominational schools through a special allocation, which was made for each child in an elementary school and which was to be used to improve facilities and salaries. Their situation remained acute, however, because of the steadily increasing numbers in the schools. Premier Debré first provided emergency financial help to the Catholic schools in mid-1959 through an advance of the special allocation and then, despite the resignation in protest of his Minister of Education, a former Socialist, brought in comprehensive legislation at the end of that year that passed by a large majority, despite hot opposition by the anticlerical Radicals and Socialists.

This legislation offers the denominational schools a choice among four different relationships with the state. Two of these relationships represent extremes: complete integration in the public school system, on the one hand, or complete independence without government aid, on the other. The arrangement accepted by most Catholic schools is called the "simple contract," according to which the state pays qualified teachers on condition that the school meets national standards on the length of the school year (190 class days), number of students, and sanitary conditions. The fourth and less popular relationship is called a "contract of association," under which public school regulations and curriculum are fully instituted in the classes covered; the teachers, who are paid by the state, are drawn either from the state schools or through contract, and the state assumes all expenses of operating the classes. Either of these last two arrangements is undertaken on a nine-year basis and may be renewed under stated conditions.

Despite a threat by the Socialists that any parochial school accepting aid will be made a part of the state school system if the Socialists ever form a government, the arrangement is a reasonable resolution of a complicated problem. In keeping with the gradual transformation of the educational system as a whole into a democratic entity, the primary goal of the system is to maintain (or establish) standards and to remain responsive to the needs of France's people.

2. WELFARE SERVICES

There are major differences between Great Britain and France both in the organization and the coverage of their welfare services. France has no National Health Service, although its national insurance system provides for the reimbursement of certain medical expenses. Although the French government does not administer social services directly, it supervises the operations of social security organs (concerned with social insurance and family allowances) and local authorities (which provide public assistance, hospital care, and so forth). The end result is a complex series of agencies providing a wide range of relatively generous benefits, particularly in the form of family allowances. The system is, in practice, a unified one, despite the absence of a unitary authority.

The French have an exceptionally interesting and complicated system of social security, which has been strongly affected both by its historical development and by a basic concern for the family as a unit. Although it is less well integrated than the amazingly comprehensive but relatively simple system of social welfare established in Great Britain after World War II, the French system of social administration interrelates social insurance, family allowances, and public assistance with a wide range of preventive and welfare services. The unique feature of the French social security system is that it is administered by a series of private institutions called "the Funds," which have financial autonomy. Since, however, the Funds have the responsibility of directing important public services, they are supervised and ultimately controlled by government officials.

In some respects France was slow in introducing measures of social welfare, and there have always been powerful voices charging that the economy could not and should not stand the burden of such expenditures. Child labor was not curbed until 1874; factory inspection began some time later; and compensation for industrial accidents was only introduced at the turn of the century. Compulsory social insurance (including provisions for old age, sickness, maternity, and workmen's compensation) was first established in 1930, and then only for those earning less than a certain amount. Trade unions opposed the establishment of a state-administered system. Instead, a decentralized system of self-administered funds (*caisses*) was set up. Workers could join these funds directly or through mutual-aid societies. Employers and employees both contributed, and the government established scales of benefits for sickness and retirement. This system was extended in 1945 to cover most employed persons and their families, and it became part of the comprehensive Social Security Code of 1956.

The French social security system is in principle self-supporting, although the state aids certain classes of persons. Whereas in Great Britain there is a flat rate of contributions, in France they are graduated according to earnings. Employers must contribute approximately 10 percent and employees 6 percent of wages up to a maximum annual wage of about $2,000, and deductions are made at the source. Benefits include reimbursement of specified levels of medical expenses (official scales are established by a committee of civil servants set up in 1960; though they are published, they are not binding on doctors), sick pay, disability benefits, retirement and widows' pensions, and death benefits. In general, benefits are proportionate to earnings and do not cover full expenses or previous earnings. There is no provision for unemployment benefits, for which there has never been the pressing need in France that has existed at times in Great Britain.

Family allowances in France have a more important place in the social welfare system than in any other country. France was a pioneer in introducing family allowances, which date back to 1884 in private industry and were already a feature of public assistance before 1914. Family allowances were significantly expanded during and after World War I. They were made a charge on all employers in industry and commerce by a law of March 1932 and were further extended in 1939.

Although the French family allowance system is self-financing, the money comes entirely from employers, who contribute approximately 14 percent of their total wage bill. Allowances are not restricted to employees, however, but are available to everyone and are not related to income. They include children's allowances (the amount rises with the third and again with the fourth child) and allowances for the nonworking mother, for maternity, and for housing. Together with a wide range of advantages for large families in income tax rebates and reduced fares on public transport, the family allowance system is intended to encourage the rising birth rate and to provide social justice. While in Great Britain the social security system is primarily designed to provide protection during illness or unemployment, in France it is a major means of redistributing income. Indeed, for the less well paid, social security benefits may bring almost as much as their pay check and may be regarded as an integral part of their regular income. Social security charges, including those for family allowances, add approximately 30 percent to the total wage bill.

The general administration of the social security system is in the hands of the management boards of the Funds, which are found on the local, regional, and national level. Three-quarters of the members of the local social security boards are workers' representatives and one-quarter are employers' representatives; the ratio on the boards of the family allowance Funds is one-half workers, one-quarter employers, and one-quarter self-employed. Unlike the local and regional Funds, the National Security Fund is a public body. It includes, therefore, not only worker and employer members elected from the local and regional Funds, but also civil servants.

Candidates for these positions are put forward by trade unions and employers' organizations, but since there is so sharp and antagonistic a division among the French trade unions —the CGT, FO, and CFTC—the decision about who shall represent the workers in the social security boards is made by direct election. These elections, oddly enough, reflect political sympathies rather than different points of view on how the social security system should be run. The Communist-dominated CGT tends to obtain nearly half the employees' votes (44 percent in 1962, compared with 21 percent for the Catholic CFTC and 15 percent for the Socialist FO), and its representatives have used their position for political purposes. Such political abuse of board powers was curtailed in 1960 by an extension of ministerial control and by a sharper distinction between the functions of the boards and the managers of the Funds. The boards now vote the budget, supervise administration, and decide discretionary programs within prescribed limits. The director handles day-to-day administration and occupies a position roughly comparable to that of the managers of nationalized industries.

Conclusion

The French are still dissatisfied with certain rigidities and inequities in their educational structure and with certain injustices in the distribution of national income, both among groups within the population and among regions. Nonetheless they are making the most determined efforts in their history to develop a more open educational system and a more rational general social policy. A notable clause in the preamble to the 1946 constitution, repeated in that of 1958, declared that "every human being who, because of his age, physical or mental state, or because of his economic situation, finds himself incapable of working, has a right to obtain the means from the community for living suitably." The first three Development Plans concentrated on stimulating the economy, but the fourth and fifth Plans have deliberately associated social objectives with economic ones.

Since 1956, a summary of social expenses known as the "Social Budget" has been a regular appendix to the Finance Bill. In 1962, the social budget was more than 20 percent of the gross national product. Like its associates in the European Economic Community, France spends between 11 percent and 14 percent of its national income on social security benefits, and the expectation is that this percentage will rise. The process has been more halting and uneven than in Great Britain, but the objectives in France are also far-reaching and the achievements increasingly impressive.

9. France and the World

Largely ignored in international relations after World War II, France under President de Gaulle has become an influential, if controversial, factor in world politics. Though overshadowed in strength by the United States and the Soviet Union, France has reasserted its dominance in Western Europe, which it is trying to shape into an independent third force. Moreover, despite the loss of its colonial empire, France continues to possess great influence in former French Africa through its economic and educational aid.

1. FROM COMMUNITY TO AFRICAN INDEPENDENCE

When de Gaulle assumed power in 1958, France had suffered a series of humiliating defeats and withdrawals from former colonial territories, notably Indo-China, Morocco, and Tunisia, and was engaged in an exhausting struggle in Algeria. Moreover, the units of its empire in West Africa and Madagascar were pressing for further self-government.

De Gaulle himself had included representatives from French Africa in the Constituent Assemblies that drafted the constitution of the Fourth Republic. But despite the efforts of the native representatives and the parties of the left to establish a federal commonwealth through extending self-government to the various units of the empire, the 1946 constitution included three types of political arrangements for the African colonies that in the end proved mutually exclusive. Following the assimilative principle so strong in France's earlier relations with its empire, the African colonies sent representatives to the French parliament throughout the Fourth Republic, as Algeria and the old colonies (Martinique, Guadeloupe, Réunion, and French Guiana) had long done. In a quasi-federal move, a new structure, the French Union, was established, whose Assembly was composed of an equal number of representatives from overseas territories and from France. The third, and ultimately the most significant, feature was to provide each colony with a local representative body. Strong and skillful pressure by the African deputies in the National Assembly led to the 1956 *loi cadre*. This measure permitted local legislatures, elected by universal franchise and directed by local African leaders, to exercise limited autonomy by the time the Fourth Republic collapsed.

The Community

De Gaulle recognized the need to provide a new basis of relationship between the African territories and France. The means proposed in the constitution was the Community, which was the substitute both for the French Union and for the representation of the African territories in the French legislature. The constitution of the Fifth Republic acknowledged the right of the African territories to choose secession and independence but offered political, economic, and cultural association with France within the Community.

Each member state of the Community was recognized as self-governing; in general, their pattern of institutions was like that in France, though commonly they had only one party. But highly important matters were reserved to the Community: foreign policy, defense, currency, common economic and financial policy, the disposition of strategic raw materials, and (except by special agreement) control of higher education, the courts, and the general organization of interstate and foreign transportation and telecommunication. These latter subjects were managed by institutions established by and common to all members of the Community: the President, who was also the President of the French Republic in whose election the overseas departments and territories shared; the Executive Council, composed of the French Premier, the heads of government of the member states, and the ministers responsible for the common affairs of the Community; the Senate, composed of delegates from the legislative assemblies of France and the other member states, whose numbers were determined both by population and responsibilities in the Community; and a Court of Arbitration to settle disputes among members of the Community.

Despite the effort to establish common institutions, the Community was clearly presidential in character. The Executive Council, over which the President presided, was not responsible to the Senate, which, in fact, was purely consultative. During its short lifetime, the Community was run, therefore, by the chief executives of its various territories with only a slight check by popular representatives.

On the vote in September 1958 on whether or not to join the Community only Guinea voted no. It associated itself with Ghana. The twelve African members voted themselves the status of autonomous republics and sometimes adopted unfamiliar names such as Voltaic Republic instead of Upper Volta, the Malagasy Republic instead of Madagascar, and, still more confusing, Central African Republic for what was formerly Ubangi-Shari.

Temporarily Senegal and Soudan formed the Federation of Mali, but this union broke up in July 1960, partly over different political philosophies, partly over personal rivalries. The Soudan took the name of Mali. Houphouet Boigny of the Ivory Coast formed the Entente, an economic and cultural association between his wealthy country and the Voltaic Republic, Dahomey, and Niger. In early 1961, the "twelve" or "the Brazzaville group" established a loose association of six French-speaking states of West Africa (all except Guinea and Mali), the states of former French Equatorial Africa—Gabon,

Chad, the Central African Republic, and the Congo Republic (Brazzaville)—the Cameroun Republic (independent in 1960), and Malagasy. By 1965, this had transformed itself into OCAM (*Organisation Commune Africaine et Malgache*), which included also the Republic of the Congo (Kinshasa, formerly Leopoldville).

Though all the former French territories in Africa except Guinea voted for the Community (French Somaliland remained an overseas territory), Senegal and Soudan, in particular, wanted to turn it into an association more like the Commonwealth, with each state controlling all its internal and external relations. Under pressure, de Gaulle reluctantly agreed to this new form of relationship within the Community —which made possible separate representation in the United Nations for what was then the Federation of Mali. Fearing to lose the nationalist initiative, Houphouet Boigny (till then the strongest advocate of the Community in its original form and probably responsible for the relevant sections in the constitution), suddenly announced in July 1960 his intention of breaking the links of the Entente with the Community and immediately seeking United Nations membership. Thus the very attenuated membership of the Community consisted thereafter only of France, Senegal, the Malagasy Republic, Gabon, Chad, the Central African Republic, and the Congo Republic (Brazzaville). Since France's relations with each of its former African territories are now determined by bilateral agreements, the Community has ceased to have significance.

Despite this development, France maintains strong ties with its former territories in Africa. The economic aid it extends to them is greater in proportion to its national income (and used to be greater in extent) than that provided for Africa by Great Britain, the United States, or the Soviet Union. Aid includes general assistance, financing specific projects, and subsidies to maintain a high price for such African crops as coffee and cotton. All former Community members—and also the Congo (Kinshasa), Rwanda, Burundi, the Somali Republic, and Nigeria—have become associate members of the Common Market. The Common Market's European Development Fund has pledged aid to the Associated States, and France has a major share in determining how this money will be used. It still prefers bilateral programs.

Perhaps still more influential in maintaining French influence with its former African colonies have been the teachers, technicians, and administrators who have served, or continue to serve, in these countries. In their first years of independence it was common to have French civil servants playing a more decisive role in decision-making than did the African ministers. Many of the French administrators and technicians have now been withdrawn; so, too, have most of the French army units in Africa. But the number of French teachers serving abroad—more than 30,000—has increased. Five thousand teach in former French African countries; 12,000 in Algeria; and 12,000 in Morocco, Tunisia, Asia, and Oceania. More than 1.5 million students are enrolled in the more than 1,500 French teaching establishments abroad, and many of them take French as well as local examinations. The universities in former French African territories are part of the French university system. Over 40,000 foreign students are studying in France. Thus have the French been able to capitalize on the spread of their language and the high esteem for their culture.

2. INTERNATIONAL RELATIONS

Though de Gaulle devotes considerable attention to France's relations outside Europe, his primary concern remains its position on the Continent. In the past, French policy was dominated by the relation to Germany, by which it had been invaded three times in three-quarters of a century. Despite the destruction in Germany during World War II and its *de facto* partition between East and West, France cannot forget that there are still over seventy million Germans in Central Europe and only forty-nine million Frenchmen, and that Germany's natural resources give it a far stronger industrial capacity than France can hope to attain. To redress the balance, France has sought at different times to exercise some control over the Saar, the Rhineland, and the Ruhr, either directly or through a joint agreement, as in the Coal and Steel Community. France's purpose, of course, is to assure an adequate supply of German coke

for its own iron ore in Lorraine so that Germany will not have unrestricted use of the products that have contributed so directly to its military resources and heavy industrial plant. France has also sought to strengthen itself through alliances, in the pattern of its policy between the wars, and to coordinate and unify Western Europe under its own leadership.

Failing after World War I to secure either the strategic control of the Rhineland or a military guarantee from Great Britain and the United States, France sought security by insisting that Germany adhere to the letter of the peace treaty of Versailles, by building a network of alliances with the countries of Eastern and Southeastern Europe, and by seeking to strengthen the League of Nations. Relations with Great Britain, though close, were frequently strained by diverging views on the German problem and on the best way of organizing peace, as well as by rivalry in the Near East. As Germany grew aggressive under Hitler, France capped its alliance structure with the Franco-Soviet Treaty. But since it was weakened by internal division, France pursued a halting foreign policy, accepting or, as in regard to Mussolini's Italy, encouraging the British appeasement policy.

Feeling ignored during World War II by the three great powers that were carrying the burden of the fighting, France at de Gaulle's insistence sought to regain its place by building up its army, keeping its claims to the fore, and reestablishing the system of alliances. This time it began with the country with which ties had been established late in the interwar period, and toward which there was nation-wide gratitude for its part in the liberation of France: the Soviet Union. On December 10, 1944, de Gaulle signed with the Soviet Union a twenty-year defensive treaty that he hoped would put France in the position of mediator between East and West. But France, despite its alliance with the Soviet Union, was not represented at the decisive Yalta Conference a little over a month later. And in neither of the international conferences that France later attended, nor in its policy toward Germany, did France find the Soviet Union prepared to lend it much support.

In the light of this disappointment, the French turned back once more to the notion of an alliance in the West. On March 4, 1947, a fifty-year alliance with Great Britain was signed at Dunkirk to guarantee joint action in case of German aggression and to assure consultation in case Germany's economic obligations were unfulfilled. Agreements with Czechoslovakia and Poland and with Belgium and Holland were also discussed. Yet increasingly, French statesmen recognized the difficulties of bridging the gulf between East and West, and saw that the Soviet military position in Central Europe could offer a serious threat to France's own security.

Side by side with questions of political alignments in Europe went the problem of economic recovery. France originally blocked the economic coordination of the four zones into which Germany was divided at the end of the war and opposed the revival of the industrial capacity of the Ruhr. In the light of France's own economic problems, however, and its initial dependence on economic aid from the United States, French statesmen gradually modified their opposition to the economic recovery of West Germany so long as this area was considered an integral part of the program for Western Europe as a whole. France then embarked on a bold program of economic and political unification in this area, in particular through the Council of Europe, plans for a European army, and the Schuman plan for the European Coal and Steel Community. Of these three, it was the last that acted as pacemaker for the remarkable moves toward economic integration of "the Six": France, Germany, Italy, Holland, Belgium, and Luxembourg.

Established by international agreement in 1949, the Council of Europe, whose function is not to make policy but rather to develop a sense of community in Western Europe, operates quietly in Strasbourg through its Secretariat, its Committee of Ministers who represent the participating governments, and its Consultative Assembly whose members are drawn from all sections of opinion—except the Communists—in the parliaments of member countries. Frenchmen, but not de Gaulle, have been among its staunchest adherents.

In August 1954, France rejected the European Defense Community—an imaginative approach to the problem of German rearmament through establishing a supranational European Army with French, German, Dutch, Belgian, Luxembourg, and Italian units—which had been proposed by its own statesmen. But when the British Conservative government suddenly took on the far-reaching military commitments of Western European Union, France agreed in October 1954 to permit the newly sovereign and rearmed West Germany to enter the North Atlantic Treaty Organization (NATO).

More influential than joint defense for progressively binding France and Western Germany together have proved to be supranational economic arrangements. Though the latter were originally designed to facilitate political integration, de Gaulle's insistence on national sovereignty has thwarted this potential by-product of supranational economic organizations. Nonetheless, the most far-reaching of Western Europe's associations, the Common Market (known more formally as the European Economic Community, EEC), has created bonds among its six members—France, Germany, Italy, Belgium, Holland, and Luxembourg—that are unprecedented in the history of Europe. To evaluate current French foreign policy, therefore, it is essential to know more about the European Coal and Steel Community, which was the first of Western Europe's supranational functional organizations, as well as about the other organizations that encourage integrated economic arrangements among the Six.

The European Coal and Steel Community

The European Coal and Steel Community, established on July 25, 1952, fuses the coal and steel production (the basis of military and industrial strength) of the same six countries—France, Germany, Belgium, Holland, Luxembourg, and Italy—under a common authority not subject to the control of any one government. Its basic purposes are to assure the efficient production of coal and steel at low cost, to organize the more than 130 million people of these six countries into a single competitive market for these products, and to pass on the economic advantages of so large a market not only to industrialists and governments but also to the workers in the form of improved standards of living. Its effect is to place under supranational control the production of the two key resources of an area as important strategically as industrially: the rich coal and iron triangle of Western Europe which, in an area only half the size of Alabama, includes Lorraine, the Saar, the Ruhr, and the Rhineland.

The supranational political structure of the European Coal and Steel Community is as complex as it is novel. The executive body is the High Authority, made up of nine members (selected by general agreement of the six governments) who are chosen not to represent particular countries or industries but "for their general competence" and who serve six-year staggered terms. The High Authority's decisions are by majority vote. It appears to have unlimited power to gather information, to prevent the growth of private cartels, and to prohibit and break up mergers that violate the nondiscriminatory aims of the treaty. It has considerable power in other areas affecting production. In practice, however, it works with the consent of its member governments rather than by issuing orders to them.

An elaborate structure of checks and balances to the power of the High Authority is provided through four other organs: the Council of Ministers, the Assembly, the Court, and the Consultative Committee. The Council of Ministers is the link between the governments and the High Authority; it consists of one member from each government, and its approval is needed for High Authority action in certain spheres defined by the treaty, notably the development of industry and the regulation of foreign trade. The Assembly (in which France, Germany, and Italy each have eighteen members, Belgium and Holland each ten, and Luxembourg four, elected either by popular vote or their national assemblies) meets annually to consider the High Authority's general report and has the supreme power of being able to force the resignation of the Authority by a two-thirds vote. The Court, composed of seven judges appointed for six-year terms by the governments acting jointly, is the final tribunal in all disputes between the Authority and governments or firms. It may order and restrain action by the High Authority insofar as empowered by the treaty. The Consultative Committee appointed by the Council gives producers, workers, and consumers equal representation, and provides advice on production programs and the "readaptation" of industry and labor to the new conditions of a larger market and more efficient organization of production.

Euratom

The second of the specialized functional agencies, Euratom, so quickly captured the public imagination that in July 1956, within a month of the drafting of the treaty, the French National Assembly approved joining the atomic energy pool, which was established in 1958. But current high coal stocks and low fuel prices have done away with much of the need for atomic energy (which seemed so urgent at the time of the Suez crisis). Euratom spreads the cost of nuclear research among a number of countries that could not afford it singly. But its importance is likely to be in the long run rather than immediately, since the high costs of production of atomic energy handicap it in competition with other types of fuel while Euratom itself faces stiff competition from the nuclear developments of Western Europe's private engineering industries.

The Common Market

Most significant and far-reaching of all Western European arrangements is the European Economic Community, or Common Market, which came into existence along with Euratom on January 1, 1958. The Common Market agreement ultimately aims to extend to the whole economy the principles that have been operating for iron and steel. The abolition of general restrictions on trade is naturally more gradual than those on iron and steel, but through extensive and often hard-fought negotiations the Six are moving toward a common external tariff and the abolition of internal trade barriers.[1] A major reason why the French economy is so healthy is that it has responded to the

[1] For a case study of how the basic agreement in agricultural policy was reached, see "The Common Market: Farmers and Foreign Policy: An Agricultural Agreement for Europe," by Michael G. Duerr in *Politics in Europe: Five Cases in European Government*, edited by Gwendolen M. Carter and Alan F. Westin (New York, Harcourt, Brace & World, Inc., 1965).

stimulus provided by the competition and opportunities offered by this larger area.

There are four institutions to manage the European Economic Community: the Commission, which is its permanent executive; the Council of Ministers, which makes policy decisions; and the Court of Justice and the Assembly (somewhat enlarged), which it shares with the Coal and Steel Community.

The extent of the authority of the Executive Commission, and particularly of its president, Walter Hallstein of Germany, has been a matter of dispute between de Gaulle and his five partners. They, like many of France's enthusiasts for European political integration, have welcomed for its political implications the prospect of independent decisions by the Commission. De Gaulle opposes the prospect for the same reason and would prefer to have the authority of the Executive Committee reduced.

The Common Market was scheduled to enter its third and final stage of economic integration in mid-1965, but France's insistence on the rule of unanimity plus a five- (rather than two-) year period of farm subsidies delayed the decision for a year, and temporarily threatened the future course of the association. The settlement in July 1966 protected France's *liberum veto* over decisions by the Executive Commission on the allocation of farm subsidies but opened the way again to continued elimination of tariffs within the area of the Six.

National tariffs on industrial products from other members of the Common Market had already been reduced by 1966 to one-fifth of their 1957 level and disappeared in 1967. Internal trade among the Six, aided by the elimination of import quotas, increased 168 percent between 1959 and 1966. Agricultural free trade within the Common Market, plus subsidies to enable the exporting countries' farmers (and especially those of France) to compete with lower world prices, resulted from the 1966 agreement. Thus France moved closer to a major objective: relative self-sufficiency in food supplies of Western Europe.

Basic to de Gaulle's economic, financial, and political policies is his determination that France shall be able to make its own final decisions on specific as well as general issues. Coupled with this overall objective are his efforts (which run counter to what his Common Market partners desire) to reduce or eliminate American influence from Western Europe, where he insists France must be dominant. Both purposes are intimately bound up with de Gaulle's reluctance to admit Great Britain to the Common Market, for he recognizes that the British not only want the economic stimulus of association with the Six but also a closer relationship between them and the United States.

France and the World

In international affairs, de Gaulle bases his policies on the simple traditional principle that the world is composed of sovereign states. For France to play an independent role determined by its self-interest, requires, in de Gaulle's view, the executive's (in practice, his own) undisputed control of foreign policy. As far as international organization is concerned, he refuses to agree that the United Nations is more than a forum in which each state presents its own point of view and determines how far it will cooperate with other members. Thus de Gaulle not only refuses to participate in the peacekeeping operations of the United Nations but also to share in paying for them. At the same time he supports the admission of Communist China, regardless of its policies, because it is a sovereign and highly populous state.

On several counts de Gaulle pits France against the United States. First, he believes that France can dominate Western Europe only if American influence is neutralized or eliminated. Thus he has forced American troops and installations out of France, thereby impairing the strategic unity of NATO. Second, he resists American efforts to secure universal sharing of United Nations responsibilities and debts. Third, his insistence on converting American financial obligations into gold has complicated American monetary policy. Fourth, he capitalizes on opposition to American policies, for example, in Vietnam. Yet the instant support afforded the United States at the time of the Cuban crisis demonstrates that de Gaulle is not anti-American. His guiding rule is to put and keep France in the front rank of world powers. Thus he exploits every situation for France's interest, particularly those situations affecting the United

States and Great Britain, of whose ultimate support in time of need he has no doubt.

That de Gaulle refused to allow Great Britain to enter the Common Market is a further example of his determination to keep France the dominant influence in Western Europe. Whether he is making the right decisions to fulfill his purposes is another matter. A closer economic and political alignment with Great Britain might strengthen France and help to create a more stable third force by lessening British dependence on the United States. By weakening NATO and depending on Western European union and France's own nuclear *force de frappe,* he may be undercutting the strategic unity of the West. He might be mistaken in his estimates that the Soviet Union is no longer expansionist, that German reunification is not possible, and that Great Britain and the United States are basically his allies despite their irritation at his policies. But de Gaulle appears to have no doubts that his policies are the best for France, and the vast improvement in its international position since he assumed power in the Fifth Republic provides him with ample evidence that he is correct.

Conclusion

For the first time in half a century France is neither at war nor in fear of the coming of war. Coupled with the political stability and economic prosperity of the Fifth Republic, this freedom from fear has created a mood of confidence and security unknown to earlier generations.

The removal of the nightmare of an aggressive Germany, and of France's traditional fear of lacking essential energy resources, is the chief external factor creating the new spirit. The partition of Germany, plus France's close relation with West Germany in the Common Market, has eliminated the former anxiety. The development of hydroelectric power and the flow of oil from North Africa, supplemented by the arrangements of the Coal and Steel Community, have made France's scarcity of coal far less important.

Internally, the economic advance that is now spreading more evenly throughout the country has done much to reduce the former social barriers between the working class and the bourgeoisie. The modernization of agriculture and the consequent shift of peasants into industry have strengthened the equilibrium of French society. The newer industries—electronics, chemicals, and oil—into which many of the new workers have gone are those in which the influence of the Communist-dominated CGT is weak. Partly for this reason, though more because of prosperity, strikes have been relatively infrequent. Another reason for the unprecedented atmosphere of optimism in France is the increasing youthfulness of France's population, created by its high birth rate (higher than the German and above the European average).

The biggest question mark in France's future concerns de Gaulle. Rarely has a democratic regime in an established country depended so completely on a single individual. It is hard to imagine that the UNR would maintain its cohesion in response to another leader. Since the chances are slight that France can develop a two-party system apart from the Communists, the old problem of devising political stability out of disparate and antagonistic parties may return if the dominant force of de Gaulle leaves the scene. Yet perhaps the electorate has acquired more sense of responsibility for casting its votes for those who intend to work within the constitutional system and will also curb its anarchic tendency to support splinter groups rather than the larger parties that have a chance to support or constructively oppose governmental policies.

France has great elements of strength. It is well balanced between agriculture and industry, town and country. It is growing in numbers and output. It has an excellent civil service, technological competence, and useful experience in public planning for further development. More now than for many decades, France is in a position to make use of the great heritage it possesses.

Bibliography

PREPARED BY LOUISE W. HOLBORN

Radcliffe Institute for Independent Study, Cambridge, Mass.

ABBREVIATIONS

AJCL: American Journal of Comparative Law, Ann Arbor, Mich., quarterly.
AJS: American Journal of Sociology, Chicago, bimonthly.
Annals: The Annals of the American Academy of Political and Social Science, Philadelphia, bimonthly.
APSR: American Political Science Review, Washington, D.C., quarterly.
BIS: Bulletin of the Institute for the Study of the USSR, Munich, monthly.
CH: Current History, Philadelphia, monthly.
CLR: Columbia Law Review, New York, monthly.
COI: Central Office of Information, London.
DSB: Department of State Bulletin, Washington, D.C., biweekly.
E: The Economist, London, weekly.
FA: Foreign Affairs, New York, quarterly.
Hansard: Hansard Society for Parliamentary Government, London.
HICOG: High Commission for Germany.
HLR: Harvard Law Review, Cambridge, Mass., monthly (Nov.–June).
IA: International Affairs, London, monthly.
IC: International Conciliation, New York, monthly, except July and August.
ICFTU: International Confederation of Free Trade Unions.
IJ: International Journal, Toronto, quarterly.
ILO: International Labor Office, Geneva.
ILR: International Labour Review, Geneva & Washington, D.C., monthly.
IO: International Organization, Boston, quarterly.
IPSA: International Political Science Abstracts, Oxford, quarterly.
ISSJ: International Social Science Journal, Paris, quarterly.
J: Journal.

JCH: Journal of Contemporary History, London, quarterly.
JIA: Journal of International Affairs, Columbia U., New York, 3 issues annually.
JP: The Journal of Politics, Gainesville, Fla., quarterly.
JPC: Journal of the Parliaments of the Commonwealth, London, quarterly.
Lib: Library.
LR: Law Review.
MIT: Mass. Institute of Technology, Cambridge, Mass.
Oceana: Oceana Publications, New York.
P: Press.
PAR: Public Administration Review, Chicago, quarterly.
Parl. Aff.: Parliamentary Affairs, London, quarterly.
Pbk: Paperback.
PEP: Political and Economic Planning, London.
POQ: The Political Opinion Quarterly, Princeton, quarterly.
PS: Political Studies, Oxford, 3 issues annually.
PSQ: Political Science Quarterly, New York, quarterly.
Pub: Publisher.
Pub. Ad.: Public Administration, London, quarterly.
Pub. Pers. Rev.: Public Personnel Review, Chicago, quarterly.
R: Review.
RIIA: Royal Institute of International Affairs, London.
RP: Review of Politics.
SR: Social Research, New York, quarterly.
SS: Soviet Studies, Oxford, quarterly.
U: University.
WP: World Politics, Princeton, quarterly.
WPQ: The Western Political Quarterly, Salt Lake City, quarterly.
YBE: The Yearbook of Education, London, annually.
YLR: Yale Law Review, New Haven, quarterly.
YR: Yale Review, New Haven, quarterly.

FRANCE

GENERAL WORKS

Aron, Raymond, *France, The New Republic*, Oceana, 1959, 114 pp.

Brogan, Denis W., *The French Nation, from Napoleon to Pétain, 1814–1940*, Harper, 1957, 328 pp, pbk.

Cairns, John Campbell, *France*, Prentice-Hall, 1965, 180 pp, pbk.

Furniss, Edgar S., Jr., *France, Troubled Ally, de Gaulle's Heritage and Prospects*, Praeger, 1960, 559 pp, pbk.

Guérard, Albert Léon, *France*, Michigan UP, 1964, 616 pp.

Hoffmann, Stanley S. et al., *In Search of France*, Harvard UP, 1965, pbk.

Laponce, J. A., *The Government of the Fifth Republic, French Political Parties and the Constitution*, U California P, 1961, 415 pp.

Macridis, Roy C. and Bernard E. Brown, *The de Gaulle Republic, Quest for Unity*, Dorsey, 1960, 400 pp.

———, *Supplement to the de Gaulle Republic*, Dorsey, 1963, 141 pp.

Pickles, Dorothy, *The Fifth Republic, Institutions and Politics*, 3rd ed., Praeger, 1965, 261 pp, pbk.

Thomson, David, *Democracy in France Since 1870*, 4th ed., Oxford UP, 1964, 350 pp, pbk.

Williams, Philip M., *Crisis and Compromise*, 3rd ed., Anchor, 1964, 546 pp.

Wright, Gordon, *France in Modern Times, 1760 to the Present*, Rand-McNally, 1962, 621 pp.

Chapter 1. THE FRENCH PEOPLE AND THEIR POLITICS

Aron, Raymond, *France, Steadfast and Changing, The Fourth to the Fifth Republic*, trans. by T. J. Irwin and Luigi Einaudi, Harvard UP, 1960, 201 pp.

Bosworth, William, *Catholicism and Crisis in Modern France, French Catholic Groups at the Threshold of the Fifth Republic*, Princeton UP, 1961, 408 pp.

Brogan, Denis W. and the editors of *Life*, *France*, Time, 1960, 176 pp.

Camp, Wesley D., *Marriage and the Family in France Since the Revolution, An Essay in the History of Population*, Bookman, 1961, 203 pp.

Curtius, Ernst Robert, *The Civilization of France, An Introduction*, Allen & Unwin, London, 1932, 247 pp.

Earle, Edward Mead, ed., *Modern France, Problems of the Third and Fourth Republics*, Princeton UP, 1959, 522 pp.

Fauvet, Jacques, *The Cockpit of France*, trans. by Nancy Pearson, Harvill, London, 1960, 159 pp.

Hayes, Carlton J. H., *France, A Nation of Patriots*, Columbia UP, 1930, 487 pp.

Joll, James, *Intellectuals in Politics*, Weidenfeld & Nicolson, London, 1960, 217 pp.

Luethy, Herbert, *France Against Herself*, trans. from German by Erich Mosbacher, Praeger, 1955, 476 pp.

McKay, Donald C., *The United States and France*, Harvard UP, 1951, 334 pp.

Metraux, Rhoda and Margaret Mead, *Themes in French Culture, A Preface to a Study of French Community*, Stanford UP, 1954, 120 pp.

Morazé, Charles, *The French and the Republic*, Cornell UP, 1958, 214 pp.

Park, Julian, ed., *The Culture of France in Our Time*, Cornell UP, 1954, 345 pp.

Peyre, Henri, *The Contemporary French Novel*, Oxford UP, 1955, 363 pp.

Schram, Stuart R., *Protestantism and Politics in France*, Corbière & Jugain, Alençon, 1954, 288 pp.

Sieburg, Friedrich, *Who Are These French?* Macmillan, 1932, 303 pp.

Siegfried, André, *France, A Study in Nationality*, Yale UP, 1930, 122 pp.

Valery, Paul, *Dialogues*, trans. by William McCausland Stewart, Pantheon, 1964, 195 pp.

Wright, Gordon, "Catholics and Peasantry in France," *PSQ*, 68(4), Dec. 1953:526–51.

———, *Rural Revolution in France, The Peasantry in the Twentieth Century*, Stanford UP, 1964, 271 pp.

INTEREST GROUPS

Ambler, John Steward, *The French Army in Politics, 1945–1962*, Ohio State UP, 1966, 427 pp.

Brown, Bernard E., "Alcohol and Politics in France," *APSR*, 51, Dec. 1957:976–94.

———, "The Army and Politics in France," *JP*, 23(2), May 1961:262–78.

Brown, Bernard E., "Pressure Politics in the Fifth Republic," *JP*, 25(3), Aug. 1963:509–25.

———, "Pressure Politics in France," *JP*, 18, Nov. 1956:702–19.

Domenach, Joan-Marie, "The French Army in Politics," *FA*, 39(2), Jan. 1961:85–95.

Ehrmann, Henry W., "Bureaucracy and Interest Groups in the Decision-Making Process of the Fifth Republic," Festschrift für Ernst Fraenkel, Berlin, 1963.

———, *French Labor from Popular Front to Liberation*, Oxford UP, 1947, 342 pp.

———, "The French Trade Associations and the Ratification of the Schuman Plan," *WP*, 6(4), July 1954: 453–81.

———, *Organized Business in France*, Princeton UP, 1957, 514 pp.

Kelly, George Armstrong, *Lost Soldiers, The French Army and Empire in Crisis, 1947–1962*, MIT P, 1965, 404 pp.

Lorwin, Val R., *The French Labor Movement in Postwar France*, Harvard UP, 1931, 346 pp.

Chapter 2. THE FRENCH POLITICAL HERITAGE

THE THIRD REPUBLIC AND BEFORE

Armstrong, Hamilton Fish, *Chronology of Failure, The Last Days of the French Republic*, Macmillan, 1940, 202 pp.

Barthélemy, Joseph, *The Government of France*, Allen & Unwin, London, 1924, 222 pp.

Brogan, Denis W., *France Under the Republic*, Harper, 1940, 744 pp.

———, *The French Nation, from Napoleon to Pétain*,

1814–1940, Harper, 1958, 328 pp.

Chapman, Guy, *The Dreyfus Case, A Reassessment*, Viking, 1955, 400 pp.

Cobban, Alfred, *The Decline of the Third Republic*, Chatto & Windus, London, 1960, 127 pp.

———, *A History of Modern France*, Penguin, 3 vols: *Old Regime and Revolution, 1715–1799*, 1957, 287 pp; *From the First Empire to the Fourth Republic, 1799–1945*, 1961, 287 pp; *France of the Republics, 1871–1962*, 1965, 272 pp.

———, *The Social Interpretation of the French Revolution*, Cambridge UP, 1964, 178 pp.

Colton, Joel, *Léon Blum, Humanist in Politics*, Knopf, 1966, 512 pp.

Darby, Louise Elliott, *Léon Blum, Evolution of a Socialist*, Yoseloff, London, 1963, 447 pp.

De Tocqueville, Alexis, *The Old Regime and the French Revolution*, trans. by Stuart Gilbert, Doubleday, 1955, 300 pp.

Gooch, Robert K., *Parliamentary Government in France, Revolutionary Origins, 1789–1791*, Cornell UP, 1960, 253 pp.

Graham, B. D., "Theories of the French Party System Under the Third Republic," *PS*, 12(1), Feb. 1964:21–32.

Guérard, Albert Léon, *France, A Modern History*, U Michigan P, 1959, 563 pp.

Halasz, Nicholas, *Captain Dreyfus, The Story of a Mass Hysteria*, Simon & Schuster, 1956, 274 pp.

Jackson, J. Hampden, ed., *A Short History of France from Early Times to 1958*, Cambridge UP, 1959, 222 pp.

Joll, James, ed., *The Decline of the Third Republic*, Praeger, 1959, 127 pp.

Maurois, André, *A History of France*, rev. ed., Farrar, Straus, 1957, 598 pp; Grove, 1960, pbk.

Micaud, Charles A., *The French Right and Nazi Germany, 1933–1939*, Duke UP, 1943, 255 pp.

Paul-Boncour, Joseph, *Recollections of the Third Republic*, Vol. 1, trans. by George Marion, Jr., Speller, 1958, 269 pp.

Pinkney, David H., *Napoleon III and the Rebuilding of Paris*, Princeton UP, 1958, 245 pp.

Romier, Lucien, *A History of France*, trans. and completed by A. L. Rowse, Macmillan, 1953, 487 pp.

Seignobos, Charles, *The Evolution of the French People*, Knopf, 1932, 382 pp.

Weber, Eugen, *Action Française, Royalism and Reaction in Twentieth-Century France*, Stanford UP, 1966, 594 pp.

———, *The Nationalist Revival in France, 1905–1914*, U California P, 1959, 237 pp.

Werth, Alexander, *France in Ferment*, Harper, 1935, 309 pp.

———, *France and Munich*, Harper, 1939, 447 pp.

———, *The Twilight of France, 1933–1940*, Harper, 1942, 368 pp.

———, *Which Way France?* Harper, 1937, 414 pp.

Zeldin, Theodore, *The Political System of Napoleon III*, Macmillan, 1958, 196 pp.

THE VICHY REGIME AND THE FREE FRENCH

Aron, Robert, *De Gaulle Triumphant, The Liberation of France, August 1944–May 1945*, Putnam, 1964, 360 pp.

———, *France Reborn, The History of the Liberation, June 1944–May 1945*, trans. by Humphrey Hare, Scribner's, 1964, 490 pp.

——— and George Elgey, *The Vichy Regime, 1940–1944*, trans. by Humphrey Hare, Macmillan, 1958, 536 pp.

Blum, Léon, *Léon Blum Before His Judges*, Routledge, London, 1943, 159 pp (a transcript of Blum's statement at the Riom Trial).

Brogan, Denis W., *French Personalities and Problems*, Knopf, 1947, 241 pp.

Cole, Hubert, *Laval, A Biography*, Putnam, 1963, 314 pp.

Géraud, André (Pertinax), *The Gravediggers of France*, Doubleday, 1944, 612 pp.

Hytier, Adrienne Doris, *Two Years of French Foreign Policy, Vichy 1940–1942*, Drosz, Geneva, 1958, 402 pp.

Langer, William L., *Our Vichy Gamble*, Knopf, 1947, 412 pp.

Laval, Pierre, *The Diary of Pierre Laval*, Scribner's, 1948, 240 pp.

Maurois, André, *Tragedy of France*, Harper, 1940, 255 pp.

Paxton, Robert O., *Parades and Politics at Vichy, The French Officer Corps Under Marshal Pétain*, Princeton UP, 1966, 432 pp.

Pickles, Dorothy M., *France Between the Republics*, Love & Malcolmson, London, 1946, 247 pp.

Reynaud, Paul, *In the Thick of the Fight, 1930–1945*, trans. by James L. Lambert, Cassell, London, 1955, 694 pp.

Spears, Edward, *Assignment to Catastrophe*, A. A. Wyn, 2 vols: *Prelude to Dunkirk, July 1939–May 1940*, 332 pp; *The Fall of France, June 1940*, 336 pp; 1954–55.

Tissier, Pierre, *The Government of Vichy*, Harrap, London, 1942, 347 pp.

Viorst, Milton, *Hostile Allies, FDR and Charles de Gaulle*, Macmillan, 1964, 280 pp.

White, Dorothy Shipley, *Seeds of Discord, De Gaulle, Free France, and the Allies*, Syracuse UP, 1964, 471 pp.

THE FOURTH REPUBLIC

Duverger, Maurice, *The French Political System*, U Chicago P, 1958, 227 pp.

Friedrich, Carl Joachim, "The Political Theory of the New Constitutions," *RP*, 12(2), Apr. 1950:215–24.

Goguel, François, *France Under the Fourth Republic*, Cornell UP, 1952, 198 pp.

Matthews, Ronald, *The Death of the Fourth Republic*, Praeger, 1954, 318 pp.

Meisel, James J., *The Fall of the Republic, Military Revolt in France*, U Michigan P, 1963, 320 pp.

Mendès-France, Pierre, "The Crisis of France, 1945–1959," *IA*, 35(3), July 1959:285–94.

Pickles, Dorothy M., *French Politics, The First Years of the Fourth Republic*, Oxford UP, 1953, 302 pp.

Romains, Jules, *A Frenchman Examines His Conscience*, Essential, London, 1956, 118 pp.

Schoenbrun, David, *As France Goes*, Harper, 1957, 341 pp.

Taylor, O. R., *The Fourth Republic of France, Constitution and Political Parties*, Oxford UP, 1951, 216 pp.

Werth, Alexander, *France, 1940–1956*, Holt, 1956, 764 pp.

Wright, Gordon, *The Reshaping of French Democracy*, Reynal, 1948, 277 pp.

——, *France in Modern Times, 1760 to the Present*, Rand McNally, 1960, 621 pp.

THE FIFTH REPUBLIC

Aron, Robert, *An Explanation of de Gaulle*, Harper, 1966, 202 pp, pbk.

Campbell, Peter and Brian Chapman, *The Constitution of the Fifth Republic, Translation and Commentary*, Blackwell, Oxford, 1958, 60 pp, pbk.

The French Constitution Adopted by Referendum of Sept. 28, 1958, and Promulgated on Oct. 4, 1958, French text and English trans., French Embassy, Press and Information Division, 1958, 75 pp.

Friedrich, Carl Joachim, "The New French Constitution in Political and Historical Perspective," *HLR*, 72(5), Mar. 1959:801–37.

Harrison, Martin, "The Constitution of the Fifth Republic, A Commentary," *PS*, 7(1), Feb. 1959:41–62.

Hoffmann, Stanley H. and Nicholas Wahl, "The French Constitution," Part 1, "The Final Text and Its Prospects," Part 2, "The Initial Draft and Its Origin," *APSR*, 53(2), July 1959:332–82.

Johnson, D., "The Political Principles of General de Gaulle," *IA*, 41(4), Oct. 1965:650–62.

Kirchheimer, Otto, "France from the Fourth to the Fifth Republic," *SR*, 26(4), Winter 1958:379–414.

Loewenstein, Karl, "The Constitution of the Fifth Republic, A Preliminary Report," *JP*, 21(2), May 1959: 211–33.

Werth, Alexander, *The de Gaulle Revolution*, Hale, London, 1960, 404 pp.

Williams, Philip M. and Martin Harrison, *De Gaulle's Republic*, 2nd ed., Longmans, London, 1961, 279 pp.

POLITICAL IDEAS

Becker, Carl L., *The Heavenly City of the Eighteenth Century Philosophers*, Yale UP, 1932, 168 pp.

Binion, Rudolph, *Defeated Leaders, The Political Fate of Callou, Jouvenal and Tardieu*, Columbia UP, 1960, 425 pp.

Buthman, William C., *The Rise of Integral Nationalism in France*, Columbia UP, 1939, 355 pp.

Caute, David, *Communism and the French Intellectuals 1914–1960*, Macmillan, 1964, 413 pp.

Charlton, D. G., *Positivist Thought in France During the Second Empire, 1852–1870*, Oxford UP, 1959, 251 pp.

Curtis, Michael, *Three Against the Third Republic, Lorel, Barres, and Maurras*, Princeton UP, 1959, 313 pp.

Elbow, Matthew H., *French Corporative Theory, 1789–1948, A Chapter in the History of Ideas*, Columbia UP, 1954, 222 pp.

Graham, B. D., *The French Socialists and Tripartisme, 1944–1947*, Toronto UP, 1965, 299 pp.

Hayes, Carlton J. H., *The Historical Evolution of Modern Nationalism*, R. R. Smith, 1931, 327 pp.

Howell, Ronald F., "The Philosopher Alain and French Classical Radicalism," *WPQ*, 18(3), Sept. 1965:594–614.

Lichtheim, George, *Marxism in Modern France*, Columbia UP, 1966, 212 pp.

Manuel, Frank E., *The New World of Henri Saint-Simon*, Harvard UP, 1956, 423 pp.

Martin, Kingsley, *The Rise of French Liberal Thought, A Study of Political Ideas from Bayle to Condorcet*, 2nd ed., ed. by J. P. Mayer, New York UP, 1954, 316 pp.

Micaud, Charles A., *Communism and the French Left*, Weidenfeld & Nicolson, London, 1963, 308 pp.

Muret, Charlotte, *French Royalist Doctrines Since the Revolution*, Columbia UP, 1933, 326 pp.

Pierce, Roy, *Contemporary Political Thought*, Oxford UP, 1966, 288 pp, pbk.

Rémond, René, *The Right Wing in France, from 1815 to de Gaulle*, trans. by James M. Laux, U Pennsylvania P, 1966, 425 pp.

Soltau, Roger, *French Political Thought in the Nineteenth Century*, Yale UP, 1931, 500 pp.

Soucy, R. J., "The Nature of Fascism in France," *JCH*, 1(1), Jan. 1966:27–55.

Chapter 3. FRENCH PARTIES AND ELECTIONS

Almond, Gabriel A., "Political Ideas of Christian Democracy," *JP*, 10(4), Nov. 1948:734–63.

Andrews, William, "By-Election System of the Fifth Republic," *WPQ*, 17(2), June 1964:690–702.

Barnes, Samuel H., "The Politics of French Christian Labor," *JP*, 21(1), Feb. 1959:105–22.

Blum, Léon, *For All Mankind*, Viking, 1946, 186 pp.

Bouscaren, Anthony, "The European Christian Democrats," *WPQ*, 2(1), Mar. 1949:59–75.

Cairns, John C., "Notes and Comment, France, December 1965, End of the Elective Monarchy," *IJ*, 21(1), Winter 1965–66:93–100.

Campbell, Peter, *French Electoral Systems and Elections Since 1789*, 2nd ed., Faber, London, 1965, 155 pp.

Cantril, Hadley, *The Politics of Despair*, Basic Books, 1958, 269 pp.

Cook, Geoffrey C., "De Gaulle and the R.P.F.," *PSQ*, 65(3), Sept. 1950:335–52.

DeTarr, Francis, *The French Radical Party from Herriot to Mendès-France*, Oxford UP, 1961, 264 pp.

Ehrmann, Henry W., "Direct Democracy in France," *APSR*, 57(4), Dec. 1963:883–901.

Einaudi, Mario and François Goguel, *Christian Democracy in Italy and France*, U Notre Dame P, 1952, 229 pp.

"The French Election of 1956," *PS*, 4(2), June 1956: 139–75; 4(3), Oct. 1956:250–82.

Godfrey, E. Drexel, Jr., "The Communist Presence in

France," *APSR,* 50(2), June 1956:321–38.

——, *The Fate of the French Non-Communist Left,* Doubleday, 1955, 79 pp.

Goldey, David B., "The French Presidential Election of 5 and 19 December, 1965, Organization and Results," *PS,* 14(2), June 1966:208–15.

——, "The French Referendum and Elections of 1962, The National Campaigns," *PS,* 11(3), Oct. 1963:287–307.

Harrison, Martin and Uwe Kitzinger, "The French General Election, 1958, Two Constituencies: (1) Paris 5: Safe Seat; (2) Personal, Regional, and Religious Factors: Strasbourg Nord-Sud," *PS,* 7(2), June 1959:147–73.

Larmour, Peter J., *The French Radical Party in the 1930's,* Stanford UP, 1964, 327 pp.

Laponce, Jean A., *The Government of the Fifth Republic, French Political Parties and the Constitution,* U California P, 1961, 415 pp.

Lichtheim, George, "The Stranded Whale, On the French Communist Left," *Encounter,* 23(5), 1964: 31–35.

McLellan, David S., "The French and Italian Communist Parties and the Decisions of the Twentieth Congress, C.P.S.U.," *WPQ,* 10(2), June 1957:446–47.

MacRae, Duncan, Jr., "Religious and Socio-economic Factors in the French Vote, 1946–1956," *AJS,* 64(3), Nov. 1958:290–98.

Marcum, John A., "French Party Literature," *WPQ,* 12(1), Part 1, Mar. 1959:168–77.

Marcus, John T., *French Socialism in the Crisis Years, 1933–1936, Fascism and the French Left,* Praeger, 1958, 216 pp.

Nicholas, H. G. and Philip M. Williams, "The French Election of 1956, I. Electoral Law and Machinery; II. The Campaign," *PS,* 4(2), June 1956:139–75.

Noland, Aaron, *The Founding of the French Socialist Party, 1893–1905,* Harvard UP, 1956, 248 pp.

Osgood, Samuel M., *French Royalism Under the Third and Fourth Republics,* Nijhoff, The Hague, 1960, 228 pp.

Pierce, Roy, "De Gaulle and the RPF—A Post Mortem," *JP,* 16(1), Feb. 1954:96–119.

Rieber, Alfred, "Communist Tactics in France, 1945–1953," *JP,* 16(1), Spring 1954:73–85.

Rossi, Angelo, *A Communist Party in Action, An Account of the Organization and Operations in France,* Yale UP, 1949, 301 pp.

Schlesinger, Joseph A., "The French Radical Socialist Party and the Republican Front of 1956," *WPQ,* 11(1), Mar. 1958:71–85.

Thorez, Maurice, *France Today and the People's Front,* Intern. Pub., 1936, 255 pp.

Williams, Philip M., "The French Presidential Election of 1965," *Parl. Aff.,* 19(1), Winter 1965:14–30.

——, "The French Referendum, 1960," *Parl. Aff.,* 14(3), Summer 1961:335–52.

——, "The French Referendum and Election of October–November 1962," *Parl. Aff.,* 16(2), Spring 1963:165–73.

——, "Party, Presidency and Parish Pump in France," *Parl. Aff.,* 18(3), Summer 1965:257–65.

——· and Martin Harrison, "The French Referendum of April, 1962," *Parl. Aff.,* 15(3), Summer 1962: 294–306.

Zariski, Raphael, "Problems and Prospects of Democratic Socialism in France and Italy," *JP,* 18(2), May 1956:254–80.

Zartman, I. William, "French Communist Foreign Policy, 1952–1954, A Propaganda Analysis," *WPQ,* 9(2), June 1956:344–62.

Chapter 4. THE FRENCH PARLIAMENT

Gooch, Robert K., *The French Parliamentary Committee System,* Appleton-Century-Crofts, 1935, 259 pp.

Howard, John E., *Parliament and Foreign Policy in France,* Cresset, London, 1948, 172 pp.

King, Jere Clemens, *Generals and Politicians, Conflict Between France's High Command, Parliament and Government,* U California P, 1951, 294 pp.

Leites, Nathan, *On the Game of Politics in France,* Stanford UP, 1959, 190 pp.

Lidderdale, D. W. S., *The Parliament of France,* Hansard, London, 1951, 296 pp.

Mavrinac, Albert, *Organization and Procedure of the National Assembly of the Fifth French Republic,* Hansard, London, 1960, 39 pp.

Chapter 5. THE FRENCH EXECUTIVE

Aron, Robert, *An Explanation of de Gaulle,* trans. by Marianne Sinclair, Harper, 1966, 210 pp.

Barrés, Philippe, *Charles de Gaulle,* Doubleday, 1941, 260 pp.

Burgess, W. Randolph, "The Economic and Political Consequences of General de Gaulle," *PSQ,* 78(4), 1963:537–47.

Campbell, Peter, "The Cabinet and the Constitution in France," *Parl. Aff.,* 5(3), Summer 1951:341–61.

——, "The Cabinet and the Constitution in France, 1951–1956," *Parl. Aff.,* 9(3), Summer 1956:206–306.

Deferre, Gaston, "De Gaulle and After," *FA,* Apr. 1966:434–45.

De Gaulle, Charles, *The Edge of the Sword,* Criterion, 1960, 128 pp.

——, *Speeches,* Oxford UP, 1944, 189 pp.

——, *War Memoirs,* Simon & Schuster, 3 vols: *The Call to Honor, 1940,* 1942, 319 pp; *Unity, 1942–1944,* 1959, 378 pp; *Salvation, 1944–1946,* 1960, 404 pp.

De Lamothe, A. Dutheillet, "Ministerial Cabinets in France," *Pub. Ad.,* 43, Winter 1965:365–81.

Funk, Arthur Layton, *Charles de Gaulle, The Crucial Years, 1943–1944,* U Oklahoma P, 1959, 336 pp.

Furniss, Edgar S., Jr., *De Gaulle and the French Army, An Appraisal of a Civil Military Crisis,* Twentieth Century Fund, 1964, 331 pp.

——, *The Office of the Premier in French Foreign Policy-Making, An Application of Decision-Making Analysis,* Princeton UP, 1954, 67 pp.

Gaudemet, P. M., "The Relationship Between the President and the Prime Minister in France," *Scots Law Times,* Edinburgh, July 22, 1961:117–20.

Harrison, Martin, "The French Experience of Exceptional Powers, 1961," *JP*, 25(1), Feb. 1963:139–58.

Hayward, J. E. S., "Presidentialism and French Politics," *Parl. Aff.*, 18(1), Winter 1964–65: 23–39.

Herriot, Edouard, *In Those Days Before the First World War,* trans. by Adolphe de Milly, Old and New World Pub., 1952, 276 pp.

Hoffmann, Stanley, "De Gaulle's Memoirs, The Hero as History," *WP*, 8(1), Oct. 1960:140–55.

——, "Succession and Stability in France," *JIA*, 18(1), 1964:86–103.

Johnson, Douglas, "The Political Principles of General de Gaulle," *IA*, 41(4), Oct. 1965:650–62.

Lacouture, Jean, *De Gaulle,* New Amer. Lib., 1966, 188 pp.

McCormick, Donald, *Mr. France, The Life and Times of France's Dynamic Postwar Premier,* Jarrolds, London, 1955, 240 pp.

Macridis, Roy C., ed., *Implacable Ally,* Harper, 1966, 248 pp.

Mauriac, Francois, *De Gaulle,* Doubleday, 1966, 229 pp.

Melnik, Constantin and Nathan Leites, *The House Without Windows, France Selects a President,* trans. by Ralph Manheim, Row, Peterson, 1958, 358 pp.

Mendès-France, Pierre, *The Pursuit of Freedom: An Autobiography,* Longmans, London, 1956, 256 pp.

Mengin, Robert, *No Laurels for de Gaulle,* trans. by Jay Allen, Farrar, Straus & Giroux, 1966, 402 pp.

Merle, Marcel, "The Presidency of the Fourth Republic," *Parl. Aff.*, 3, Summer 1954:287–302.

Pickles, William, "Making Sense of de Gaulle," *IA*, 42(3), July 1966:410–20.

Pickles, William, "Special Powers in France, Article 16 in Practice," *Pub. Law*, Spring 1963:23–50.

Schoenbrun, David, *The Three Lives of Charles de Gaulle,* Atheneum, 1966, 373 pp.

Thomson, David, *Two Frenchmen, Pierre Laval and Charles de Gaulle,* Cresset, London, 1951, 256 pp.

Viansson-Ponte, Pierre, *The King and His Court (Les Gaullistes),* Houghton Mifflin, 1965, 250 pp.

Werth, Alexander, *De Gaulle, A Political Biography,* Penguin, 1966, 391 pp.

——, *Lost Statesman, The Strange Story of Pierre Mendès-France,* Abelard-Schuman, 1958, 428 pp.

Wright, Gordon, *Raymond Poincaré and the French Presidency,* Stanford UP, 1942, 271 pp.

Chapter 6. THE FRENCH ADMINISTRATION: NATIONAL AND LOCAL

NATIONAL ADMINISTRATION

Baum, Warren C., *The French Economy and the State,* Princeton UP, 1958, 391 pp.

Brown, J. C., "Education of the New French Administrative Class," *Pub. Pers. Rev.*, 16(1), Jan. 1955:17–27.

Clough, Shepard C., "Economic Planning in a Capitalist Society, France from Monnet to Hirsh," *PSQ*, 71(4), Dec. 1956:539–68.

Cohen, Stephen, *French Economic Planning,* Weidenfeld & Nicolson, London, 1965.

Crozier, Michel, *The Bureaucratic Phenomenon,* U Chicago P, 1964, 320 pp.

De Vries, Henry P. and Berthold H. Hoeniger, "Post Liberation Nationalizations in France," *CLR*, May 1950:629–56.

Einaudi, Mario et al., *Nationalization in France and Italy,* Cornell UP, 1955, 260 pp.

Feyzioglie, T., "The Reforms of the French Higher Civil Service," *Pub. Ad.*, 33(1), Spring 1955:69–93 and 33(2), Summer 1955:173–89.

Grégoire, Roger, *The French Civil Service,* trans. from French, rev. ed., Intern. Inst. Admin. Sciences, Brussels, 1965, 363 pp, pbk.

Hackett, John and Anne-Marie, *Economic Planning in France,* Harvard UP, 1963, 418 pp.

Mendès-France, Pierre and Gabriel Ardan, *Economics and Action,* Columbia UP, 1955, 222 pp.

Parris, Henry, "Twenty Years of l'Ecole Nationale d'Administration," *Pub. Ad.*, 43, Winter 1965:395–411.

Perroux, Francois, *The IVth French Plan, 1962–65,* trans. by Bruno Leblanc, Nat. Inst. Ec. and Social Res., London, 1965, 84 pp, pbk.

Peterson, Wallace C., *The Welfare State in France,* U Nebraska Studies, Lincoln, 1960, 115 pp.

Piquard, Michel, "Organization and Planning of the Paris Region," *Pub. Ad.*, 43, Winter 1965:383–93.

Ridley, F. and J. Blondel, *Public Administration in France,* Routledge, London, 1964, 336 pp.

Robson, William, ed., *The Civil Service in Britain and France,* Macmillan, 1965, 191 pp.

Sheahan, John B., *Promotion and Control of Industry in Postwar France,* Harvard UP, 1963, 301 pp.

Sturmthal, Adolf, "The Structure of Nationalized Enterprises in France," *PSQ*, 67(3), Sept. 1952:357–78.

Sweetman, L. T., "Prefects and Planning, France's New Regionalism," *Pub. Ad.*, 43, Spring 1965:15–30.

Waline, Marcel, "The Constitutional Council of the French Republic," *AJCL*, 12, Autumn 1963:483–93.

Wilson, John Stuart Gladstone, *French Banking Structure and Credit Policy,* Harvard UP, 1957, 453 pp.

LOCAL ADMINISTRATION

Blondel, Jean, "Local Government and the Local Offices of Ministries in a French Department," *Parl. Aff.*, 37(2), Spring 1959:65–74.

Chapman, Brian, *Introduction to French Local Government,* Allen & Unwin, London, 1953, 238 pp.

Kaminsky, Elija Ben-Zion, "The Reorganization of Metropolitan Paris," *Pub. Aff. Bull.*, Arizona State U, 4(1), 1965, 4 pp.

Marshall, A. H., "Wide Powers Vested in Prefects and Mayors, Aspects of Central Administration and Local Government in France," *Mun. J*, Nov. 23, 1956:2273–74 and Dec. 7, 1956:2878–79.

Chapter 7. FRENCH LAW AND COURTS

CIVIL LAW AND COURTS

Amos, Sir Maurice Sheldon and F. P. Walton, *Introduction to French Law,* Oxford UP, 1935, 393 pp.

David, René and Henry P. de Vries, *The French Legal System, An Introduction to Civil Law Systems,* Oceana, 1958, 152 pp.

King, Jerome B., "Constitutionalism and the Judiciary in France," *PSQ,* 80(1), March 1965:62–87.

Lewy, Claude et al., *Essays on French Law,* Washington Law Society, 1958, 96 pp.

Rabel, Ernst, "The French Civil Code," *Louisiana LR,* 1949–50:107–19.

ADMINISTRATIVE LAW AND COURTS

Alibert, Ralph, "French Conseil d'État," *Modern LR,* London, Apr. 1940:257–71.

Chapman, Brian, "The French Conseil d'État," *Parl. Aff.,* 12(2), Spring 1959:164–73.

Colliard, C. A., "Comparison Between English and French Administrative Law," *Grotius Society Transactions,* London, 1940:119–33.

Diamant, Alfred, "The French Council of State, Comparative Observations on the Problem of Controlling the Bureaucracy of the Modern State," *JP,* 13(4), Nov. 1951:562–88.

Freedman, Charles E., *The Conseil d'État in Modern France,* Columbia UP, 1961, 205 pp.

Garner, James W., "Judicial Control of Administrative and Legislative Acts in France," *APSR,* 9(4), Nov. 1915:637–65.

Hamson, C. J., *Executive Discretion and Judicial Control, An Aspect of the French Conseil d'État,* Stevens, London, 1954, 222 pp.

Koch, Gerald L., "The Machinery of Law Administration in France," *U Pennsylvania LR,* 108, 1959–60: 366–86.

Schwartz, Bernard, *French Administrative Law and the Common-Law World,* New York UP, 1954, 367 pp.

Chapter 8. FRENCH SOCIETY IN CHANGE

EDUCATION

Aron, Raymond, "Some Aspects of the Crisis in the French Universities," *Minerva,* 2, Spring 1964:477–83.

Fraser, W. R., *Education and Society in Modern France,* Humanities, 1963, 140 pp.

"French Education, Why Jeannot *Can* Read," Yale French Studies, 22, Winter–Spring 1958–59.

Hoyt, N. Deming, "Educational Reform in France," *Harvard Educ. R,* 18(4), Fall 1948:220–27.

Ridley, F., "The French Educational System, Policy and Administrative Aspects," *PS,* 11(2), June 1963:178–202.

Weber, Eugen, "Current Control of French Education," *CH,* 40(238), June 1961:327–33.

SOCIAL POLICY

Galant, Henry C., "France, A Comprehensive Health Plan," *CH,* 44(262), June 1963:351–58, 368.

Lorwin, Val R., "Collective Bargaining in Postwar France," *Annals,* 310, Mar. 1957:66–74.

Mares, V. E., "The French New Deal," *CH,* 45(267), Nov. 1963:276–82, 303.

Peterson, Wallace C., *The Welfare State in France,* Nebraska UP, 1960, 115 pp.

Rodgers, Barbara, "Social Security in France," *Pub. Ad.,* 31(4), Winter 1953:377–98 and 32(1), Spring 1954:99–116.

Social Security in France, Ministry of Labor and Social Security, Paris, 1965, 79 pp.

Chapter 9. FRANCE AND THE WORLD

FROM EMPIRE TO COMMUNITY

Andrews, William G., *French Politics and Algeria, The Process of Policy Formation 1954–1962,* Appleton-Century-Crofts, 1962, 217 pp, pbk.

Beloff, Nora, *The General Says No, Britain's Exclusion from Europe,* Penguin, 1963, 181 pp.

Berg, Elliot J., "The Economic Basis of Political Choice in French West Africa," *APSR,* 54(2), June 1960: 391–405.

Brace, Richard M. and Joan, *Ordeal in Algeria,* Van Nostrand, 1960, 450 pp.

Cady, John F., *The Roots of French Imperialism in Eastern Asia,* Cornell UP, 1956, 322 pp.

Camps, Miriam, *What Kind of Europe? The Community Since de Gaulle's Veto,* Oxford UP, 1965, 140 pp, pbk.

Catroux, Georges, "The French Union," *IC,* 495, Nov. 1953:193–256.

Clark, Michael, *Algeria in Turmoil, A History of the Rebellion,* Praeger, 1960, 480 pp.

Delavignette, Robert, *Freedom and Authority in French West Africa,* Oxford UP, 1950, 152 pp.

Fisher, Sidney Nettleton, ed., *France and the European Community,* Ohio State UP, 1964, 176 pp.

Gillespie, Joan, *Algeria, Rebellion and Revolution,* Praeger, 1960, 208 pp.

Gordon, David C., *The Passing of French Algeria,* Oxford UP, 1966, 265 pp.

Grosser, Alfred, *Foreign Policy of the Fifth Republic,* Little, Brown, 1966, 189 pp.

———, "France and Germany, Divergent Outlooks," *FA,* 44(4), Oct. 1965:26–36.

Hammer, Ellen J., *The Struggle for Indo-China,* Stanford UP, 1954, 342 pp.

———, *The Struggle for Indo-China Continues, Geneva to Bandung,* Stanford UP, 1955, 40 pp.

Hodgkin, Thomas and Ruth Schachter, "French-Speaking West Africa," *IC,* 528, 1960.

Kraft, Joseph, *The Struggle for Algeria,* Doubleday, 1961, 263 pp.

Pickles, Dorothy, *Algeria and France, from Colonialism to Co-operation,* Methuen, London, 1963, 215 pp.

Robinson, Kenneth, "Alternative to Independence," *PS,* 4(3), Oct. 1956:225–49.

———, "The End of Empire: Another View," *IA,* 30(2), Apr. 1954:186–95.

———, "A Survey of the Background Material for the Study of Government in French Tropical Africa," *APSR,* 50(1), Mar. 1956:179–98.

Sulzberger, Cyrus Leo, *The Test, de Gaulle and Algeria,* Harcourt, Brace & World, 1962, 228 pp.

Thompson, Virginia and Richard Adloff, *French Equa-*

torial Africa, Stanford UP, 1961, 595 pp.

———, *French West Africa*, Stanford UP, 1958, 626 pp.

Tillon, Germaine, *Algeria, The Realities*, Knopf, 1958, 128 pp.

———, *France and Algeria, Complementary Enemies*, Knopf, 1961, 184 pp.

Willis, F. Roy, *France, Germany, and the New Europe, 1945–1963*, Stanford UP, 1965, 397 pp.

INTERNATIONAL RELATIONS

Aron, Raymond and Daniel Lerner, eds., *France Defeats EDC, Studies in an International Controversy*, Praeger, 1957, 225 pp.

Cowan, Laing G., *France and the Saar, 1680–1948*, Columbia UP, 1950, 247 pp.

Deniau, J. F., *The Common Market, Its Structure and Purpose*, Barrie-Rockliff, London, 1960, 143 pp.

France and Britain, A Report by a Chatham House Study Group, RIIA, London, 1945, 110 pp.

France and the European Community, PEP, London, 1961, 41 pp.

Furniss, Edgar S., Jr., *Weaknesses in French Foreign Policy-Making*, Princeton UP, 1954, 52 pp.

Gooch, G. P., "Franco-German Coexistence at Last?" *FA*, 37(3), Apr. 1959:432–42.

Heckscher, August and Raymond Aron, *Diversity of Worlds*, Viking, 1957, 178 pp.

Hoffmann, Stanley S., "De Gaulle, Europe, and the Atlantic Alliance," *IO*, 18(1), Winter 1964:1–28.

Jordan, W. M., *Great Britain, France, and the German Problem, 1918–1939, A Study of Anglo-French Relations in the Making and Maintenance of the Versailles Settlement*, Oxford UP, 1944, 235 pp.

Lauret, René, *France and Germany, the Legacy of Charlemagne*, trans. by Wells Chamberlin, Regnery, 1964, 272 pp.

Lieber, Robert J., "The French Nuclear Force, A Strategic and Political Evaluation," *IA*, 42(3), July 1966:421–31.

Marcus, John T., *Neutralism and Nationalism in France*, Bookman, 1959, 207 pp.

Reynaud, Paul, *The Foreign Policy of Charles de Gaulle, A Critical Assessment*, Odyssey P, 1964, 160 pp.

———, *Unite or Perish*, Simon & Schuster, 1951, 214 pp.

Salvin, Marina, "Neutralism in France and Germany," *IC*, 472, June 1951:283–318.

Wolfers, Arnold, *Britain and France Between Two Wars, Conflicting Strategies of Peace Since Versailles*, Harcourt, Brace & World, 1940, 467 pp.

Index